New
Territories,
New
Perspectives

New Territories, New Perspectives

THE RELIGIOUS IMPACT OF THE LOUISIANA PURCHASE

Edited with an Introduction by

Richard J. Callahan, Jr.

UNIVERSITY OF MISSOURI PRESS
COLUMBIA AND LONDON

Library of Congress Cataloging-in-Publication Data

   New territories, new perspectives : the religious impact of the Louisiana Purchase /
edited with an introduction by Richard J. Callahan, Jr.
      p.   cm.
   Summary: "Marking the first study to take the Louisiana Purchase as the focal point for
considering development of American religious history, this collection of essays takes up
the religious history of the region including perspectives from New Orleans and the
Caribbean and the roots of Pentecostalism and Vodou"—Provided by publisher.
   Includes index.
   ISBN 978-0-8262-1784-4 (alk. paper)
   1. United States—Church history—19th century. 2. Louisiana Purchase. 3. United
States—History—1801–1809. I. Callahan, Richard J., 11/13/67–
   BR525.N49 2008
   200.973'09034—dc22

                                                                            2007052623

 ♾™ This paper meets the requirements of the
American National Standard for Permanence of Paper
for Printed Library Materials, Z39.48, 1984.

Designer: FoleyDesign
Typesetter: FoleyDesign
Printer and binder: Integrated Book Technology, Inc.
Typeface: ITC Usherwood Book and Minion

Contents

The Shifting Nature of Reform
Envisioned on the Mississippi Steamer
Exchanges, Masks, and Charities in
Herman Melville's *The Confidence-Man*
CAROLE LYNN STEWART

Mixed-Race Ecstasy across a Single Line
The Deep South Roots of Pentecostal
Tongue Speaking
ELAINE J. LAWLESS

Vodou Purchase
The Louisiana Purchase in
the Caribbean World
PAUL CHRISTOPHER JOHNSON

Spirituality and Resistance
among African-Creoles
JOHN STEWART

New Orleans as an American City
Origins, Exchanges, Materialities,
and Religion
CHARLES H. LONG

Contributors

Index

Acknowledgments

———+———

T HE CHAPTERS IN THIS BOOK EMERGED FROM A CONFERENCE titled "Moving Boundaries: American Religion(s) through the Louisiana Purchase" that was held in February 2004 at the University of Missouri–Columbia. In addition to the authors of these chapters, Philip Arnold, Richard Bradley, Larry Brown, Steve Friesen, Joel Hartman, Mark Hulsether, Miriam Levering, Mary Jo Neitz, Jacqueline Peterson, Alan T. Terlep, and Betty Winfield also presented papers at the conference, and I would like to thank them for their participation and their interest in exploring the religious history of the Louisiana Purchase. In addition, I would like to thank everyone at the Department of Religious Studies at the University of Missouri–Columbia for their enthusiasm and aid with the project; Cheryl Smith, Steve Friesen, Paul C. Johnson, and Trish Beckman deserve special mention. The conference received support from a variety of sources, without whom it would not have been possible to gather such a diverse, interdisciplinary, and distinguished group of scholars. I would like to thank the Missouri Humanities Council (with support from the National Endowment for the Humanities) and the American Academy of Religion (Midwestern Region) for their financial assistance. Generous funding also came from several sources at the University of Missouri–Columbia, including the Office of the Chancellor, the Office of the Provost, the Student Organization Allocation Committee through the Religious Studies Club, the Rufus Monroe and Sophie Paine Lectureship in Religion, the Center for Arts and Humanities, and the College of Arts and Sciences Symposium Fund. I am grateful to all who contributed.

The process of turning a selection of conference papers into a book has been a long one, and I must thank the contributors for their unwavering support, their patience, and their willingness to see the project through. At the University of Missouri Press, Beverly Jarrett and Sara

Davis merit great thanks for their encouragement and careful reading of the manuscript. I would also like to thank the anonymous reviewers for their helpful comments and suggestions.

Finally, I thank my wife, Melissa, and my son, Trey, for their patience and support.

New
Territories,
New
Perspectives

Introduction

———+———

A Reorienting View from the Center of the Country

RICHARD J. CALLAHAN, JR.

———+———

ON APRIL 30, 1803, THE BOUNDARY OF THE UNITED STATES MOVED west to include the "Louisiana Territory." The Louisiana Purchase doubled the size of the still-young nation and critically impacted its political and economic development. More than that, however, the addition of this vast territory to the interior of the country substantially transformed America's self-identity.[1] For despite its image as empty, unsettled, wild land, the territory included occupants, experiences, and histories that differed from that known by those of Anglo descent who now tried to define and possess the land. Native Americans, Africans, African Americans, and others competed and at times cooperated with the new nation, as space, authority, and identity were refigured into the story of the United States. Both tempting and threatening—full of promises and full of dangers—the region that became, over the course of the nineteenth century, the "wild west" captured the American imagination.[2] The concrete and symbolic labor that was involved in transforming the Louisiana Territory into *American* territory in turn transformed America itself.

Most Americans today would recognize the story of the United States told as a movement from east to west, starting from the

1. See Peter J. Kastor, *The Nation's Crucible: The Louisiana Purchase and the Creation of America* (New Haven: Yale University Press, 2004).

2. See William H. Goetzmann and William N. Goetzmann, *The West of the Imagination* (Norman: University of Oklahoma Press, 2005); Richard Slotkin, *Fatal Environment: The Myth of the Frontier in the Age of Industrialization, 1800–1890* (Norman: University of Oklahoma Press, 1985); and Henry Nash Smith, *Virgin Land: The American West as Symbol and Myth* (Cambridge: Harvard University Press, 1950).

English colonies on the east coast that formed the young republic, then moving westward. The first significant barrier to westward expansion was the Appalachian Mountains, and the space between this range and the Mississippi River was the first "western frontier." With the Louisiana Purchase, the frontier moved to include the "wild west," bordered by the Rocky Mountains. Heroes including Meriwether Lewis and William Clark led expeditions to explore and map the landscape that was, according to the American story, heretofore unknown. The Louisiana Purchase figures into the narrative as the inevitable growth of an already planted seed, the addition of "elbow room" to an already established and growing nation, cast by the 1840s as America's "Manifest Destiny." By the 1890s, historian Frederick Jackson Turner was able to offer an interpretation of American history guided by this notion of the frontier, arguing that the nation was actively shaped and constituted by the frontier experience. According to Turner's "frontier thesis," the Louisiana Purchase was yet another in a succession of frontiers that American pioneers settled, each one a movement away from Europe and an advancement of the American character. "It is like the steady growth of a complex nervous system for the originally simple, inert continent," Turner wrote.[3]

Narratives of the history of religion in the United States likewise have tended to follow this westward trajectory.[4] They locate their origins in New England's Puritans, or at least, again, in the English colonies, each of which, more or less, was dominated by one or another form of Christianity. As the story goes, the Great Awakenings—the first in the mid-eighteenth century, the second in the early-nineteenth—helped to meld these different Christianities and communities into something of a shared American style of Protestantism, just as the American Revolution melded the separate colonies into a shared American national identity. From there

3. Frederick Jackson Turner, "The Significance of the Frontier in American History," in *Rereading Frederick Jackson Turner,* ed. John Mack Faragher (New Haven: Yale University Press, 1994), 41. Turner's essay was originally published in the *Annual Report of the American Historical Association for the Year 1893* (Washington, D.C., 1894).

4. I am referring to histories that have become somewhat "canonical" in the field of American religious history, and the narrative structure that often shapes the trajectory of courses taught on the subject. Thomas A. Tweed makes a similar point in his introduction to *Retelling U.S. Religious History* (Berkeley and Los Angeles: University of California Press, 1997), 13.

everything moved to the west as America grew and spread into the uncharted territories.

Although the Louisiana Purchase is central to the story of American westward expansion, it rarely appears in narratives of American religious history. In one sense, this is not surprising. The Purchase itself was not a religious event, at least not in any overt way that was recognized as such. It did not directly involve churches or doctrines or religious authorities. However, the transfer of the Louisiana Territory to the United States did have consequences that were crucial to the development of religion in North America, and to conceptions of American identity and purpose. The process of making the Louisiana Territory into U.S. territory—the political labor of nation building—meant shaping the space to conform to American cultural, social, and religious identity. That process took place both on the ground, through physical possession and transformation of land and people, and ideologically, through the writing of history. These two aspects of the production of "America" buttressed each other. By the mid- to late nineteenth century, the contours of the narrative of American religious history familiar to most Americans today was constructed.[5] The content of the narrative was shaped by two important overarching story lines that held it together. First, it was overwhelmingly a Protestant story. Despite attempts in recent years to represent more experiences, the touchstones and concerns that make up the familiar plot and drive the narrative forward are predominantly Protestant. Second, it was a nationalist story, its contours defined by the political borders of the United States and the activities of its citizens. That is to say, French and Spanish and Native American presence in North America did not fit smoothly into traditional narratives of American religious history. To be sure, Protestant missionaries to western indigenous peoples have found a place in American religious history. But what of the long histories of other human religious activity in the West? They tended to be excluded, or they have been included as part of a disconnected story not joined to the national narrative except insofar as they concern assimilation.[6] National identity defines the story line, and French and Spanish

5. Henry Warner Bowden, "The Historiography of American Religion," in *Encyclopedia of the American Religious Experience: Studies of Traditions and Movements,* 3 vols., ed. Charles H. Lippy and Peter W. Williams (New York: Scribner's 1988).

6. See, for example, Sidney Ahlstrom's canonical *A Religious History of the American People* (New Haven: Yale University Press, 1972).

experiences are written out of the American story. However, national identity did not come fully formed. The boundaries between "us" and "them" did not simply appear, cleanly and uncontested. Both boundaries and identities were formed through physical and symbolic labor that involved negotiations and exchanges, suggesting that the story of "us" cannot be so simply isolated from the story of "them." These categories only emerged through dynamic interaction in fields of power and interest. Moreover, the Protestant story and the national story have tended to merge in the United States, the national story becoming one of divine providence and the religious history following the unfolding of particular Protestant communities and dilemmas as the nation's central religious narrative. These issues beg for exploration of the experiences and processes of the transformation of the Louisiana Territory into U.S. territory, on any number of levels. Against this background, the present volume begins to investigate continuities, disruptions, and changes relating to religion in the context of the Louisiana Purchase.

A Matter of Perspective

In February 2004, scholars from across North America and from a variety of disciplines convened at the University of Missouri–Columbia to explore American religious history through the lens of the Louisiana Purchase. The event was occasioned by the 2003 bicentennial of the Purchase, which had given rise to a host of conferences and memorial events throughout the Midwest. The organizers of the University of Missouri conference noticed that very little attention had been paid to the role of religion in the Louisiana Purchase, or to the impact of the Purchase on religion in America. Nor, indeed, as already noted, did the event that was receiving so much commemorative attention appear in common narratives of American religious history. However, the bicentennial celebration did bring into focus a number of issues that were relevant to the study of American religion. First, the anniversary itself raised questions about the fashioning of national history, and its myths of founding and origin, in the process of selecting events that are marked and celebrated as formative. Second, the celebrations begged for critical reflection about how the event was represented, including how diverse experiences and impacts of the Purchase were included or excluded, and why its diverse religious effects and influences were never a part of the story. Third, we realized that the Purchase itself involved important work of reorientation—such as shifting the boundaries of identity and ideology, for instance, or possessing, encountering, and mapping new landscapes and new peoples, and fashioning values and community out of such experiences—that are themselves part of the work of religion as it is coming to be understood by contemporary scholars of religion. Finally, revisiting the Louisiana Purchase served as a reminder that the European governance of the Louisiana Territory was seated in New Orleans, and that this location situated the middle of what would become the United States in a Caribbean network of exchange that was international, diverse, and quite different from the picture of U.S. society with which most Americans are familiar. For these reasons, we organized a conference with the title "Moving Boundaries: American Religion(s) through the Louisiana Purchase," to explore how we might approach the religious impact of the Louisiana Purchase.

Recent scholarship has raised questions about the traditional east-to-west spatial orientation of American religious history, asking what the story would look like from different perspectives. The *Retelling U.S. Religious History* volume edited by Thomas A. Tweed offers two such examples. William Westfall's "Voices from the Attic: The Canadian Border and the Writing of American Religious History" explores how the view from Canada "reveals new things about history and suggests new ways of telling the story" of religion in America. At the border, the work of defining national identities and ideologies is illuminated, and the role of religious history in this work becomes more clear. Laurie R. Maffly-Kipp's "Eastward Ho! American Religion from the Perspective of the Pacific Rim" shifts our common orientation by reversing the direction of the familiar narrative, beginning with European colonial activities in the Pacific in 1513. From this perspective, an entirely different set of religious concerns appears to shape the history of the western edge of the United States, deeply troubling the standard east-to-west narrative. As Maffly-Kipp points out, "it is easy enough, of course, to find fault, particularly with grand narratives. It is much harder to propose a narrative that takes all of these criticisms into account and corrects them."[7]

7. William Westfall, "Voices from the Attic: The Canadian Border and the Writing of American Religious History," in Tweed, *Retelling*, 184; Laurie R. Maffly-Kipp, "Eastward Ho! American Religion from the Perspective of the Pacific Rim," in Tweed, *Retelling*, 130.

Taking heed of her warning, this volume does not propose to *correct* the grand narrative, but rather to shift the perspective, to ask what American religious history might look like from the perspective of the Louisiana Purchase territory. Indeed, despite efforts to tell the story of American history from alternative perspectives, the New England–centered east-to-west story does not appear to be in any danger of going away. This is the strength of a founding myth. It has insinuated itself into American culture through history, folklore, holidays, and so many other means that it has become a basic part of the fabric of American life. Simply asserting a different perspective cannot transform the national orientation. However, the Louisiana Purchase, occurring as it did only a relatively short time after the mythic revolutionary founding of the United States and doubling the size of its territory, offers a profound opportunity to revisit the nation's origins from an alternative, but connected, line of sight. Moreover, the Purchase was overseen by Thomas Jefferson, a "founding father" himself. Placing the Louisiana Purchase at the center of our gaze not only returns us to the nation's founding period with "new eyes" but also has the potential to reorient us, unsettling the familiar narrative and our expectations just enough to rediscover ourselves. It makes the story of American "internal" expansion an international story, one of religious, national, and ethnic diversity. The Louisiana Territory was firmly positioned in the geopolitical nexus of the United States, France, and Spain. Its original indigenous inhabitants were joined by Catholic missionaries, both French and Spanish, whose interactions with Native peoples began a process of refiguring the material and religious landscape of the New World. Added to this mix were Africans, primarily brought as slaves to the Caribbean Islands and North America. The transference of the Louisiana Territory to the United States necessitated new social, political, and economic relationships with cultural and religious ramifications that have remained largely unexamined by American religious historians. Focusing on this transformation provides one way to reposition American religious history in a global context.

Internally, the religious labor that took place in the space of the Louisiana Territory following the Purchase, both physical and conceptual, was instrumental to the ways that religion developed in America. In their possession of this space, and in their movements across and through it, Americans created and enacted meanings of freedom and possibility. Discovering and possessing the region became modes of activity that merged with ideas of destiny, while settling it meant shaping it according to ideals of purity and order. Conflict and transgression encouraged the language of providence and theodicy. It was here that the issue of slavery came to a head as the territory was carved into states. Here, also, was the laboratory for new forms of interactions with indigenous peoples and, ultimately, the creation of the reservation system. Clearly, as some Americans were imagining the new territory as an expansive location of freedom, others were experiencing the region as a violent site of oppression and constraint. In the midst of these plays of power, religious communities produced often innovative ways to make a place for themselves and fashion identity from resources both traditional and newly found. The dynamics of possession and dispossession and the boundary marking of self and other on this frontier helped to shape the contours of identity and value in the still-forming nation, the repercussions of which are still being felt today. They also refigure the issues that shape our understanding of the landscape of religion in America.

Organization of the Book

The chapters that follow are loosely grouped into two sections. The first several chapters offer new material and perspectives on the activity of possessing and peopling the Louisiana Purchase territory by those who moved into it primarily from the east and, at times, the south. While problematizing the idea that the territory was empty space, these papers explore the religious impact of the dynamics of possession (and dispossession) in the process of making Louisiana into America. Carole Lynn Stewart's essay, "The Shifting Nature of Reform Envisioned on the Mississippi Steamer: Exchanges, Masks, and Charities in Herman Melville's *The Confidence-Man*," then acts as a crossroads, the Mississippi River marking both an east/west axis that defined the frontier's westward expansion and a north/south axis that marked growing conflict over slavery in the United States that also played out in the possibilities of the Louisiana Purchase. Moving down the Mississippi River with Melville's steamer, we arrive at the point where the river empties into the ocean: New Orleans. The final set of essays take up the religious history of the Louisiana Purchase from the perspective of New Orleans and the Caribbean.

An important aspect of possessing the Louisiana territory and making it into American space involved the literal transformation of the landscape through the planning and construction of buildings, homes, towns, and cities. Peter W. Williams begins the collection with an exploration of the built religious environment of the Louisiana Purchase. He finds that the architecture of New Orleans, at the southern tip of the Louisiana territory, reflects the "multilayered" history of the city, including French, Spanish, and Catholic influences not typical of American cities in the Northeast. But as he moves northward and westward, he finds that the landscape quickly changes, resembling most other regions of the United States where settlers from the east exhibited "a pattern of constructing religious, as well as most other, buildings in patterns that originated in Europe and were subsequently scaled-down and adapted to frontier purposes." Indeed, most came to the middle of the country by way of East Coast centers that had themselves imported and adapted European styles. Describing and analyzing the built environments of the frontier camp meetings, communitarian societies, Mormons, Native Americans, and the cities of the plains and prairies, Williams traces the construction of a familiar American landscape as settlers and planners from the East Coast possessed and inhabited the West. While the influences shaping the built religious spaces of the Louisiana Purchase area were decidedly European by way of the eastern United States, the landscape and experiences of the western region produced significant innovations, such as the Prairie Gothic style of church design and the intensely creative symbolic structures materialized in Mormon architecture.

If the built environment tells a history of East Coast dominance over the space of the Louisiana Purchase, in her essay "Conflicting Destinies: Religion, Sex, and Violence in the Louisiana Purchase," Amanda Porterfield asks us to look closely at another aspect of this dominance, this time in the more abstract realm of conceptions of destiny. The Louisiana Purchase, Porterfield explains, fueled profoundly powerful ideas of destiny on the part of a variety of communities. The place of the West in Victorian Protestant ideas of America's destiny are well-known, but the Purchase and subsequent events in its spaces also impacted Mormon and Native American ideas of destiny, and all of these orientations interacted with and clashed with each other in the process of making the Louisiana Territory a part of the United States. Together they "added up to a sense of destiny more enormous and pervasive than any particular point of view," argues Porterfield, creating "new expectations about American hegemony." Intriguingly, views of gender, sex, and marriage were especially important elements of these conflicting ideals, and cultural conflicts over these issues motivated—and acted as justification for—acts of extreme violence. Therefore, she asserts, "attention to the interplay of violence, sex, and gender" in this space and its conflicts "is essential to understanding the construction of American power." Porterfield's history is a complex one, pushing readers to consider not only how some of what we continue to extol as "American values" promoted and obscured very real violence and terror but also how the physical, cultural, and religious labors of possessing the ambivalent spaces of the Louisiana Purchase were profoundly instrumental in creating American values and expectations. "Some of the most salient aspects of American culture today," she writes, "coalesced in the context of the Louisiana Purchase."

Important to Porterfield's method of historical analysis and interpretation is the attention she pays to the interrelations of diverse peoples and interests in the space of the Purchase. Rather than identifying several parallel histories, or a story line where one national, cultural, or religious group takes center stage, Porterfield finds that a more inclusive and revealing history includes the intersections and interactions between groups where identities are fashioned and boundaries are constructed and maintained, or challenged and transgressed.

In a different way, Michael J. Zogry also takes up the issue of how intersecting stories are, or are not, told in American religious history by exploring the relationship between the voluntary trail blazed by Lewis and Clark's Voyage of Discovery and the involuntary Trail of Tears endured by Cherokees in the 1830s. While these two trails were both geographically and ideologically linked, they are treated as unrelated events in textbooks of both American history and American religious history, and in public commemoration. Zogry finds the reason for this in the influence of a pervasive national mythology or "cultural narrative" shaped by providential views of American history that continue to frame ostensibly secular historical writing. A triumphant story line of America's westward expansion "obscures events of a place . . . and the complex history of all its inhabitants, past and present." As a result, the country cannot reconcile and recognize with equal significance the multiple experiences of its development. Zogry's essay identifies Anthony F. C. Wallace's concept of "revitalization movements" as being particularly influential in the writing of American religious history through its reformulation by William G. McLoughlin. The idea, developed in the context of studying Native American religions, becomes in the hands of McLoughlin and subsequent historians an explanatory model of American religious development that isolated revivals and awakenings from their larger historical contexts and obscured related events. Employing Paul Gilroy's concept of "the chronotope of the crossroads," Zogry suggests that historians would be better served if they concerned themselves with the intersections of peoples and cultures and histories in a particular place. "The Trail of Tears needs to 'stand' next to the Louisiana Purchase as well as the Second Great Awakening in the narrative," argues Zogry. "Only then can scholars begin to write a postfrontier, postcolonial, postmodern history."

African Americans increasingly populated the spaces of the Louisiana Purchase region over the course of the nineteenth and twentieth centuries, moving primarily into urban areas. Douglas Henry Daniels explores an unrecognized but religiously significant aspect of African American life in these urban spaces in his essay "Crossroads, the Cosmos, and Jazz in the Heartland: Oklahoma City's Deep Deuce and Kansas City's Vine Street." Scholars have explored the folk religious expressions of the rural South, Daniels argues, but "the continuation of other African, West Indian, and specific Louisiana cultural retentions within twentieth-century urban settings should cause us to reconsider both the history of religion and the culture" in the Louisiana Purchase area. In particular, Daniels asks us to consider the history of African American music and dance (jazz and blues in particular) as an important part of African American religious heritage, and the sites of music and dance halls in Oklahoma City and Kansas City, situated at crossroads, as overlooked sites of African diasporic religious heritage. Congo Square in New Orleans, in this account, becomes a prototype of black possession of space. The embodied sociality of dance and celebration at these famous crossroads may not be considered as religious events in the eyes of either observers or participants, but Daniels argues that they bear the traces of a religious heritage fragmented by social and historical forces. They continue to function in significant ways by tying together community, producing alternative history, and linking community to ancestors. Furthermore, they have become increasingly important locations for the recovery and commemoration of cultural heritage through festivals, urban preservation, and educational programs.

The next essay, Carole Lynn Stewart's "The Shifting Nature of Reform Envisioned on the Mississippi Steamer: Exchanges, Masks, and Charities in Herman Melville's *The Confidence-Man*," takes up Melville's novel as a remarkable exploration of the dilemmas posed by the appropriation of the Louisiana Purchase by the United States. The question of how to possess and occupy this space, Stewart notes, raised a number of ambiguities concerning "freedom, race, and religious meaning in the construction of an 'American' identity and the dominant civil faith or religion." Melville's *The Confidence-Man*, published in 1857, is set on a steamer traveling down the Mississippi River. The Mississippi can be understood as something of an American crossroads. It formed the eastern edge of the Louisiana Purchase, and therefore it demarcates a familiar east/west axis of national expansion and movement. But the river also runs from north to south, another meaningful axis in America. In the nineteenth century, and certainly by Melville's time, *south* connoted slavery while, for many, *north* implied freedom. North and south have been defining cultural coordinates for most of the nation's history, as have east and west. Both of these axes have also defined American dilemmas—African American slavery and the relocation and devastation of Native Americans. The Louisiana Purchase's doubling of the size of the American nation highlighted these issues by forcing a series of decisions and compromises relating to how the United States would deal with racial diversity. According to Stewart's reading, Melville's novel asserts that these were ultimately questions about the source and meaning of human value, and value itself in an increasingly diverse, increasingly commercial nation. Stewart takes Melville's book as a serious expression and analysis of the ambiguities produced by the Louisiana Purchase several decades into its incorporation, finding this literary source to be an important resource for understanding and interpreting the effects of the Louisiana Purchase on American religion and culture. Ultimately, she writes, "the confidence game itself has become the new religion of the west, a structure that persists in the culture and language of the United States."

Following Melville's steamer south along the river, we arrive in New Orleans, the cornerstone of the Louisiana Territory. The remaining papers reorient the discussion of American religion through the Louisiana Purchase by shifting our gaze from the inland territory to the Caribbean matrix.

In "Mixed-Race Ecstasy across a Single Line: The Deep South Roots of Pentecostal Tongue Speaking," Elaine J. Lawless revisits the history of Pentecostalism to find formative roots in the mixture of black and white cultures around the Mississippi Delta and the Deep South. According to Lawless's revision, which proceeds from a focus on religious verbal art and performative practices, the practice of "speaking in tongues" that is central to Pentecostalism began as a mixed-race religious performance in the Deep South. In this setting, African and Haitian-based possession practices, African American "shouts," and white "camp meeting" revivals merged under the sign of "speaking in tongues." Tracing reports of early Pentecostal experience, Lawless suggests that tongue speaking derived from the verbalizations of possession trances. As the practice traveled into the Louisiana Purchase territory—northward up the Mississippi River and westward to Kansas and, eventually, to California's Asuza Street—it distanced itself from these origins (and from any connection with "possession"). Narratives of Pentecostalism's origins that trace the movement to Kansas or California thus obscure its complex roots that were deeply planted in the diverse religious soil of the African-Caribbean-Southern U.S. matrix. The story that Lawless presents, of Pentecostalism's messy birth and the subsequent revision of its origin tale, in some ways parallels the story of the Louisiana Territory's transformation into American space.

Paul Christopher Johnson begins his chapter, "Vodou Purchase: The Louisiana Purchase in the Caribbean World," with a discussion about the writing of history. Why, he asks, should we consider the Louisiana Purchase to be an American story, rather than a Caribbean one? Furthermore, if the Purchase, which doubled the size of the United States, can be seen through a Caribbean lens, then perhaps the story of America itself can be told as part of a Caribbean story. His purpose is one of initial disorientation and subsequent reorientation that usefully places the United States in a more global context. "I hope not only to pull the Caribbean into the purview of the United States' historical frame, but also to pull the United States into the Caribbean story," he writes. "The Louisiana Purchase, as will become clear, is less the story of a land deal followed by unidirectional human traverse than a complex confluence of contingencies, ideas, and bodies." Johnson also interestingly shifts the religious framework of the Louisiana Purchase from the Protestant-based sense of providence and destiny so prevalent in the national mythology of the United States (and in works of American religious history, as Michael Zogry earlier noted) to the possibility that the event was instead the result of a vodou ceremony in Haiti. By placing the stories of Jefferson and Napoléon, and of Louisiana and Saint-Domingue, in tandem, then adding the important figure of Toussaint-Louverture, a central player in the Haitian revolution, to the mix, Johnson convincingly argues that the "nation-building stories" of Haiti and the United States "are not freestanding; they lean against each other."

Vodou certainly links Haiti and New Orleans. But John Stewart looks to another New Orleans tradition to find a hidden history of religious innovation and survival that is the product of the Louisiana Purchase and the forces that produced it. In Mardi Gras, particularly the African-Creole performances of Mardi Gras Indians, Stewart finds the fragments of African-Creole spirituality and an alternative history of power and presence. In "Spirituality and Resistance among African-Creoles," Stewart carefully explains that the Louisiana coast, prior to the Louisiana Purchase, was an integral part of a Caribbean culture zone under the control of French and Spanish Catholics. Creoles emerged in this zone with a culture that amalgamated European, African, and Native American elements. The African-Creole variant of this culture drew heavily on incidences of marronage, a communal form of resistance against slavery, and the cultivation of an African-styled spirituality. According to Stewart's keen analysis, Mardi Gras Indian performances are essential parts of African-Creole identity that link an American community to a transnational history of resistance. "At its salient core," he writes, "Creole culture constructs, or resurrects perhaps, the resource for developing alternative spiritualities where such constructions elaborate meanings of themselves that might be otherwise constrained." Stewart complicates and deepens his argument by comparing New Orleans Mardi Gras performances and history with Carnival in Trinidad. While both emerged from a similar cultural matrix, the comparison illustrates how differently this heritage developed following the Louisiana Purchase's disruption of the Caribbean cultural zone. Stewart's essay reveals effects of the Louisiana Purchase on religious identity and performance that are typically invisible in studies of American religious history.

Finally, Charles H. Long's essay, "New Orleans as an American City: Origins, Exchanges, Materialities, and Religion," is a fitting close to the volume. Long follows Johnson and Stewart in placing New Orleans in its international, Caribbean context, but he recognizes it as an "American" city as well. Not just any American city, but an especially intriguing one that might serve as a "space where new meanings and data regarding a meaning of American civil religion might be forthcoming." In revisiting the concept of American civil religion, Long argues that the familiar New England– and Virginia-based national mythology is problematically restrictive, effectively encompassing only people of a European background. However, the United States has always been more diverse and complex than that. Contending that "the culture of the United States of America is an Aboriginal-Euro-African culture," Long proposes that New Orleans, which became a part of the United States with the Louisiana Purchase, shortly after the birth of the nation and doubling its size, is a place that is neglected in our founding myths but necessary for understanding America more completely. "My interest in New Orleans as a meaning and locus for the renewal of the discussion about civil religion is related to another possibility of our common origins," he remarks. "While we like to characterize ourselves as now concerned about diversity and multiculturalism, there is no fundamental structure of our culture that has ever affirmed either diversity or the multicultural as constituting an empirical situation in the country." New Orleans offers such a situation, and the context of its incorporation into the United States further invites critical reflection upon American foundings and origins. In a sense, Long brings the volume full circle, returning to initial concerns about the possession of the Louisiana Territory, European and East Coast dominance, and the dilemmas and ambiguities of diversity.

Into the Future

So at the end of the day, is anything gained by viewing American religion(s) through the Louisiana Purchase? The essays making up this volume suggest that such a perspective does open new questions and possibilities. In particular, it compels us to take account of intersecting histories and dynamics of power that are often neglected in the way that we understand and relate America's religious development.

It also pushes us to consider new ways to engage our familiar narratives and models critically so that they can take account of the religious causes and effects of nation building.

This volume is only a start, a hint at some of the rich religious history of the Louisiana Purchase territory. Readers may note that the essays included here do not touch on many obvious issues and traditions that are part of the religious history of the Louisiana Territory region. Among the important topics that one might expect to find in such a book, but that are not included here, are a more thorough exploration of the history of Catholicism in the region, which predates Protestant settlement by over one hundred years; countless aspects of Native American history; missionary work among Native and African Americans; itinerant preachers and the settling of local churches and denominations; denominational conflicts in frontier towns; religious music developed and performed in frontier towns; the mythology of the West, and its performance in Wild West shows; and the list could continue.

Indeed, most of the essays in this volume do not focus on "church history," or even on the expected forms of religion that spring to mind when one is asked about religion in the Louisiana Purchase area. Rather, in the main the authors have chosen to explore the unexpected—stories, practices, and issues that might not be part of a "traditional" history of religion in the Midwest. There is a reason behind this madness: the purpose of the volume, and of the conference where these papers originated, is to provoke readers to reimagine American religious history from the viewpoint of the Midwest and the Purchase territory. We hope that the more "obvious" studies already exist or may be called into existence through this provocation. We further hope that the essays included here compel readers to imagine different ways of thinking about religion in America through the lens of the Louisiana Purchase and, we hope, American religious history as a whole.

The Religious Landscape of
the Louisiana Purchase

PETER W. WILLIAMS

W HAT IS THE RESULT, THE SYMPOSIUM THAT PRODUCED THESE essays asked, if the development of American religious culture is viewed from the point of view of New Orleans rather than the more traditional cultural hearths of Boston, New York, or Philadelphia? Does this shift in viewpoint produce a decentering similar to those that have resulted from earlier shifts of interpretive viewpoint away from that of white male Protestants? In the following essay, in which the architecture and built environment of religion are the major focus, the answer to the second question is not a resounding affirmative. Although a close look at the area of the Louisiana Purchase does illuminate aspects of American religious history and its building that are often neglected from more traditional perspectives, the patterns of influence thereby revealed tend more than anything to reinforce a perspective that antedates even Frederick Jackson Turner and William Warren Sweet: namely, that religious building patterns—at least among Euro-Americans—have tended to flow southward and westward from the northeast rather than in opposing directions. New Orleans itself is a partial exception to this rule, but even then, it is only a partial one.

An early classic of American studies scholarship was John William Ward's *Andrew Jackson: Symbol for an Age*, first published in 1955. Although Ward's brand of "myth and symbol school" analysis is no longer in fashion, his evocation of Jackson and his symbolic resonance in the early republic provides a good starting point for this reflection on the development of religion during the two centuries since the dramatic expansion of U.S. territory that resulted from the purchase of Louisiana—the vast environs of the Louisiana Purchase.

The public space now known as Jackson Square in New Orleans features a striking equestrian statue of "Old Hickory" by Clark Mills; exact replicas can be found near the Tennessee statehouse in Nashville and at the White House in Washington, D.C., two other Jackson-related locales. This Jacksonian presence, at once verbal and material, marks the spot as a decidedly *American* place, incorporated into the canon of civil religion by reference to a national political and military hero and continuously frequented by an ongoing flow of tourists through the French Quarter *(Vieux Carré)*—who are more attracted, most likely, to the picturesque cityscape and fabled cuisine than by any desire to pay homage to a leader whose reputation is tarnished by a rather dismal record of treatment of Native Americans.

The square itself—known in earlier eras as the Plaza de Armas and the Place d'Armes—bespeaks in its onomastic history the multilayered character of the city's ethnic and religious identity. Only antebellum Charleston in South Carolina and the Miami of the twentieth century and beyond can rival New Orleans as a center of cultural ferment in a region known more for ideological homogeneity and racial bifurcation than its diversity or exoticism. Although its role as a point of contact between North America and the Caribbean has been eclipsed by southern Florida, and although its distinctive cultural attractions, such as Dixieland jazz and the annual Mardi Gras celebration, have become highly commercialized, the city still retains a distinctive sense of "otherness" in the broader context of regional and even national culture. New Orleans is a city of Catholic rather than Protestant origins and one in which African Americans played a far more visible role in shaping an urban culture than elsewhere in a South that was predominantly rural and in which Africanisms had to be cultivated in secret for fear of suppression and reprisal. The devastation caused by Hurricane Katrina in 2005 has added yet another layer to the city's mystique of doom and decadence, developed in recent years by vampire-obsessed writer Anne Rice.

Although the Catholic presence is a major, even a dominant, part of the religious landscape of many American cities, especially in the Northeast, that church's role as a relative latecomer worked against its material centrality as Boston, New York, and Philadelphia developed their early and distinctive senses of place. In New Orleans, the dominance of the Cathedral of St. Louis, which serves as a backdrop for Mills's statue of Jackson, provides an important visual clue that this was not the case here. That it represents the Roman Catholicism that was the established faith of the two colonial powers who dominated its early existence is itself significant, but the story does not end here. The very fabric of the cathedral, like the various names that have graced the square on which it fronts, has a multilayered history that reveals something of the city's social evolution. Earlier churches had been built on the site by the French in 1721 and 1727. When the 1727 church burned in 1788, a local Spanish magnate and government official, Don Andrés Almonester y Roxas, financed what would become the basis for the present cathedral, designed by Don Gilberto Guillemard—a name exhibiting both French and Spanish origins—in a neoclassical style reflecting Spanish practice.

The cathedral was remodeled in 1820 by Benjamin Henry Latrobe, the Protestant architect of the first Catholic cathedral in the United States in Baltimore, and then again in 1851 by J. N. B. de Pouilly, who substituted hexagonal spires for Latrobe's cupolas. The result is a pleasing but oddly hybrid structure that clearly "reads" as a Catholic cathedral but is not easily described with the standard vocabulary of architectural stylistic morphology. ("Romantic Classic revival" was one attempt.) In any case, the St. Louis Cathedral provides striking visual evidence of a blending of national traditions and period fashions that might serve as a metaphor for the culture of the city more broadly. It is flanked, significantly, by the Cabildo (1795–1799), which was the seat of Spanish administration, and the Presbytère (1795, 1847), whose name is French for a house for clergy—yet another illustration of the piling on of layers of cultural apparatus.[1]

The Roman Catholic Church has historically built not only houses of worship but also a variety of other institutions for carrying out a program of cradle-to-grave care for its membership. The Ursuline convent in the French Quarter is the oldest of such facilities in the city, and it is the only building surviving from the French period. Dating from 1745, it reflects the classicism of French provincial design of the era and has been used for a variety of ecclesiastical

---

1. New Orleans Chapter, American Institute of Architects (AIA), *A Guide to New Orleans Architecture* (New Orleans: AIA, 1974), 18–120; Kenneth Severens, *Southern Architecture* (New York: E. P. Dutton, 1981), 86–89; R. Warren Robison, *Louisiana Church Architecture: 350 Years of Distinctive American Buildings* (Lafayette, La.: Center for Louisiana Studies, University of Southwestern Louisiana, 1984), 2–3, 16–18.

purposes over the years.[2] Even more distinctive is the system of cemeteries that the extremely high water level under the city necessitates. Built aboveground, they are better described as necropolises—"cities of the dead"—than as burial grounds, since earth is in scant supply. In the 1840s, St. Louis Number One, the oldest of these cemeteries, became the object of an aesthetic upgrading, and its tombs were rebuilt in a uniform neoclassical style—some by the same de Pouilly who remodeled the cathedral.[3]

Although French and Spanish influences were formative during the city's colonial era, subsequent immigration of a variety of groups has paralleled to some degree the sort of urban demographic development exhibited in many other American cities. This can be seen in the proliferation of ethnic Catholic churches as Irish, Germans, Italians, and others arrived during the nineteenth century, as well as in others designated for African American congregations. (German-born Archbishop Joseph F. Rummel ordered the desegregation of archdiocesan institutions in the early 1960s.) In some cases, architecture reflected ethnicity. St. Mary Assumption Church (1858–1860) incorporates German Baroque motifs into a structure erected for parishioners primarily of that origin. Other Catholic churches simply reflect styles fashionable in the period in which they were built. Although Catholic churches not surprisingly dominate the religious cityscape, other religious structures can be easily found as well, ranging from the predictably Gothic Christ Church Episcopal Cathedral (1886) to the Byzantine-inspired Touro Synagogue of 1909.[4]

Although Catholic, mainline Protestant, and Jewish houses of worship are the most visible and architecturally conspicuous manifestation of the city's "churchscape"—as they are in most American cities—many of New Orleans's historically substantial African American population worship in hundreds of less-conspicuous buildings. These are (or were, given the as-yet-unknown ultimate impact of Hurricane Katrina) sited on less-traveled streets and seldom designed by professional architects. They often originated as the homes of white congregations or as "storefronts" built for

2. Jeremy duQuesnay Adams, "New Orleans," in Mary Kupiec Cayton and Peter W. Williams, eds., *Encyclopedia of American Cultural and Intellectual History* (New York: Scribner's, 2001), 2:629–39, 635; AIA, *Guide*, 24–25.

3. Adams, "New Orleans," 636.

4. Robert W. Heck (text) and Otis B. Wheeler (photographs), *Religious Architecture in Louisiana* (Baton Rouge: Louisiana State University Press, 1995), 93, 103, 104.

commercial rather than religious purposes and were subsequently adapted for reasons of convenience and economy.

Distinctive to New Orleans are the city's "spiritual" churches— African American congregations with varying origins and rituals but collectively constituting a loose but distinctive movement dating to the twentieth century. These churches in varying ways combine aspects of Roman Catholic liturgical apparatus, such as statues of saints, with "sanctified" (Holiness-Pentecostal) practices such as speaking in tongues, prophecy, and faith healing during worship. Behind these practices are murky but plausible linkages with both the Spiritualist movement of the later nineteenth century, involving contact by the living with spirits of the departed, and Voodoo (Vodun or Voudou), a movement of primarily Haitian origin involving a series of correspondences between Roman Catholic saints and traditional African deities. The physical setting of these churches in New Orleans is evoked by the two anthropologists who have conducted a major study of the movement:

> [M]ost Spiritual churches are rather unimpressive from the outside. Some are even completely unrecognizable as churches and almost disappear into the fabric of the community. At times, churches are simply rooms in someone's house that have been set aside for the worship of God, or old stores that have been refashioned into temples and dedicated to the saints. Occasionally, they are found in some of the small, frame church buildings that dot the New Orleans landscape. In a few instances, they occupy larger, more substantial brick buildings, such as the Israelite Church. Regardless of the kind of structure, the exteriors usually have no significant architectural details. There is nothing to prepare the visitor for what awaits within—the elaborate altars, statues of the saints, images of Native American Indians, incense and ministers in colorful vestments.[5]

The French beyond New Orleans

Much of the rest of southern Louisiana was also settled by Catholics of French origin, but by a very different route and with different cultural consequences. The Cajuns who settled the bayou country

5. Charles F. Jacobs and Andrew J. Kaslow, *The Spiritual Churches of New Orleans: Origins, Beliefs, and Rituals of an African-American Religion* (Knoxville: University of Tennessee Press, 1991), 12.

received their name from a vernacular pronunciation of the French "Acadiens," who had settled in Nova Scotia and been expelled by the English, after that nation's acquisition of the territory from France, when they refused to conform to British cultural expectations in 1755–1757. Catholic church building here reached its most intense period during the first three decades of the twentieth century and was characterized by brick churches built on a grand scale in a variety of medieval-derived styles. These might be called "semivernacular" creations, designed by local clergy and laity and built with the help of imported architects and engineers.[6]

Although Catholics are not absent in northern Louisiana, for which Baton Rouge rather than New Orleans is the local metropolis, the religious and cultural complexion of this area is much closer to that of its neighboring states than are the atypically French-derived Cajun and Creole enclaves further south. (*Creole* is a word with a variety of meanings; in New Orleans it describes the distinctive local cultural mix embodied especially in the famed cuisine, which reflects a coming together of French, Spanish, African, and Native American influences.) In northern Louisiana, as in much of the American South, evangelical Protestantism is the religious norm and is expressed in a mixture of Baptist, Methodist, Holiness, and Pentecostal denominations and in independent congregations, both black and white.

As we move northward from Louisiana along the Mississippi River and further west, to the mountains that constituted the western boundaries of the Louisiana territory, we rapidly lose almost all but a few faint traces of the rich cultural gumbo that the port of New Orleans traditionally constituted. Reminders of Nouvelle France remain in several cities along the Mississippi River in Missouri, the names of which indicate an obvious French provenance. Two clusters arose: the first around present-day St. Louis, including Florissant, St. Charles, and Carondelet; the other about forty miles along the river to the south, including Ste. Genevieve, Missouri, and Kaskaskia and Prairie de Rocher, Illinois. A few religious buildings dating from the early nineteenth century still exist in these towns, including the Church of St. Ferdinand in Florissant, the Ste. Genevieve Church in the town of the same name, and the Sacred Heart Convent in St. Charles.[7]

6. Robison, *Louisiana Church Architecture,* 29, and passim.
7. Workers of the Writers' Program of the Works Projects Administration of the State

Foremost of these, of course, is St. Louis, founded in 1764 along the route explored a century earlier by the Jesuit Père Jacques Marquette, as a French trading post. A series of churches began in 1770 with the erection of what was little more than a log hut during the time of Spanish hegemony in the region. Six years later this was replaced with a slightly more substantial log structure, distinguished by a curved roofline that extended slightly beyond the building's sides, where the ends met a series of wooden posts. (Its prototype can probably be found in the vernacular French colonial housing of the era.)[8] Louis du Bourg, who became the bishop of Louisiana in 1815, moved the episcopal seat to St. Louis, and built the city's first cathedral, a vernacular brick structure with round-arched windows and a central tower, in 1820. His successor, Joseph Rosati, built the more monumental "Old Cathedral," which still endures as a basilica, in 1834. Built of limestone, it consists of a rectangular body with round-arched windows, a four-columned Doric portico, and a two-staged square tower with spire, similar to the somewhat later St. Peter in Chains Cathedral in Cincinnati.[9]

This handful of architectural survivals from the period of French Catholic colonization along the Mississippi is emblematic for understanding the subsequent pattern of religious building in the broader Louisiana territory. For practical purposes, the region was materially a tabula rasa, since the only lasting artifacts of the aboriginal peoples consisted of long-abandoned mounds such as those at Cahokia Mounds State Park near East St. Louis, Illinois.[10] Subsequent Euro-American settlement would bring with it a pattern of constructing religious (as well as most other) buildings in patterns that originated in Europe and were subsequently scaled down and adapted to frontier purposes. These could be "high-style" structures such as the St. Louis Cathedral or vernacular forms that will appear later in our survey. It would soon become most common for styles to originate not in Europe, as in the earliest generations of settlement, but rather

---

of Missouri, *Missouri: A Guide to the "Show Me" State* (New York: Duell, Sloan and Pearce, 1941), 266, 340; Marion Rawson Vuilleumier and Pierre DuPont Vuilleumier, *America's Religious Treasures* (New York: Harper and Row, 1976), 176.

8. Gregory M. Franzwa, *The Old Cathedral* (St. Louis: Archdiocese of St. Louis, 1965), 18, 20; Virginia McAlester and Lee McAlester, *A Field Guide to American Houses* (New York: Knopf, 1984), 120–23.

9. Franzwa, *Old Cathedral,* 31, 33, 40, 46; Workers of the Writers' Program, *Missouri,* 311.

10. Vuilleumier and Vuilleumier, *America's Religious Treasures,* 133.

in the East Coast centers of fashion that had in their own turn imported and adapted styles from London and other European cultural centers. New Orleans and the remainder of Louisiana would have little if any part to play in this process. Much of the history of the built environment beyond the narrow reach of French influence followed a similar pattern, in which early vernacular adaptations were successively replaced by provincial versions of high-style structures from Europe and the American East Coast.

Tradition and Adaptation on the Frontier

The frontier camp meeting, such as that which took place in Cane Ridge, Kentucky, in 1801, is one of the best examples of religious building—or, more broadly, use of available space—to arise directly from the circumstances of the frontier. Although this phenomenon was most intense in the early part of the century in areas east of the Mississippi, it also took place somewhat later in the Louisiana Purchase territory, sometimes in conjunction with that other uniquely Methodist phenomenon, the circuit rider. The camp meetings were originally nondenominational frontier "happenings," in which scattered settlers would come from considerable distances to camp out for several days to listen to extemporaneous preaching and participate in the at times frenzied "exercises" it provoked. As time passed and more routinized forms of religious life arose, the Methodists in particular institutionalized these camp meetings into fixed compounds, to which adherents would come for perhaps weeks at a time during the summer for a sustained stint of religion and recreation.[11]

The Methodist circuit rider was another example of the innovative genius of this popular new denomination, which in its American incarnation had divorced itself from the weight of Anglican institutionalism that had kept its founder John Wesley within the Church of England to the end of his life. The circuit rider required no manmade structures whatever to carry out the swift completion of his appointed rounds. Equipped only with horse and saddlebag, these

11. For background on the camp meeting, see Dickson D. Bruce Jr., *And They All Sang Hallelujah: Plain-Folk Camp-Meeting Religion, 1800–1845* (Knoxville: University of Tennessee Press, 1974); and Steven D. Colley, "Manna and the Manual: Sacramental and Instrumental Constructions of the Victorian Camp Meeting during the Mid-Nineteenth Century," *Religion and American Culture* 6, no. 2 (summer 1996): 131–60.

ardent young men preached—and slept—in the open air, gathering small audiences where they could and frequently dying early from exhaustion. In the twilight of his life, the legendary Peter Cartwright would lament, as elders are wont to do, that the newer generation of Methodists, now numerous and wealthy enough to build churches and engage settled, educated clergy, had "gone soft" and lost the heroic faith of their predecessors.

A description of the origins of organized religion at Lake Creek, near Smithton, Missouri—billed as "the oldest continuous Camp-meeting West of the Mississippi River"—is illustrative of the combination of Methodist form and ethnic matter that sometimes characterized trans-Mississippi settlement:

> Beginning in the 1830s and 1840s a steady stream of German immigrant settlers began to come to Pettis, Benton and Morgan counties in Missouri. . . .
>
> As early as the year 1839 some of the families felt a need for religious services. Both Methodists and Lutherans worshipped together for a while. A Methodist Lay Preacher by the name of Francis Walkenhorst helped organize the people together for worship. . . . The services were irregular and were held in homes. The fact that some organization had been done prior to the sending of the first missionary helps us understand why the Lake Creek Society was so quickly organized.
>
> The families of Cord Kahrs, Jacob Timken and Gerhard Ringen sent a petition to Dr. William Nast, leader of the German Methodist Movement, asking for a missionary to be sent to them. In the fall of 1843 Sebastian Barth was sent to organize the Osage Mission.
>
> A generally accepted method of organizing a society was to hold a campmeeting and gather new converts and supporters together. The first campmeeting at Lake Creek was held in the fall of 1843 and by the end of the year Barth had organized 15 preaching points. The fact that this was done so quickly lends credence to the advance lay preacher, Walkenhorst, laying the groundwork before him. It took three weeks for Barth to travel the circuit on horseback to all preaching points. They reached from Jefferson City to Lexington, Missouri.[12]

The subsequent history of this foundation involves the organization of the Lake Creek Methodist Episcopal Church following the first camp meeting in 1843. This congregation initially met in local homes

---

12. Lake Creek Campmeeting, "History of the Lake Creek Campmeeting," http://www.lccampmeeting.org/LCHistory.html (accessed November 12, 2007).

and then in a log cabin, followed by a log church in 1844. In 1883 a Prairie Gothic wooden church was built on a new site. In addition, a camp meeting ground with cabins was maintained at the old location, then rebuilt on a new site in 1891.[13]

The sequence of events in the early history of this trans-Mississippi Methodist congregation is illustrative of the dominant pattern of religious building in the region, namely, the adaptation of European and East Coast–derived building forms to the needs of the region. The log cabin—such as that now enshrined at Cane Ridge, Kentucky, as a historical site—was itself a European (German and Swedish) import.[14] The first Catholic chapel in Kansas was the log cabin of a fur company's agent, and sod churches were constructed on the plains of Nebraska where wood was in short supply.[15] These forms of folk design were short-lived by both necessity and intention and were only built to last until they could be replaced by more permanent facilities.

The earliest religious buildings that were designed to last beyond temporary use were usually adaptations of older patterns derived from eastern patterns that were themselves usually adaptations of European prototypes. In Missouri, for example, are two of the oldest examples of Presbyterian and Episcopal churches west of the Mississippi. For example, the Bonhomme or "Old Stone" Church that stands today in Chesterfield, Missouri, is cited variously as the oldest or second-oldest church of that denomination in the region.[16] This church replaced earlier log structures used for temporary worship and is clearly in the meetinghouse style that characterized worship in the Reformed tradition. It is an unornamented stone rectangle with a gently pitched roof, rectangular windows, and a small chimney stack. As such, it resembles a scaled-down version of similar structures in Pennsylvania rather than something novel.

The same general pattern of adaptation can be observed in St. John's Episcopal Church, built in Eolia, Missouri, in 1856 by Anglican migrants from Virginia and regarded as the oldest Episcopal

13. Lake Creek Campmeeting, "History of the Lake Creek Church," http://www.lccampmeeting.org/LCChurch.html (accessed November 12, 2007).

14. John DeVisser and Harold Kalman, *Pioneer Churches* (New York: Norton, 1976), 131.

15. Edward Robert De Zurko, *Early Kansas Churches* (Manhattan: Kansas State College, 1949), 10–12; DeVisser and Kalman, *Pioneer Churches,* 166.

16. DeVisser and Kalman, *Pioneer Churches,* 164; Bonhomme Presbyterian Church, "What Is Bonhomme's Old Stone Church?" http://www.bonpres.org/oldstonechurch/oscwhat.html (accessed November 12, 2007).

church west of the Mississippi. Although its general contours evoke the tradition of Anglican church building in colonial Virginia, its combination of disparate stylistic features, such as the Greek revival pediment and pointed-arch Gothic style windows, are more characteristic of the eclecticism of the frontier periphery than of a well-established architectural "pedigree."[17]

As members of eastern-based denominations and immigrants from Europe began to settle the prairies and plains during the latter half of the nineteenth century, a characteristic style of religious building began to emerge in the region that rapidly gained iconic status. This style is sometimes dubbed "Prairie Gothic" and is immortalized in the background of Grant Wood's widely parodied painting *American Gothic*. The basic form of such prairie churches consisted of a rectangular box about thirty by eighty feet at the base, with clapboard siding, a gable roof, and a small steeple, with a tower serving as an entry sometimes added to the facade.[18] Wood was the nearly universal medium of construction, generally painted white. (One exception is the prototype of the sentimental song "The Little Brown Church in the Vale," a Congregational church in Bradford, Iowa. According to local folklore, brown paint was cheaper than other colors.) Exterior style, always in highly simplified forms, reflected contemporary eastern modes, especially the Greek and Gothic revivals. A good example of bare-bones Greek revival can be found in the First Methodist Church in Taylors Falls, Minnesota, built in 1860.[19]

Although many of these prairie and mountain churches were built by local folk directed by clergy, who designed according to their memories of prototypes "back East," a "high church" version of the Prairie Gothic style was popularized by the Anglican architect Richard Upjohn, who was responsible for Manhattan's Trinity Church (1845) and countless other churches, mostly Episcopal, that were erected from that decade onward under the influence of the Cambridge Camden (Ecclesiological) Society in England. In addition to designing these "high-style" churches, mostly found in East Coast cities, the English-born architect published in 1852 his

17. DeVisser and Kalman, *Pioneer Churches*, 144, 164; Pike County Tourism, "Pike County, Missouri," http://www.pikecountytourism.com/history.htm (accessed November 12, 2007).

18. Ferenc Morton Szasz, *The Protestant Clergy in the Great Plains and the Mountain West, 1865–1915* (Albuquerque: University of New Mexico Press, 1988), 22–23.

19. DeVisser and Kalman, *Pioneer Churches*, 164, 166, 238–39.

Upjohn's Rural Architecture, which provided low-cost plans for the construction of small-scale churches in board-and-batten, a method of construction in which thin vertical boards overlapped broader ones.[20] These and other simplified wooden churches, which first became popular in upstate New York, spread westward and were adapted by the entire panoply of Christian traditions represented in the Canadian prairies, plains, and mountains as well as their American counterparts. More liturgical denominations such as the Roman Catholic and Russian Orthodox enhanced these wooden boxes on the exterior with features such as the iconic Russian onion dome and, on the inside, with altars and liturgical ornament far more extensive than the spare pulpits, tables, and benches found in a typical Congregational or Methodist church.[21]

Communitarian Societies

Although the communitarian impulse expressed itself most numerously in the quadrant of the nation north of the Mason-Dixon Line and east of the Mississippi, settlers from central Europe in the prairies and plains also set about, on a smaller scale, to establish communities based on religious—usually German Pietist—principles in contrast to the individualism of the mainstream of settlers in the region. The most significant and lasting of these were the Amana Colonies, seven small villages in the Iowa River valley that are maintained today through the combined motives of economic productivity, historical tourism, and the persistence of a number of descendants of the original colonists who, though following a modernized lifestyle, nevertheless maintain some of the community's traditions of worship.

The Amana colonies originated in the ferment of German Pietism in the early eighteenth century. What distinguished this particular sectarian impulse was the belief that prophecy on the Old Testament model continues in modern time through *Werkzeuge:* latter-day humans utilized by God as "instruments" for proclaiming his continuing message. After various vicissitudes, the movement, now based in Hesse and numbering some thousand adherents, was motivated

---

20. Ibid., 141–42; Everard M. Upjohn, *Richard Upjohn* (1939; reprint, New York: Da Capo, 1968), 117 ff.
21. DeVisser and Kalman, *Pioneer Churches,* 138–43.

by adverse political and economic conditions in Germany to emigrate to the United States, and in 1843 they founded a community near Buffalo, New York, named Ebenezer. Economic and social motives led to a move to Iowa in 1855, where the Community of True Inspiration, as the movement had hitherto been known, incorporated as the Amana Society. (*Amana* means "believe faithfully.")

The development of the built environment of the Amana Colonies nicely illustrates some of the construction principles that characterized American development more generally. The original Amana village followed medieval European patterns, with usage and topography determining the arrangement of buildings and streets. The subsequent villages—each named "Amana" with a spatial qualifier, such as "Middle Amana" and "South Amana"—followed the rectilinear scheme characteristic of nineteenth-century American town planning. In the same fashion as in medieval Europe (and perhaps also in early New England), these villages resembled to a degree the *Landschaft* paradigm described by John Stilgoe: a cluster of residential buildings with barns and other agricultural buildings at the periphery, surrounded by orchards, vineyards, and gardens.[22] Supplementing the traditional agricultural pursuits, however, the Amana colonies began to add modern industries, especially woolen and calico factories, which provided income for the purchase of goods from outside. The Amana lifestyle was communal: goods were owned and meals taken in common, while families occupied individual residences. Community-owned and -operated kitchens, bakeries, and other facilities provided food so that individuals could pursue a variety of tasks assigned by elders.

Worship followed the sectarian tradition: each community possessed a house of worship that resembled a house more than a church, and parts of such buildings were sometimes used as residence facilities. The Homestead Church, built in 1865 of local brick, is a long, one-story rectangular structure with a gently pitched roof lined with chimneys and dormer windows. Two narrower extensions on each end were originally used for living quarters. The central area was known as the *Saal* (hall) and has two sets of doors, one each for men and women, who were traditionally seated on opposite sides of a central aisle that connected the hall's longer sides. Plainness was their

22. John R. Stilgoe, *Common Landscape of America, 1580 to 1845* (New Haven: Yale University Press, 1982), 12 ff.

custom, and furnishings were restricted to simple pine benches and a table for the minimal apparatus needed for worship. Services in the traditional mode are still held today, led by members of the community living in the area but occupied in various "worldly" callings.

Another notable feature of the Amana landscape is its cemeteries, which are similar to those of other communitarian groups in their order and simplicity. Each is surrounded by a hedge of pine trees, a traditional symbol of eternal life. Graves were originally designated by wooden markers, which were later replaced with more durable ones of concrete. The markers face east, the supposed direction of the Second Coming of Jesus. Believers were buried in uniform fashion in order of death, with the remains of children, nonmembers, and suicides placed elsewhere. The emphasis, in death as well as life, was on simplicity and equality.

By the time of the Great Depression, the Amana communities were experiencing the pressures of modernization as well as economic stress, and in 1932 the religious arm of the community was separated from the business sector, which became a joint-stock company known as the Amana Society, Inc. This transformation, similar to that which occurred in the Oneida Community in upstate New York, is still referred to as "the Great Change" and was probably inevitable if the colonies were to survive in any recognizable form. As is also the case in Oneida, descendants of the original colonists continue to live in the area and participate not only in the commercial but also in the religious life of the continuing enterprise as well.

The Mormon Landscape

The saga of the Church of Jesus Christ of Latter-Day Saints (the LDS, also called the Mormons) began, as did much of American religious life in the earlier nineteenth century, in that cultural extension of New England known as the "Burnt-Over District" of upstate New York. Joseph Smith, the movement's prophet and original leader, was born in Vermont and raised in Palmyra, New York, where he claimed to discover a set of golden tablets revealed to him by an angel named Moroni. On these tablets were described the stories of a group of ancient Hebrews who crossed the ocean and settled in Central America. Jesus appeared to them as well as in the Old World, but they fell into factions and eventually either killed off one another or became assimilated into what became the ancestors of the Native peoples of North America. Smith received supernatural aid in translating these tablets into what he published as the Book of Mormon, the foundational scripture of the church that would take its unofficial name from its title.[23]

Smith and his early followers established their first settlement in Kirtland, Ohio, now a southern suburb of Cleveland. There they built their first temple for the performance of the complex rituals that had also been revealed to Smith. The Kirtland Temple, now maintained by a group long split from the "Utah Mormons" and today known as the Community of Christ, was basically a New England meetinghouse in overall shape that eclectically featured pointed-arch windows in the Gothic style, a vernacular blending that Smith may have observed on some churches in New York City.[24]

After hostile "gentile" neighbors forced Smith and his followers to flee Kirtland, Smith determined that the Garden of Eden had existed near Independence, Missouri—at a place Mormons call Adam-Ohndi-Ahman—and that a second temple should be built at this spot, where the Second Coming of Jesus was to take place as well. Hostility similar to that experienced at Kirtland led to a rapid abandonment of these plans. The place still enjoys a privileged position in Mormon history, however, and the Community of Christ—the name recently adopted by what was previously known as the Reorganized Church of Jesus Christ of Latter Day Saints—in 1994 dedicated a ziggurat-like temple as headquarters for their version of the Mormon faith.[25]

The next attempt at a Mormon community was launched in Nauvoo, Illinois, on the Mississippi. Nauvoo was laid out on an extensive grid, following the urban planning techniques of the day. In addition to substantial brick houses for the faithful, the city featured a structure known as Nauvoo House, which contained both Smith's residence and a hotel, and an elaborate temple, based on Sir James Gibbs's widely imitated Church of St.-Martin-in-the Fields in

---

23. A lengthier version of the following discussion of Mormon (LDS) architecture and landscape is found in Peter W. Williams, *Houses of God: Region, Religion, and Architecture in the United States* (Urbana: University of Illinois Press, 1997), 216–22.

24. Laurel B. Andrew, *The Early Temples of the Mormons* (Albany: State University of New York Press, 1978), 37–38, and passim.

25. Ibid., 8; Alma P. Burton, *Mormon Trail: Vermont to Utah*, rev. and enlarged ed. (Salt Lake City: Deseret Book, 1966), 57–60.

London with some Greek revival features. A new iconography of celestial symbols, influenced by the Freemasonry in which Smith was involved, helped give this structure a distinctively LDS identity. After Smith's assassination in 1844, the Nauvoo settlement was abandoned along with the temple, which was later burned by arsonists and the remains demolished. The temple was later rebuilt and dedicated in 2002 as a functioning LDS temple.[26]

Although the movement divided after Smith's death and various factions formed, including the Community of Christ based in Independence, Missouri, a large majority of the Mormons in Illinois chose to follow Smith's deputy, Brigham Young, on an epic trek to Salt Lake City, Utah, which has to this day remained the world headquarters for the LDS. The monumental temple built here between 1853 and 1892 evokes in its general contours the power and presence of a Gothic cathedral, but the symbolism derives not from medieval Christianity but from the distinctive LDS iconography introduced at Nauvoo. Subsequent temples erected at St. George, Manti, and Logan in Utah echo the Salt Lake temple in overall configuration and in the way in which they dominate the landscape, asserting Mormon hegemony in this territory initially named "Deseret."[27]

In addition to the building of temples as well as local houses for worship, a distinctive Mormon approach to shaping the regional landscape emerged in Utah and environs. Richard Francaviglia has cataloged in detail its features, which included, among other things, wide streets; roadside irrigation ditches; barns, granaries, and substantial brick houses within the town limits; distinctive fencing; and simple, Georgian-revival chapels. Thus the Mormon landscape that became characteristic of nineteenth-century Utah and the adjacent "Mormon corridor" combined monumental religious buildings incorporating elements of a variety of traditional and some not-so-traditional styles, with distinctive, though hardly unique, domestic and agricultural structures intentionally arranged and sited. This combination of iconographic and practical strategies was intended to convey the message that this was not the realm of characteristic American individualism but rather the culture of a particular religious

---

26. Andrew, *Early Temples,* 56 ff., 71–73, 82–83; Dolores Hayden, *Seven American Utopias: The Architecture of Communitarian Socialism, 1790–1975* (Cambridge, Mass.: MIT Press, 1976), 110 ff.

27. Andrew, *Early Temples,* 97 ff. and 158 ff.

community that had claimed a desert land that no one else had heretofore coveted, and that they alone had made to bloom.[28]

Cities on the Prairies and Plains

Although a few New World cities like Boston followed medieval practice in allowing roads to develop from patterns of use, the logic of the grid has dominated American urban planning from the time of William Penn's "green country town" and the orthogonal pattern imposed on development in Manhattan by the Commissioners' Plan of 1811. The same rectilinear logic prevailed in the platting of the Old Northwest territory, which soon became the states of Ohio, Michigan, Indiana, Illinois, and Wisconsin. The land here was laid out in six-mile-square townships, a pattern that would later be applied to the division of lands further west.[29]

As cities developed in the Louisiana Purchase territory, they, too, followed what had become the American tradition. Almost all cities followed the orthogonal grid mode, which lent itself readily to the needs of commercial development.[30] Although less confined by natural obstacles than in many eastern cities, those of the West expanded in familiar ways, with central business districts surrounded by vicinally differentiated residential neighborhoods and, eventually, suburbs. The location and design of houses of worship similarly followed that of eastern prototypes, though in some cases, such as that of Jewish synagogues and temples, the pattern more closely resembled that prevalent in southern cities, where Jews and other minorities were considerably scarcer than in the urban Northeast.

Briefly, downtown commercial areas in the larger cities were interspersed with churches—usually those of what are now known as the "mainline" Protestant denominations, as well as Roman Catholic churches and cathedrals. Since many of these cities grew up in the period between the Civil War and World War II, a period of intense urban development throughout the nation, many of the

28. Richard V. Francaviglia, *The Mormon Landscape: Existence, Creation, and Perception of a Unique Image of the American West* (New York: AMS Press, 1978), 25, 63, 67, 69, 81, 83, 89–90.

29. Stilgoe, *Common Landscape*, 99.

30. Witold Rybczynski, *City Life: Urban Expectations in a New World* (New York: Simon and Schuster, 1995), 44–46, 147.

religious structures that grew up with them reflect both the denominational configurations and architectural styles that were dominant in the period.

Denver is a midsized regional city (with a population of about 550,000 in 2000) that had its origins in the discovery of gold in the South Platte River in 1858. It has three adjacent central areas: the downtown itself, the Civic Center (which includes the state capitol—a domed neoclassical affair representative of the genre—and other governmental, civic, and cultural buildings), and the surrounding residential and commercial area known as Capitol Hill. These constitute the heart of the original city, and most of the city's oldest and largest religious sites lie in the Civic Center and Capitol Hill. On Capitol Hill are found the "First Baptist Church, a neo-colonial revival structure built in 1938"; the "Central Presbyterian Church, a red sandstone auditorium church in Romanesque revival style dating from 1892"; the "former Temple Emanuel (1899), a good example of the 'Jewish Victorian' love of Middle Eastern exotic decorative elements such as towers resembling minarets, copper domes in the Turkish mode, and 'arabesque' floral and geometric motifs"; the "St. John's Episcopal Cathedral (1911), a twin-towered English Gothic affair designed by the New York firm of Gorton, Tracy, and Swarthout"; and the "Roman Catholic Basilica of the Immaculate Conception, in the French Gothic mode, built from 1906 to 1912 of gray Indiana limestone. This monumental structure is the diocesan cathedral."[31]

Nearby, in the downtown area, are the "Trinity United Methodist Church (1888), an even more monumental example of the auditorium church style than its Presbyterian counterpart on higher ground with seating for 1200"; and the "Holy Ghost Catholic Church (1943), in the Lombardesque mode, which sold its parish plant to the developers of an adjoining commercial building in the 1980s to build a homeless shelter."[32]

Other religious buildings, most of them long gone, had been built in these areas during the early period of Denver's history but had their properties sold for commercial use as their congregations

31. Thomas J. Noel, *Buildings of Colorado* (New York: Oxford University Press, 1997), 78, 79, 81–82, 78.

32. Jeanne Halgren Kilde, *When Church Became Theatre* (New York: Oxford, 2002), 92–95; Noel, *Buildings of Colorado*, 54–55, 57.

drifted to the suburbs, where they built churches and temples in the period styles of the 1900s.

A similar story could be told of the history of the religious architecture and landscape of most cities in the former Louisiana territory for the period from roughly the Civil War to the present. Some once-popular but now-antiquated forms such as the downtown auditorium church have sometimes survived longer in the West than in the region east of the Mississippi, in part, perhaps, because cities tended to stay smaller and because pressures for land reuse were less intense. The basic forms of design, siting, and scale of these city's "churchscapes," however, demonstrate little that is original or regionally distinctive. Overall, they are the continuation of patterns established in the East and adapted in not-too-startling ways to the specific conditions of western urban development.

Native American Building: Adaptation and Innovation

The topic of the built religious environment of the aboriginal peoples of the Louisiana Territory might well have come first in this series of architectural vignettes but, when placed at the end, it emphasizes the complicated character of the Native American experience in the region. Long prior to the arrival of Europeans, Native peoples had come and gone over the Great Plains, but the introduction of horses by the Spanish set off a new era of Native life characterized by increased mobility and more effective utilization of the area's resources, especially in hunting the bison.[33] This era of semi-nomadic settlement would come to an end in the 1880s, when the Plains peoples would be forced to adopt Euro-American patterns of settlement and construction.

The three most common building forms of the Plains Indians were the tepee and the grass house, although earth lodges were still in use to some extent into the nineteenth century among the Mandan in the Dakotas.[34] These archetypal structures could be used for a variety of purposes, from residence to sacred ceremonial.

33. Peter Nabokov and Robert Easton, *Native American Architecture* (New York: Oxford University Press, 1989), 123. This and subsequent references are from chapter 3, "Earth Lodge, Grass House, and Tipi," which deals with the building patterns of the Plains Indians.
34. Ibid., 127–28, 135.

Whatever the purpose, however, they were usually made not with a purely utilitarian intent, but rather according to a prototype revealed either primordially to the group or in individual vision quests to contemporaries. Shelter, like other aspects of life, was part of a cosmological routine in which all aspects of individual and communal existence were sacralized.

The most prevalent shelter type on the Plains was the tepee, the semiconical shape of which has become iconic in American popular culture as symbolic of Native Americans. Typically, sacred medicine bundles would be hung on tripods within or tied onto the exterior of the skins that formed the tepee's covering. When the Cheyenne assembled as a nation or for tribal councils, special painted tepees were erected that would house sacred objects for ritual use. Similarly, the seven sacred pipes of the Oglala Sioux were kept in special tepees at sites designated by tradition.[35]

In addition to tepees designated for communal ritual use, individual Cheyenne who had received visions in fast-induced initiatory trances replicated scenes from these spirit journeys onto the sides of their individual tepees. These tepees thus would become part of what have been called "sacred kits," together with the vision-quest narratives themselves and the sacred songs and objects associated with the vision. Such tepees and their accompanying kits could be passed along over the generations, together with the prestige and spiritual power that adhered to them.[36]

Another important example of a Plains sacred structure was a sort of open-air tepee built by the Cheyenne as lodges for their Sun Dance, a ceremony that for a time was outlawed by the federal government because of the self-mutilation that was part of this ritual. Such a lodge was demarcated by a circular fence that ranged from forty to fifty feet in diameter. At its center was a pole made from a specially cut tree—usually a cottonwood—from the apex of which radiated long rafters. The pole was an *axis mundi*, a cosmic center that, as was often the case among the mobile Plains peoples, was not associated with a fixed object, such as a mountain, but rather was re-created ritually as the occasion arose. (The Oglala Sioux Black Elk is said to have observed that "anywhere is the center of the world"— meaning, presumably, that any place can be ritually transformed

---

35. Ibid., 158, 168.
36. Ibid., 158.

into such a center.)[37] A "thunderbird nest," fashioned from willow branches or buffalo grass, was placed on the top of the pole, confirming its symbolic character. In the Arapaho variant on this structure, an altar with ceremonial apparatus was placed at its center.[38]

Still other types of ceremonial building are employed today by Plains people in rituals that have sometimes originated or been adapted in response to the particular exigencies of their situation. The tepee, for example, is utilized by the Native American Church, the very loosely organized set of practitioners of an accommodationist ritual that combines to varying degrees traditional rites involving peyote-induced visions with Christian symbolism and interpretation. The sweat lodge, which resembles a sort of sacred sauna in its shape and use, is another widely dispersed structure that is still in frequent use in various places.[39]

The subjugation of the Plains peoples by the American government late in the nineteenth century brought about the end of traditional patterns of life and residence. In 1887 they were forced to accept 160-acre individual allotments on which Anglo-style log cabins or frame houses were to replace the traditional tepee, and churches and schools on the Euro-American pattern were added to promote assimilation.[40] These impositions continue to shape contemporary patterns of residence, with the mobile home as a frequent alternative.

Sweat lodges still exist, often located in the backyards of private homes and constructed from brightly colored plastic. Christian churches of various denominations follow Euro-American building patterns, although traditional Native symbolism is sometimes introduced as well, especially among Catholics. Powwows—tribal and intertribal homecomings—are a new vehicle for reasserting communal solidarity, bringing those living far away back to the reservation for a few days of dancing and celebration. The facilities in which these are conducted, however, resemble rodeo or state fairgrounds and often consist of a central oval area for dancing and ceremonies with bleacher seating and concession stands along the periphery. Ritual gift exchanges, such as those ending a period of mourning,

37. John G. Neihardt, *Black Elk Speaks: Being the Life Story of a Holy Man of the Oglala Sioux* (1932; reprint, New York: Pocket Books, 1975), 36.
38. Nabokov and Easton, *Native American Architecture*, 168, 169, 171.
39. Ibid., 171.
40. Ibid., 142.

combine traditional forms with new contents: the gifts might have been purchased at the nearest Wal-Mart rather than being hand-crafted. Likewise, the food sold at concession stands consists of items such as buffalo burgers and fry bread, both the result of enforced exposure to Euro-American foodways. The result is a *tertium quid:* neither wholly traditional nor Euro-American, but a blending of the two into new patterns indicative of the complex character of contemporary Native American life.[41]

Some Concluding Thoughts

Reevaluating the course of American religious life from the vantage point of the Louisiana Purchase can take two directions. First, if we look at New Orleans itself, we do find some interesting perspectives in a city at once American, Southern, and Caribbean. Its religious history is unique in the United States, at least for the decades preceding the Civil War; the most fruitful comparisons might be with Miami, New York, or Los Angeles as sites of dramatic multiethnic contact in the twentieth and twenty-first centuries. Since New Orleans has never had much of a geographical periphery, though, lines of approach involving the dissemination of cultural influence do not lead very far; even the Cajun/Acadian territory of southern Louisiana is not culturally continuous with New Orleans itself.

From the point of view of the religious built environment, New Orleans is best seen as part of a string of colonial French settlements ranging up to Detroit. Except for a few churches and other religious buildings dating from the late eighteenth or early nineteenth centuries, little of interest remains. The French impact on the culture of the United States has never been extensive—the Protestant Huguenots as well as the Catholic French Canadians have all proven adept at adaptation, and outside of Quebec, they have never shown a great deal of interest in or aptitude for cultural survival (or, as the Quebecois themselves might say, *survivance*).

The pattern of religious building in the remainder of the Louisiana Territory—in the vast majority of which no French influence was ever exerted—the pattern was almost universally one of

---

41. Examples drawn from the author's visit to a Winnebago powwow and the neighboring Omaha reservation in northeastern Nebraska during the late 1990s.

adaptation of building modes that originated elsewhere, generally in
Europe or along the eastern seaboard of North America. This is not
to say that there are no characteristic religious landscapes in this
area, especially in its extensive rural reaches. The "Prairie Gothic"
phenomenon still provides a stunning punctuation of the oceanic
reaches of wheat or corn on the plains, and it has attained iconic status in Dorothea Lange's 1941 photograph of three such churches,
each of a different denomination, within a very short distance of one
another in South Dakota. Similarly, the Mormon built environment
in Utah and contiguous areas is certainly distinctive, both in its
monumental temples and the everyday agricultural landscape that
arose from the movement's genius with irrigation. In both cases,
however, the building prototypes originated much further eastward
and took on new adaptive form in the proverbial wide open spaces
of the prairies and plains. If Frederick Jackson Turner and William
Warren Sweet were correct in their argument that the frontier held
the key to understanding American society and culture, the record of
the religious built environment of the American West would not
have given them much comfort.

Conflicting Destinies
Religion, Sex, and Violence in the Louisiana Purchase

AMANDA PORTERFIELD

I N THE EARLY WINTER OF 1816, A GROUP OF SKIDI PAWNEE KIDNAPPED an Ideo Comanche "girl" as part of a ceremonial plan to make her into Evening Star, the celestial deity associated with the earth's soil, and the winds, clouds, and storms. The Pawnee relied on the stars and explained things in terms of their activities and demands. As a Skidi man later explained, the sacrifice of a captive girl was an obligatory rite performed to appease Morning Star, the celestial war god who conquered Evening Star after other male gods tried and failed. Life and light came into the world because he and his partner the Sun succeeded in penetrating Evening Star's realm of darkness. The sexual union between Morning and Evening stars also produced the first human being—a girl. To produce vitality anew, and to ensure bountiful crops and victory in hunting, horse raiding, and warfare, Morning Star had to be placated with the sacrifice of a new girl. At the culminating moment in an elaborate ceremonial process during the time of spring planting, the Skidi tied the captive girl to a scaffold in preparation for dismemberment.[1]

As the Skidi informant recalled, the warrior leading the kidnapping raid learned of his destiny as the agent of Morning Star in a

---

1. Gene Weltfish, *The Lost Universe: Pawnee Life and Culture* (Lincoln: University of Nebraska Press, 1965), 80–81, 106. Weltfish's principal informant from 1928 to 1936 was Mark Evarts, who had grown up on the Pawnee reservation in Nebraska between 1861 and 1875, when the U.S. government closed that reservation and established a new Pawnee reservation in Oklahoma. For Weltfish's account of her methodology and informant, see ix–xiii.

dream. The raiders knew that the girl's kinsmen would take revenge later, and the girl knew her fate was sealed. Her kinsmen would take their time to retaliate, but not to save her, and the kidnappers would get away without much of a fight.[2] In other words, this was a world governed by strict rules of reciprocity, and a pervasive sense that human destiny proceeded in harmony with the stars.

For participants, the sacrifice would certainly have driven home a point about male dominance and emphasized men's control over women. But other aspects of the ritual reflected an ongoing contest between women and men and acknowledged women's essential although subordinate role in Pawnee culture. According to early-twentieth-century accounts of the creation story, Morning Star's conquest of Evening Star was not easy, and great forces were hers to command—"wolf in the southeast, who had the power of the clouds; wildcat in the southwest, with power of the winds; mountain lion in the northwest, with lightning power; and bear in the northeast, with his power of thunder." Sharp teeth encircled her vagina, "like the mouth of a rattlesnake with teeth around." If the attribution of terrible power to Evening Star rationalized violence against women, it also attested to female strength. Of course, men controlled the ceremonies, but female visionaries played a part, and coinciding rites instructed girls in their powers and responsibilities alongside rites that prepared boys for manhood.[3] The whole ceremonial complex was a cooperative process celebrating sexual union and village solidarity. The sacrificial victim was an *enemy* girl, not anyone from the village. In 1816, she was an Ideo Comanche. In 1838, the year of the last recorded sacrifice, she was Sioux, a member of the Pawnee's most hated enemy group, whose warriors invaded Pawnee territory and repeatedly laid in wait in the cornfields to scalp Pawnee women.

The Pawnee farmed along the Platte and Loup rivers in what is now Nebraska. During buffalo hunts, whole villages decamped for months at a time, and raiding parties ventured as far south as Mexico to steal horses. The Skidi rode south more often than the other Pawnee groups and maintained stronger ties with Caddoan-speaking groups in the Southwest, where the Pawnee had originated centuries before. The Skidi represented an older way of life typical, in important respects, of village life on the plains before the

---

2. Ibid., 106–9.
3. Ibid., 79–85, 95–100, quotations from 82.

nineteenth century. Because their village was the farthest from the Missouri and its increasing traffic, the Skidi knew less about Americans, French, and Canadians than other Pawnee people. After vicious wars against them in the late eighteenth century, the other Pawnee groups treated the Skidi as primitive, distant, and hostile relations. The Skidi, for their part, took pride in their own cultural integrity, disciplined bravery, and general superiority.[4]

The Pawnee were old-timers in the Plains Indian economy of rivalry and exchange, which expanded with the infusion of horses, European goods, and new people and then narrowed and collapsed in the drive for buffalo and overwhelming tides of predators, refugees, adventurers, salesmen, soldiers, emigrants, and missionaries who descended on the plains. Other Indians credited the Pawnee with originating the calumet, the long pipe passed around in a circle as a way of establishing oases of peace between rival groups for purposes of trade, talk, and religious performance. This custom had been part of Plains Indian culture since at least the early seventeenth century, when the French explorer Marquette carried a calumet up the Missouri as a "safe conduct pass through alien territory."[5]

Two centuries later, a constellation of forces jeopardized the Pawnee way of life. Epidemics of smallpox generated by fur traders along the Missouri during the eighteenth century had drastically diminished the Pawnee population. In 1805, shortly after the United States acquired the vast territory of Louisiana, both American and Spanish officials took sudden interest in the Pawnee as part of their grander schemes against one another. Meanwhile, the destructiveness of revenge warfare escalated as Indians from east of the Mississippi moved in and worked out their destinies, competing for the hunting territories and buffalo herds on which the Pawnee depended.[6]

Gruesome as the Skidi rite of girl sacrifice must have been, the pain and blood the Sioux exacted from the Pawnee were greater. And as brutal and unrelenting as the Sioux were in their forays against the Pawnee, the destruction brought upon the Pawnee by Americans was exponentially more devastating. The Americans undermined the structural dynamics of Pawnee culture, much as they undermined the cultures of other Native peoples who hunted, farmed, and raised

---

4. George E. Hyde, *The Pawnee Indians* (Norman: University of Oklahoma Press, 1974), 123–25, 154, 168–69.

5. Ibid., 8–9, 31, quotation from 175.

6. Ibid., 149–56, 165–73.

horses and dogs on the plains. And they did so with a sense of destiny no less forceful than the Pawnee sense that their destiny lay with the stars. For all their differences with one another, Americans believed that their own activity as explorers, settlers, missionaries, and entrepreneurs was part of history's providential course and that, like it or not, traditional Indian lifeways were destined for extinction. While slaveholders vied with abolitionists, missionaries vied with Indian-haters, Protestants vied with Catholics (as well as with each other), and Mormons vied against almost everyone, they all carried ideas about destiny. Compounded together, these ideas, although diverse and conflicting in many of their aspects, added up to a sense of destiny more enormous and pervasive than any particular point of view. In this essay, I show how particular notions of destiny current in the Louisiana Purchase conflicted with one another but also combined in a process that created new expectations about American hegemony. The doom almost universally assigned to Indians was a crucial and telling part of this process. I also want to argue that sex and gender, especially in their relation to violence, figured importantly in the process of making America out of Louisiana, and that attention to the interplay of violence, sex, and gender is essential to understanding the construction of American power.

The Louisiana Purchase raised to a massive, continental scale the conflicting destinies of various groups.[7] As conflicts with and among Native groups multiplied and coincided with escalating tension over race and slavery, the Louisiana Purchase opened up an enormous territory for playing out the dreams and ambitions of people back in the states. With little overarching government, and few constraints on violence, the Louisiana Purchase was a vast, bloody ground where American identity as a singular phenomenon took shape, an identity ultimately more powerful than the sectional divide between North and South. By focusing on forces of sex, gender, and violence that intersected in powerful ways, I hope to reconstruct the gathering sense of destiny that created America out of what, prior to 1803, was foreign land.

7. Jon Kukla makes a similar point in the concluding pages of *A Wilderness So Immense: The Louisiana Purchase and the Destiny of America* (New York: Alfred A. Knopf, 2003), 289–340. In addition to discussing how the expansion of U.S. territory intensified sectional conflict already existing in the states, Kukla shows how the ratification of the Louisiana Purchase Treaty by the U.S. Congress required an expansive understanding of national sovereignty that prompted use of the term *empire* to describe U.S. territorial holdings.

Even Americans sympathetic to Indians were convinced of the inevitable overtaking of the American continent by people like themselves. The ethnographer Lewis Henry Morgan, for example, took keen interest in the kinship structures of Indian societies, and in visits to numerous Indian tribes in Kansas and Nebraska in 1859, he came to admire Indian leaders. But the best he could hope for these people was rapid assimilation to American culture, and that, he believed, would be possible only for a select few. Observing the progress in adopting American forms of agriculture made by some of the Delaware people in Kansas, he predicted that "their children will intermarry respectably with our white people, and thus the children will become respectable and, if educated, in the second and third generations will become beautiful and attractive. This is to be the end," he concluded, "of the Indian absorption of a small portion, which will improve and toughen our race, and the residue run out or forced into the regions of the mountains."[8]

Morgan was a loving husband and father who practiced law in Rochester and built a tomb there for his family. If it occurred to him that any relationship existed between the sweet insularity of his Victorian family life and the overrunning of Indian tribes on the Great Plains, he never wrote about it. His scientific insight into Native kinship structures was pathbreaking. At the same time, he held essentially mythical assumptions about American destiny. And like everyone else invested in the noblest aspects of American culture, Morgan failed to see that his culture enabled the deregulation of violence outside the charmed circles of nuclear family life. Commitment to the narrowly focused kinship structure supporting the stability and tranquility of nuclear family life gave relatively free rein to violence in other sectors of life.

While family ties constructed society for both middle-class Americans and Plains Indian villagers, Plains Indian concepts of family were thicker and more intertwined. The Pawnee's reenactment of creation in their springtime ceremonies is one example of the kind of collective ritual practice that celebrated the interlocking kinship ties holding Plains Indian village societies together. Thus the Skidi chiefs representing particular lineages kept sacred bundles, one representing Morning Star, another Evening Star, and others representing

---

8. Lewis Henry Morgan, *The Indian Journals, 1859–62*, ed. Leslie A. White (Ann Arbor: University of Michigan Press, 1959), quotation from 55.

ten more celestial deities. Priests renewed the powers of the twelve lineages and their sacred bundles each spring, and the spring ceremonies that ensued recalled and celebrated the cosmic aspects of these lineages and their interactions.[9]

Kinship arrangements varied from one tribe to another and also changed in response to environmental factors. As the buffalo economy became paramount, female lineages associated with agriculture weakened, and male lineages associated with hunting and warfare became more dominant. In the late eighteenth and early nineteenth centuries, rites of male aggression increasingly dominated religious life on the plains as horses, guns, and European trade made buffalo hunting and revenge warfare all consuming, and as the stresses induced by epidemic disease, increased warfare, and declining populations of wild animals made ritual violence seem insufficient. The status of women declined with the decline of traditional farming, which women typically controlled, and women worked harder lugging baggage around as families traveled increasing distances in search of buffalo. As women lost control over a means of economic production, they became viewed more as property and were more subject to abuse. In his observations of the Blackfeet in 1833, the Belgian Prince Maximilian estimated that for every twelve tents, there were seven or eight women whose noses had been cut off as punishment for adultery.[10] At the beginning of his trip in 1859, Morgan recorded his horror at seeing a Delaware girl with sores all over her face from syphilis. Later he noted, with more dispassion, that Pawnee women were notorious for being prostitutes.[11]

It may be obvious to us now that the degradation of women was part of a larger process of social stress and demoralization in Native cultures resulting from European and American trade, settlement, and militarism. But while many Americans back east expressed outrage at the treatment of women in Native cultures, most of them believed that brutality toward women was typical of Indian life. Few comprehended the extent to which their own culture contributed to the brutality they decried.

9. Weltfish, *Lost Universe*, 80.

10. Maximilian, Prince of Wied-Neuwied, *Travels in the Interior of North America*, vols. 22–25, *Early Western Travels, 1748–1846*, ed. R. G. Thwaites (reprint, New York: AMS Press, 1966), 23:110; Alan M. Klein, "Plains Economic Analysis: The Marxist Complement," in *Anthropology on the Great Plains*, ed. W. Raymond Wood and Margot Liberty (Lincoln: University of Nebraska Press, 1980), 129–40, esp. 134.

11. Morgan, *Indian Journals*, 28, 66.

For example, reaction to the Pawnee girl sacrifice revealed eagerness to interpret Indian life in American terms, along with incomprehension of the religious meaning of the rite and its importance for communal solidarity. Newspapers incorporated descriptions of the ritual in a sensational story about the young warrior who made a successful attempt, in the spring of 1817, to save the Ideo girl that the Skidi priests were preparing to sacrifice. One of the older leaders, Knife Chief, had met with the Indian superintendent William Clark in St. Louis, who made it clear that the people of the United States could not abide human sacrifice and demanded an end to the practice. Knife Chief got the message and urged the priests not to kill the Ideo girl. But the priests and many of the Skidi people feared that canceling the sacrifice would jeopardize their crops, as well as their success in hunting and war, and went ahead with the ceremony. With the girl bound to the scaffold, Knife Chief's son Pitalesharo stepped out from the crowd and announced that he had come to take her away or die trying. He took the girl and rode south with her for several days, in the direction of her people, and left her with a supply of food. When that story circulated in the East, romantically inclined Americans depicted Pitalesharo as a heroic savior. Championed especially by young ladies, he journeyed to Washington to receive a large silver medal from a group of students representing Miss White's Select Female Seminary. The medal bore an inscription, "To the bravest of the brave," along with etchings depicting the rescue. At the ceremony in Washington, Pitalesharo thanked the girls for calling him brave, but he said he had not thought he was brave when he freed the Ideo girl. From a Pawnee perspective, a more traditional form of courage involved sacrifice in behalf of the community.[12]

The thrilled reception greeting Pitalesharo in Washington says as much about the relationship between sex and violence in American culture as it does about the difficulties the Pawnee faced in maintaining their economic and religious life. From the sentimental perspective, Pitalesharo's freeing of the captive girl was a gallant act signifying respect for female virtue. Sentimental codes of feeling revolved around the protection of female sexual purity and thus required some threat of sexual violence, or at least the suggestion of

---

12. Hyde, *Pawnee Indians,* 160–63; Weltfish, *Lost Universe,* 115–16. Weltfish describes Pawnee courage in a similar way, emphasizing the courageous restraint of anger involved in endurance of humiliation; see Weltfish, *Lost Universe,* 13–14.

it, against which that purity could be defined and defended. Perceptions of Indian men were incorporated in that context, partly as wild men that helpless females had to be rescued from, and partly as untutored noblemen with a natural instinct for moral feeling and gallantry.[13] Heroes like Pitalesharo appeared to bridge Native and Christian cultures, standing up against the savage elements of Native culture and its brutality toward women, while at the same time manifesting a prelapsarian goodness that involved adulation of female beauty and virtue. In this sentimental variant of Christian mythology, untamed aggression and sexual violence epitomized sin. Regulation of male aggression pleasing to and protective of women epitomized redemption.

Sentimental notions of gentility hid a good deal of injustice and violence and encouraged the false impression that the violent behavior so obvious in the Louisiana Purchase was essentially at odds with American life. In other words, the exaltation of female purity may have done as much to rationalize male aggression as to hold it in check. In the South especially, a romantic culture of honor, gallantry, and devotion to female purity worked as a cover for slavery, obscuring its dehumanization and brutality from those who benefited from it economically. Romantic images of Indians as noble savages

13. For more on sentimental culture in nineteenth-century America, see Eva Cherniavsky, *That Pale Mother Rising: Sentimental Discourses and the Imitation of Motherhood in Nineteenth-Century America* (Bloomington: Indiana University Press, 1995); Ann Douglas, *The Feminization of American Culture* (New York: Avon Books, 1978); and Amanda Porterfield, "The Domestication of Theology" and "Witchcraft and Sexuality in Literature," in *Feminine Spirituality in America: From Sarah Edwards to Martha Graham* (Philadelphia: Temple University, 1980), 51–98. The sentimental reconstruction of rescue can also be seen in Indian-captivity stories. Beginning in seventeenth-century New England, such accounts made popular reading. In relating the imprisonment and suffering at the hands of savages, these stories carried lessons about what captives learned about themselves and their relationships to God. For example, a popular narrative by Mary Rowlandson, who had been captured and freed in the 1670s, likened her plight to the suffering of Israel and represented her captivity as a chastisement from God designed to awaken Rowlandson to her sinfulness, need for repentance, and dependence on God. Varying perspectives on womanhood were expressed in this popular story form. By the early nineteenth century, fictional captivity narratives emerged expressing themes about romance and female delicacy and sexual vulnerability. See Kathryn Zabelle Derounian-Stodola, ed., *Women's Captivity Narratives* (New York: Penguin Books, 1998); Kathryn Zabelle Derounian-Stodola, "The Indian Captivity Narratives of Mary Rowlandson and Olive Outman: Case Studies in the Continuity, Evolution, and Exploitation of Literary Discourse," *Studies in the Literary Imagination* 27 (1994): 33–46; and Michelle Burnham, *Captivity and Sentiment: Cultural Exchange in American Literature, 1682–1861* (Hanover, N.H.: University Press of New England, 1997).

worked similarly to obscure the role that Americans played in the destruction of Indian people and lifeways.

Some of the violence in nineteenth-century America involved loss of control, on the part of both men and women, Indian and American, over older, more traditional means of holding communities together, managing reciprocity and revenge, and keeping aggression in check.[14] But the exaltation of female virtue in sentimental culture obscured awareness of that common thread. On the surface, nothing seemed more different than the contrast between the degradation of Indian women and the sentimental adulation of white women. And deeper down, the differences were real. In many Indian societies, women's strength and authority were in decline. By contrast, sentimental women enjoyed real advantages of health and wealth. However heartfelt their deference to male dominance, sentimental women were also enjoying new opportunities for education and self-expression and new importance as producers of culture.

The sexual arrangements associated with sentimental culture were not entirely dissimilar to those worked out in Pawnee ceremonies. In both cases, females embraced submission to males in exchange for protection and respect. But overlaying this similarity, Americans dominated Indians, forcing their submission and denying them opportunities for revenge. Americans forced Indians into subordination and often insisted that Indian men take up the humiliating work of farming, an occupation traditionally assigned, in many tribes, to women. If Indian men were torn between two destinies, Indian women lost much of their ability to command protection, even as Americans used the plight of Indian women as a foil to demarcate their own superiority.

Missionary outreach to Indians complicated these intercultural dynamics. Missionary women often looked down on sentimental culture and tended to think of sentimental women and their pursuits as frivolous.[15] But these differences may only have compounded the powerful sense of American destiny that gripped them both and contributed to the American overtaking of the continent. A terrible sense of providential doom surrounded nineteenth-

---

14. For a similar argument, see Richard Slotkin, *Regeneration through Violence: The Mythology of the American Frontier, 1600–1860* (Middletown, Conn.: Wesleyan University Press, 1973).

15. See, for example, Amanda Porterfield, *Mary Lyon and the Mount Holyoke Missionaries* (New York: Oxford University Press, 1997).

century missionary efforts on the Great Plains, and Indians felt it, too. "It is too soon to send missionaries among us," a Pawnee chief told some church people who approached him in 1817. "We are not starving yet. We wish to enjoy hunting until the wild animals are extinct. Let us use up the wild animals before you make us work and spoil our happiness."[16]

Both Catholic and Protestant missionaries were zealous on behalf of Indian welfare, and they were often outspoken against the seizure of Indian lands and the blatant manipulation of treaties, economic provisions, and government agreements that so frequently occurred. But missionary efforts to facilitate Indian welfare in the nineteenth century were not very successful. "The problems confronting the missionaries were more serious than either they or their sponsors had anticipated," wrote one sympathetic chronicler of early Protestant missions to the Osage in Kansas, who were as much invested in maintaining the economic and ceremonial life of hunting and warfare as their bitter enemies, the Pawnee.[17] The Presbyterian missionary Benton Pixley described how he was taunted by the Osage at Neosho in the late 1820s. Some of the Osage men even denounced Pixley's God "as hateful and bad." Before Pixley abandoned his post in 1829, the Osage told him they "hate" God; "he is of a bad temper," they told Pixley, and they "would shoot him, if they could see him."[18]

The Presbyterian missionary John Dunbar had little better success among the Pawnee. Although he felt "constrained to say that they are a kind-hearted, liberal people," he could not abide the Pawnee

16. Hyde, *Pawnee Indians,* 175.

17. "The trail-blazing missions did not achieve what was expected of them, but this may be classed as an error of expectation rather than as a lack of diligence on the part of the missionaries." William W. Graves, *The First Protestant Osage Missions, 1829–1837* (Oswego, Kans.: Carpenter Press, 1949), 7. See also M. L. Wardell, "Protestant Missions among the Osages, 1820–1838," *Chronicles of Oklahoma,* vol. 2 (Oklahoma City: Oklahoma Historical Society, 1924), 285–97.

18. "When I tell them I came to teach them the word of God, they sometimes sneeringly ask, 'Where is God? Have you seen him?'—and then laugh that I should think of making them believe a thing so incredible." T. F. Morrison, "Mission Neosho: The First Kansas Mission," *Kansas Historical Quarterly* 4, no. 3 (August 1935), 227–34, quotations from 232. In 1833, explaining Osage indifference to his preaching of a gospel of peace, William F. Vaill blamed a culture of war that unified families and villages, providing occasion for bravery, glory, and the display of Pawnee scalps. Graves, *First Protestant,* 225. In accounting for the failure of Pixley's mission, one historian had concluded, "The Indians were not exactly indifferent to the agricultural skill of white men, but they could not be induced to devote themselves to such pursuits. This was especially true of the men. . . . They were content with the efforts of the squaws, who . . . cultivated and produced beans, pumpkins, watermelons and corn." Morrison, "Mission Neosho," 234.

lifestyle, their division of labor, or the practice of polygamy that, in Dunbar's observation, brought younger sisters into an elder sister's marriage. "One educated in our privileged land can scarcely form a conception of the ignorance, wretchedness and degraded servitude of the Pawnee females," he wrote in his narrative about Pawnee life in the mid–1830s. "We cannot contemplate the condition of these wretched creatures without being led to feel deeply that for all that is better in the condition of females in Christian lands they are indebted to the gospel of Jesus Christ." Dunbar perceived the underlying vulnerability of women in both kinds of culture and hinted at the dire consequences for women outside the gospel's protective embrace. "The female, no matter who she is, that makes light of the Christian religion, trifles with that which makes her to differ from the most abject slave and degraded heathen."[19]

The perfectionists from Oberlin College who followed Dunbar to the Pawnee were no less intent in eradicating heathen behavior. Lester and Elvira Platt believed that progress should be forced on the Pawnee if they would not take it up willingly, and to that end, Elvira Platt took control of the lives of as many children as she could capture. She separated those under her instruction from their families, cut off the boys' warlocks, which made them into objects of ridicule among their peers, and sent them often to the Indian soldiers for whipping or beat them herself at the slightest infraction or sign of rebellion.[20] If Platt's approach to children's sinful behavior was more draconian than that of other missionaries, she was not alone in believing that conversion involved radical submission to Christian authority. The sacrifice Christ endured on behalf of the world gave Indians the opportunity for salvation from sin, and it modeled the suffering and violence they might expect in the process of their own purification.

Catholic ideas about Christianity's relationship to Native cultures were in many ways much more accommodating than Protestant ones. Nevertheless, Catholic baptism and catechism disturbed the core structures of Native societies, even if they offered religious practices that bridged the chasm between Native and American lifeways more effectively than Protestantism. Like Protestants, Catholic

---

19. John Dunbar, "The Presbyterian Mission among the Pawnee Indians in Nebraska, 1834–1836," in *Collections of the Kansas State Historical Society, 1909–1910*, vol. 11 (Topeka: State Printing Office, 1910), 323–32, quotations from 331.

20. Hyde, *Pawnee Indians*, 226, 256–57.

missionaries devoted great energy to altering the marital and sexual customs of Native peoples, focusing on the inadequacy of Native marriage and defining Christian virtue, to a large extent, in terms of sexual behavior. Thus the Jesuit missionary Pierre-Jean De Smet instructed adult converts in the necessity of Christian marriage, and he took pride in the numerous marriages he performed during visits to tribes along the Missouri and Platte rivers and further west. He regarded polygamy as a major obstacle to conversion and found the looseness, impermanency, and lack of exclusiveness in sexual relations between Indian men and women intolerable. Traditional sex and marriage were areas of Native culture he took strongest exception to and tried most to reform. In a letter written in 1841, he declared, "We hold the principle that, generally speaking, there are no valid marriages among the savages of these countries." With respect to the relationships Indians thought of as marriage, De Smet took the position that "there has been no marriage, because they have never known well in what its essence and obligation consisted."[21]

De Smet's rejection of Indian marriage is remarkable in light of his openness to other aspects of Indian society and his friendliness toward Indian people. His gregarious bonhomie and concern for Indian happiness enabled cordial relations with Indians across the plains and northwest. His *robe noire*, ritual procedures, and religious objects represented a spiritual authority that many Indians took seriously. A flag with "the holy name of Jesus on one side and on the other the image of the Virgin Mary, surrounded with gilt stars" traveled before him when he approached a village and stood near him in council meetings, representing his religious identity and power.[22]

But De Smet's Catholic flag ultimately served American interests, as did his approach to Indian marriage. While the religious details in his flag and in his theology of marriage distinguished him from Protestants, they contributed to an underlying religious message about American destiny upon which Protestants agreed. As a naturalized

21. As an obstacle to conversion, De Smet regarded polygamy as second only to "the immoderate use of strong drink." With respect to Indian men, he wrote, "we have not found one, even among the best disposed, who, after marriage had been contracted in their own fashion, did not believe himself justified in sending away his first wife, whenever he thought fit, and taking another. Many even have several wives in the same lodge." *Life, Letters, and Travels of Father Pierre-Jean De Smet, S.J., 1801–1873*, ed. Hiram Martin Chittenden and Alfred Talbot Richardson, 4 vols. (New York: Francis P. Harper, 1905) 1:332–33, quotations from 1:125 and 332.

22. Ibid., 1:96.

citizen of the United States and a staunch patriot committed to the compatibility between the Catholic religion and American progress, the Belgian-born cleric embraced his adopted country with religious zeal. "Providence has laid out his country on a gigantic scale," he explained to friends in Europe, "its destiny is to march onward, and no power on earth can stop it."[23]

De Smet served as a U.S. Army chaplain for several years and conducted important peace missions on behalf of the U.S. government in 1848, 1851, and 1868. In 1851, he played a leading role in treaty negotiations between the U.S. government and representatives of many of the western tribes east of the Rockies. In 1868, he executed a dangerous mission to the Lakota Sioux on behalf of the U.S. government. In a formal council meeting with Sioux leaders around the northern border of Nebraska, he prayed to the Great Spirit, smoked the calumet, gave away his religious flag as a sign of good faith, and persuaded the aggrieved Chief Sitting Bull to enter into negotiations with the United States for peace.[24]

Anyone could see the difference between De Smet's religion and that of a stern Protestant like Elvira Platt. These differences stimulated a good deal of competition. But the strenuousness with which Catholics and Protestants competed against each other only compounded the sense of American destiny they shared.[25]

A similar argument can be made with respect to the followers of Joseph Smith. For the most part, Protestants and Catholics hated the Mormons more than they hated each other, not only because of unique details about American religious history that Smith claimed to have translated from revelations written on golden tablets, but also because of subsequent revelations permitting Smith and some of his followers to take plural wives. Lewis Henry Morgan, the most open-minded of all observers of unfamiliar kinship structures, wrote

23. Ibid., 1:127.
24. Ibid., 1:60–61, 96–103; see also George Tinker, *Missionary Conquest: The Gospel and Native American Cultural Genocide* (Minneapolis: Fortress Press, 1993), 69–94.
25. Mary Lyon, for example, the influential educator of numerous female missionaries (including Mary Riggs, the renowned Protestant missionary to the Sioux), established a school that would train teachers to counter the work of Catholics busy "converting this nation to the Church of Rome." Like many other supporters of Protestant missions in the 1830s and 1840s, Lyon focused on Protestant conflict with Catholic belief and practice and failed to see the similarity in their religious views of American destiny. Mary Lyon, *General View of the Principles and Design of the Mount Holyoke Female Seminary* (Boston: Perkins and Marvin, 1837), 8; see also Stephen Return Riggs, *Mary and I: Forty Years with the Sioux* (Chicago: W. G. Holmes, ca. 1880), 3.

disparagingly of the "harems" traveling with Mormon men across the plains. Francis Parkman voiced the opinion of many in his description of Latter Day Saints in the Louisiana Purchase as "blind and desperate fanatics," too well armed for anyone's good, whose peculiar doctrines and aggressive practices continually sparked violence. Commenting on the tide of Mormon emigrants passing through Missouri, Parkman wrote, "it is notorious throughout the country how much blood has been spilt in their feuds." People lived in fear, since "No one could predict what would be the result, when large armed bodies of these fanatics should encounter the most impetuous and reckless of their old enemies on the broad prairie, far beyond the reach of law or military force."[26]

Mormon leaders and missionaries made concerted efforts to win Indian converts and allies. In 1830, Smith sent Oliver Cowdery, Frederick G. Williams, and Parley Parker Pratt on a mission "unto the Lamanites" west of the Mississippi. Reaching a settlement of Delawares in Kansas, Cowdery explained that "the Great Spirit had once spoken to the Indians" but had withdrawn because of Indian wickedness and had permitted their decline. Golden tablets uncovered by Smith explained the whole story and promised Indians a chance of redemption. Pratt thought the Delawares responded positively to this message, but U.S. agents chased the missionaries off the reservation before they could set up a school.[27]

Two decades later, across the western boundary of the Louisiana Purchase, missionaries sent out by Brigham Young attempted to forge an alliance with Shoshone in the strategically important region around Green River, Wyoming. Young dispensed supplies and worked hard to develop strategic alliances with Indian groups along the Oregon Trail to protect Mormon immigrants. "Our young men are learning to speak your language," Young's messenger Orson Hyde told Chief Washakee; "they want to be united with your people and a number of our men want to marry wives from your people and live with them and live in your country." But wives were a form of wealth in Shoshone culture, and if the Mormon men could find any women willing to go with them, Washakee wanted reciprocity: "we cannot afford to give our daughters to the white men, but we are willing to

26. Francis Parkman Jr., *The Oregon Trail,* ed. David Levin (New York: Penguin Books, 1982), 379, 75.
27. Warren A. Jennings, "The First Mormon Mission to the Indians," *Kansas Historical Quarterly* 37, no. 3 (autumn 1971): 288–99, quotations from 296 and 295.

give him an Indian girl for a white girl." Perhaps to avoid antagonism, Washakee claimed lack of understanding: "I cannot see why a
white man wants an Indian girl. They are dirty, ugly, stubborn, and
cross, and it is a strange idea for white men to want such wives." But
a deal still could be made: "The white men may look around though
and if any of you could find a girl that would go with him, it would
be alright, but the Indian must have the same privileges among the
white man."[28]

The Mormons may have hoped their enthusiasm for marriage
would help them forge alliances with Native groups. But Mormon
marriage customs involved beliefs about the eternal lives of individual souls very different from the religious beliefs about ancestry
involved in Native polygamy. And Mormon stories about the Lamanites relegated Indians to very low status, as many Natives were quick
to recognize. In a council meeting around Green River in 1855, when
Mormon elders presented a copy of the Book of Mormon to Shoshone leaders following a "declaration concerning the Indian's fore-
fathers," one of the subchiefs expressed the reaction of his peers: "No
good to the Indian."[29]

Mormon supplies were welcome, and Mormon beliefs did gener-
ate some interest among Indians, but not because they represented
any real alternative to religious beliefs about destiny and progress
that Catholics and other Protestants shared.[30] Joseph Smith saw his
revelations as the capstone to the providential unfolding of American destiny and ran for president of the United States in 1844 with
that destiny in mind. After Smith was murdered and violence against
Mormons east of the Mississippi escalated, Brigham Young and his
followers established a separate state on the western boundary of the
Louisiana Purchase and enlisted the help of Indians to defend it.

28. Fred R. Gowans and Eugene E. Campbell, *Fort Supply: Brigham Young's Green
River Experiment* (Salt Lake City: Brigham Young University Publications, 1976), 78, 32.
    29. Ibid., 39. Washakee berated the subchiefs for rejecting the elders' advances: "you
are all fools for you do not understand. These men are our friends. The great Mormon
captain (Brigham Young) has talked with our father above the clouds, and he told the
Mormon captain to send these good men here to tell us the truth not a lie" (39–40).
    30. Unique aspects of the Book of Mormon aside, beliefs about America being
known in ancient times and about Indians as descendants of one of the ancient tribes
of Israel were commonplace in nineteenth-century America. According to George
Armstrong Custer, for example, "Few persons will deny that the existence of America
was believed in if not positively known centuries before its discovery by Columbus."
Custer supported the theory that "the Indians are the descendants of the tribes of Israel
that were led captive into Assyria. Many of the Indian customs and religious rites," he
confidently asserted, "closely resemble those of the Israelites." George Armstrong
Custer, *My Life on the Plains, or Personal Experiences with Indians* (1874; reprint,
Norman: University of Oklahoma Press, 1962), 16–17.

Whatever animosity Mormon separatism provoked, their Zion in Utah is better understood as a zealous variant of American culture than an exception to it. As became increasingly clear after the Mormon Church denounced polygamy in 1890, the Mormon religion only reinforced American ideas about destiny.

Beliefs about marriage played a crucial role in framing these ideas. In contrast to Native groups, Mormons and other Americans viewed marriage as the basic unit of society, more fundamental than lineage. They conceptualized marriage in terms of notions about appropriate sexuality, female purity, and male restraint, and also in terms of notions about the positive effects of women's wifely and maternal influence and the importance of that influence for America's moral development as a nation. Widespread acceptance of that importance served as the stepping-stone that enabled many nineteenth-century American women to venture beyond traditional household occupations and develop new forms of competence, status, and respect as public schoolteachers, missionaries, nurses, social activists, and religious organizers. These new skills certainly contributed to greater female equality. But commitment to male dominance in marriage defined the terms on which women could advance. For the most part, Mormons operated as much on these terms as other Americans, even if other Americans did not see it.

In other words, the empowerment of American women played a crucial role in the American sense of destiny, and in the contrast Americans were quick to draw between the degradation of Indian women and the high status of women in America's Christian culture. This contrast not only overlooked aspects of traditional Indian cultures that protected and even empowered women but also obscured the aggressiveness of American women and their role in the construction of American destiny and power. American women were not simply lucky recipients of men's respect, but forceful actors in the construction of a new cultural and religious arrangement that benefited them significantly.

To appreciate the real force operating behind the pervasive feeling of destiny that developed in the Louisiana Purchase, it is important to see how different subcultures within American society thought and acted in ways that complemented one another, thus contributing to the sense that the American overtaking of the plains was beyond human control. Even the differences and conflicts among Americans about how Indians should be treated combined with one another, in ways that the American actors themselves did not see, to create a pervasive and powerful feeling, for both Americans and Indians, of being caught up in a divine plan.

In some important and sobering ways, sex and gender contributed as much to the construction of feelings about America's manifest destiny as did beliefs about God, Christ, and the progress of history. Indeed, Americans often worked out the meaning of their destiny in terms of sex and gender, linking God and Christ to certain forms of marriage and sexual discipline, and explaining progress in terms of the elevation of women's status. This construction of American destiny involved real cooperation between men and women, especially in the context of the nuclear family enclaves that were the building blocks of middle-class culture. At the same time, it encouraged competition among religious groups who represented particular variants of this culture. It also involved strenuous efforts to convert others and a willingness to employ force against anyone or any group who stood in the way.

Some of the most salient aspects of American culture today coalesced in the context of the Louisiana Purchase. Commitment to women's high status, even when not borne out in reality, is an important aspect of this culture, as is eagerness to convert others to an American way of life. The aggression associated with American destiny in the Louisiana Purchase laid groundwork for the unilateral force, and justification of that force, that continues to characterize American society and its outreach into the world today. Despite the fact that American people were (and still are) a motley group at odds with each other in many important respects, many felt (and still feel) that the expansion of America is providential. The Louisiana Purchase played a crucial part in the emergence of that enveloping sense of destiny.

Wide Open Spaces

The Trail of Tears, the Lewis and Clark Expedition, and Gaps in the National Memory

MICHAEL J. ZOGRY

SCHOLARS HAVE DEVOTED MUCH ATTENTION TO THE FAR-RANGING effects of the Louisiana Purchase upon the United States as well as First Nations, and the recent bicentennial of the Lewis and Clark Expedition resulted in renewed scholarly attention. The effects upon First Nations communities west of the Mississippi in particular were well documented as part of the commemorative activities connected to the three-year celebration, but not surprisingly, what was *not* featured was the link between this expansion of the United States and the ensuing removal of southeastern First Nations only decades later. However, despite this omission, the trails of exploration and removal were in fact linked. As historian Jon Kukla has observed, "America's barely visible first steps along the Trail of Tears were taken in the White House as Thomas Jefferson pondered the implications of the Louisiana Purchase."[1]

Though the early-nineteenth-century policies of Thomas Jefferson that laid the groundwork for the Indian Removal Act of

I gratefully acknowledge the support of the National Endowment for the Humanities Summer Stipend for preparation of the initial publication of this chapter. Any views, findings, conclusions, or recommendations expressed in this publication do not necessarily reflect those of the National Endowment for the Humanities.

1. Jon Kukla, *A Wilderness So Immense: The Louisiana Purchase and the Destiny of America* (New York: Alfred A. Knopf, 2003), 303. Instead of using *Native American* or *American Indian,* I employ the term *First Nations* throughout this essay. For a useful discussion of this issue, see Michael Yellow Bird, "'What We Want to Be Called': Indigenous Peoples' Perspectives on Racial and Ethnic Identity Labels," *American Indian Quarterly* 23, no. 2 (spring 1999): 1–22.

1830 and the ensuing forced removals of the "Five Civilized Tribes" have received some scholarly attention recently, U.S. religious historical narratives, particularly those presented in university textbooks, routinely ignore what I argue is a necessary discussion of the relationship between the two sets of events. In this essay I approach the relationship between the voluntary trail blazed by Lewis and Clark and the involuntary trail of the forced march endured by members of the Cherokee nation in the late 1830s by employing the notion of the "chronotope of the crossroads." This is an apt concept to employ, because research has confirmed that these two trails physically crossed and because the two events were related by more than this coincidental physical crossing of paths. Equally important, it also illustrates the converging issues of historiography and the presentation of historical research that one must consider when negotiating such a busy intersection.

Cape Girardeau, Missouri, is a city of about thirty-five thousand inhabitants located in southeastern Missouri. It is on the border with Illinois, on the banks of the Mississippi River. Settled by Spanish immigrants, it was named for a French trader who established a trading post in 1733. Prior to the Civil War, the town enjoyed a prosperous river trade, and in the 1880s, railroads enabled the town to rebound with industry. Thus Cape Girardeau's landscape is marked with diverse routes—routes that reflect issues and events associated with the development and expansion of the United States.

One of the chief tourist attractions near Cape Girardeau, about ten miles north of the city, is a 3,415-acre park. This park offers the visitor forested hills, valleys, and bluffs dramatically overlooking the Mississippi. The area's wildlife includes deer, turkey, foxes, and in the winter months, bald eagles. But this park—Trail of Tears State Park—is named for other winter visitors, and unlike the birds that are our nation's symbol, these visitors were human and involuntary. In the winter of 1838–1839, Cherokee people on a forced march from Georgia crossed over the Mississippi River and through the southern part of the park on their way to the Indian Territory (what is now Oklahoma). Ice floes in the Mississippi River prevented some of the ferries from crossing, stranding and separating contingents, who had to camp on either side of the river to wait.

Evan Jones, a Baptist missionary who accompanied a detachment on their journey, described the situation in a letter from December 30, 1838:

> We have now been on our road to Arkansas seventy-five days, and have traveled five hundred and twenty-nine miles. We are still nearly three hundred miles short of our destination. . . . At the Mississippi river, we were stopped from crossing, by the ice running so that boats could not pass, for several days. Here, br. Bushyhead's detachment came up with us. . . . I am afraid that, with all the care that can be exercised with the various detachments, there will be an immense amount of suffering, and loss of life attending the removal . . . the fact that the removal is effected by coercion, makes it the more galling to the feelings of the survivors.[2]

"Brother Bushyhead" was the Reverend Jesse Bushyhead. According to one source, "Bushyhead's group and others crossed from Willard Landing in Illinois to Mocasin Springs, Missouri, on Green's Ferry," while other groups crossed "to Bainbridge [Missouri] near Cape Girardeau." The same source noted that Bushyhead's sister "died of cold and exposure at the campground"; while "[t]he white people in the area called her Princess Otahki, but family research has shown that 'Otahki' was Nancy Bushyhead Walker Hildebrand." According to the park's Web site, a memorial named for Hildebrand, whom "legend says" died and was buried in the park, stands as a "tribute to her and all the other Cherokee who died on the trail."[3]

I have never been to this area of the country, but I spent the better part of a Sunday afternoon poring over maps of the region. A call to the park visitors' center and a visit to the University of Missouri's geography department Web site confirmed what I had thought. On November 23, 1803, Lewis and Clark had passed by this place on their way to St. Louis to officially begin their journey of exploration.

2. Evan Jones, letter of December 30, 1838, "Letters, May–December 1838," in Theda Perdue and Michael D. Green, eds., *The Cherokee Removal: A Brief History with Documents,* Bedford Series in History and Culture (Boston: Bedford Books of St. Martin's Press, 1995), 167–68.

3. Joan Gilbert, *The Trail of Tears across Missouri* (Columbia: University of Missouri Press, 1996), 55, 54, 57, 58; Denise Dowling, "Resources to Explore: Trail of Tears State Park," *Missouri Resources* 16, no. 2 (summer 1999): 25–28, available online at http://www.dnr.mo.gov/magazine/1999-summer.pdf (accessed November 12, 2007). See also Missouri State Parks and Historic Sites, Trail of Tears State Park, "General Information: Remembering an American Tragedy," www.mostateparks.com/trailoftears/geninfo.htm (accessed November 12, 2007).

In fact, according to a park employee, the park was in the process of placing a permanent marker in the northern part of the park, on a bluff overlooking the river, to commemorate the event.[4]

It is this confluence of two routes that I choose as the reference point for my discussion of the relationship between the two events. In much the same way as Paul Gilroy, in *The Black Atlantic*, wrote about the products of the black Atlantic's "literature and expressive cultures," the narratives recalling these events are "narratives of loss, exile, and journeying which . . . serve a mnemonic function: directing the consciousness of the group back to significant, nodal points in its common history and its social memory." Gilroy also spoke of shifting "from the chronotope of the road to the chronotope of the crossroads," invoking Mikhail Bakhtin's concept of the "chronotope," a "unit of analysis for studying texts according to the ratio and nature of the temporal and spatial categories represented."[5]

I find Gilroy's comments useful and important, and I want to stress the physical nature of the crossroads as well as the events that took place there. In this way, as I move through such ethereal concepts as "construction of history" and "cultural narrative of the nation" ("national mythology"), I remain mindful of a crucial concept about which Charles Long has written and lectured over the course of his distinguished career: "what Gaston Bachelard described in Hegelian language as the lithic imagination." As Long wrote,

> The hardness of life or of reality was the experience of the meaning of the oppressed's own identity as opaque. Reality itself was opaque and seemed opposed to them. The affirmations "black is beautiful" or "God is Red" are more than mere slogans. They are shorthand for the agonizing history of communities that have had to face the ultimacy of reality as a daily experience in the modern world.[6]

---

4. Geographic Resources Center, Department of Geography, University of Missouri–Columbia, "Lewis and Clark across Missouri: Nov. 23, 1803: At Old Cape Girardeau," http://lewisclark.geog.missouri.edu/campsites/1804/nov23camp.shtml (accessed November 12, 2007), printed in James D. Harlan and James M. Denny, *Atlas of Lewis and Clark in Missouri* (Columbia: University of Missouri Press, 2003), 18–20; Trail of Tears State Park employee, conversation with author, February 15, 2004.

5. Paul Gilroy, *The Black Atlantic: Modernity and Double Consciousness* (Cambridge, Mass.: Harvard University, 1993), 198; M. M. Bakhtin, *The Dialogic Imagination,* ed. and trans. Michael Holquist (Austin: University of Texas Press, 1981), 426, cited in Gilroy, *Black Atlantic*, 225n2.

6. Charles H. Long, *Significations: Signs, Symbols, and Images in the Interpretation of Religion* (Philadelphia: Fortress Press, 1986), 178, 197.

By drawing attention to this particular crossroads, I want to reiterate the "hardness of reality" that characterizes events such as these that become encapsulated ideological moments in historical narratives of the United States.

The year 2003 inaugurated a three-year national commemoration of the bicentennial of the Lewis and Clark Expedition to the West, an event that has become synonymous with the history of expansion in the United States. That year also marked the publication of the first "Interpretive Plan" for the Trail of Tears National Historic Trail, to commemorate the forced removal of the Cherokee nation. As a symbol of all the forced removals of First Nations in the 1830s, this event has become synonymous with the injustices and abuses of U.S. expansion. In the corpus of U.S. cultural narratives, this series of removals has become associated primarily with the administration of Andrew Jackson and his presidential policies.[7]

Several factors are absent in this narrative. First, Jackson's policies reflected his era, were indicative of broader public opinion, and represented the culmination of at least thirty years of carefully proscribed presidential policy that included Thomas Jefferson's original concept of Lewis and Clark's expedition. Second, during this era, the land parcel that is now known as the continental United States was home to many autonomous First Nations, as well as Russian, Spanish, and French colonies. Lewis and Clark crossed international borders, as did U.S. government officials as they negotiated with First Nations such as the Cherokee. Both of these were international events at the time, but as they have become typecast in the American historical memory through a variety of mediums, this aspect often remains overlooked, as does their close relationship.[8] That these two events continue to resonate in the American historical memory, and do so as unrelated events, is a testament first to how enmeshed both

7. The term *cultural narrative* is used in the context of this essay to refer to what are commonly called "myths"; this term implies cultural significance without assigning a "truth" value.

8. I am aware of the hubris of referring to the United States as "America" and U.S. citizens as "Americans," since this designation ignores the people of every other nation on the continents of North and South America. Because I am discussing issues of idealization and cultural narratives, I retain the distinction, and use it consciously in certain contexts, though I recognize its problematic nature.

have become in the cultural narrative ("historical mythology") of the United States, and second, to the power of this narrative to overwhelm historical relationships.

I think the persistence of this narrative also reflects a dogmatic refusal on the part of individuals and communities to let go of images that have acquired a certain legendary and unassailable quality.[9] Often this stance is based on the perceived connection of these images to the traditions and history of an organization, community, nation, or some other entity in which such individuals are invested. During anniversaries, such as the one that provided the impetus for this conference, these foundational concepts are reinforced. As the historian Richard White has noted, "Americans have never had much use for history, but we do like anniversaries."[10]

Charles Long was speaking about much the same thing when discussing hundred-year "cycles of American history," which "represent dramatic rituals of the archetypes of American history and religion." While each of these "mythical cycles" brings the promise of "change of the ritual ... at each of these junctures the American revolution is aborted and clever priests of our national language and apparatus, skillful in the ways of ritual purity and manipulation, come upon the scene to ensure the repetition of the American ritual."[11] As a result, a bounded history of short duration is created that often obscures the *longue durée* (to use Fernand Braudel's term), events of a place, in this case, the partition of land now known as the continental United States, and the complex history of all its inhabitants, past and present.[12] Such a history is crammed with details, yet it still retains wide open spaces.

---

9. I argued this point with regard to religious stereotypes of First Nations peoples in Michael J. Zogry, "Lost and Found: Religious Stereotypes in Paul Green's *The Lost Colony*," paper presented at the American Academy of Religion Southeast Region Meeting, Charlotte, N.C., March 2001.

10. Richard White, "Frederick Jackson Turner and Buffalo Bill," in James R. Grossman, ed., *The Frontier in American Culture: An Exhibition at the Newberry Library, August 26, 1994–January 7, 1995* (Berkeley and Los Angeles: University of California Press, 1994), 7.

11. Long, *Significations*, 152. While I do not assert this point in such absolutist terms, the point is well taken.

12. Braudel coined the term in the context of proposing three different levels, or spans, of time. These are geographical time, that of social and cultural history, and that of events (the short span, or *courte durée*). For a cogent summary of Braudel's theories, see John Lechte, "Fernand Braudel," in *Fifty Key Contemporary Thinkers: From Structuralism to Postmodernity* (New York: Routledge, 1994), 89–93.

As a religious studies scholar who specializes in the academic study of First Nations religious systems, I constantly face issues related to negotiation of memory, construction of history, and construction of narrative ("mythmaking") in the United States. While teaching an introductory survey course on religion in the United States, I found that religious studies textbooks treating American religious history routinely noted only briefly or completely ignored the events that are the subject of this study. Even if the textbook authors included the events, they completely ignored the relationship between them. Further, a review of selected textbooks in history as well suggests that, unlike the Louisiana Purchase, the removal events still have not been adequately integrated into the U.S. historical narrative.

Two recent works that discuss the relationship between the two events are Jon Kukla, *A Wilderness So Immense: The Louisiana Purchase and the Destiny of America,* and Anthony F. C. Wallace, *Jefferson and the Indians: The Tragic Fate of the First Americans.*[13] In spite of these treatments, not surprisingly the synthetic texts about U.S. history written by committee, which are still standard issue in many universities, naturally lag behind in scholarship. The historian Paul Boyer has remarked upon the "stylistic conservatism" of the "history-textbook genre," noting that "[t]extbooks evolve with glacial slowness, as authors and publishers make incremental changes rather than radically revising."[14] Three recent examples of U.S. historical narratives will suffice here to make the point; one from the discipline of religious studies and two from the discipline of history.

In the unit on the nineteenth century in the excellent survey *Religion in American Life: A Short History,* esteemed historian of

13. Kukla, *Wilderness;* Anthony F. C. Wallace, *Jefferson and the Indians: The Tragic Fate of the First Americans* (Cambridge: Belknap Press, Harvard University Press, 1999). Patricia Nelson Limerick, *The Legacy of Conquest: The Unbroken Past of the American West* (New York: W. W. Norton, 1987), and Michael Kammen, *Mystic Chords of Memory: The Transformation of Tradition in American Culture* (New York: Alfred A. Knopf, 1991) are two examples of well-known works that have treated the issues of Jefferson laying the groundwork for the removal policy and the memory of historical events, respectively. Also significant are Frederick Hoxie, ed., *Indians in American History* (Arlington Heights, Ill.: Harlan Davidson, 1988), and Calvin Martin, *The American Indian and the Problem of History* (New York: Oxford University Press, 1987).

14. Paul Boyer, "In Search of the Fourth 'R': The Treatment of Religion in American History Textbooks and Survey Courses," in Bruce Kuklick and D. G. Hart, eds., *Religious Advocacy and American History* (Grand Rapids, Mich.: William B. Eerdmans, 1997), 127.

religion Grant Wacker mentioned the Cherokee Trail of Tears in a chapter on reformers and missionaries. He accorded it one paragraph that highlighted conversion to Christianity by Cherokee people and Christian missionaries' roles as advocates for the Cherokee cause.[15] One might have hoped for even a brief discussion of the impact of these events on the Cherokee religious system, not to mention their effects on the Cherokee communities of North Carolina and Oklahoma. In the chapter that discussed the actual time period of the Trail of Tears, entitled "Awakeners of the Heart," Wacker did not mention the Trail of Tears, as he focused on evangelicalism in the "first half of the nineteenth century," primarily the Second Great Awakening.[16] Oddly, the Cherokee Trail of Tears was inserted into a chapter that primarily concerned reform movements of the *late* nineteenth century. Again, one might have hoped for a more integrated presentation of events.

The second example I offer is *America: Past and Present,* in which the Indian Removal was accorded roughly a page. The Lewis and Clark Expedition rated two paragraphs in an earlier chapter, and this entry was preceded by roughly a page of text on the Louisiana Purchase. The narrative did take Jackson and his administration to task over the issue of Indian Removal; however, once again, little effort was made to link all of these events together.[17]

My final example is *The American West: A New Interpretive History,* by historians Robert V. Hine and John Mack Faragher. A new edition of a venerable work, this book provides an extended account of the Trail of Tears, as well as a discussion of events from 1811 to 1821 in the Cherokee nation as an "example of the revitalization movements that swept through the Indian nations of the trans-Appalachian West during the first decades of the nineteenth century." However, it was not until two chapters later that the authors discussed removal events, with the Cherokee displacement featured over the course of two and a half pages.[18]

15. Grant Wacker, "Adventurers of the Spirit," 321–22, in Jon Butler, Grant Wacker, and Randall Balmer, *Religion in American Life: A Short History* (New York: Oxford University Press, 2003).

16. Grant Wacker, "Awakeners of the Heart," in Butler, Wacker, and Balmer, *Religion in American Life,* 182–96; quotation 182.

17. Robert A. Divine et al., eds., *America: Past and Present,* vol. 1, *To 1877,* 5th ed. (New York: Addison Wesley Educational Publishers, 1999), 303–4, 243, 240–42.

18. Robert V. Hine and John Mack Faragher, *The American West: A New Interpretive*

Despite these narrative renderings, published scholarship and my own research confirm that these events are closely linked in actual fact as well as ideologically. I argue that the series of forced removals and migrations of First Nations as well as the Lewis and Clark Expedition have overt significance in the American religious history narrative, particularly in terms of but not confined to the antebellum period. As early as 1775, the Reverend John Witherspoon expressed religious justification for such sentiments, when, preaching at Princeton University, he stated, "[T]rue religion, and in her train, dominion, riches, literature, and art have taken their course in a slow and gradual manner from East to West . . . from thence forebode the future glory of America." Jedediah Morse echoed these sentiments of empire, also expressed by George Washington and James Madison, when he remarked in his 1789 textbook *American Geography* that the "Mississippi was never designed as the western boundary of the American empire." Four years later, in 1793, Thomas Jefferson gave money to a French botanist planning an expedition to the west, and "one month before his inauguration, Jefferson asked Meriwether Lewis to prepare for a major western exploration."[19]

According to the geographer John Logan Allen, there were "twin themes that were so preponderant in the images of the American Northwest at the time of the Lewis and Clark Expedition": "The Garden of the World" and the "Passage to India." As Allen noted, the second notion, building upon the first, "was as much a part of the teleological faith in the West as it was the process of logical deduction following the elimination of other unknowns from the map. The components of the conceptions of the geography of the Northwest fit the pattern of both logic and faith."[20]

In January 1803, President Thomas Jefferson sent a confidential letter to Congress requesting twenty-five hundred dollars for what would become the Lewis and Clark Expedition. This section of the letter is well-known, but the letter also outlines a strategy for gaining possession of lands east of the Mississippi, primarily those held

---

History (New Haven: Yale University Press, 2000), 121, 129–31, 176–79; see also 366–67. There was no discussion of evangelicalism until chapter 12, when the book discussed the Cane Ridge Revival, and the term "the second Great Awakening" was never invoked.

19. All quotes ibid., 3, 133, 134. Hine and Faragher remind us that 1789, the year Morse's book was published, was the year the Constitution was ratified.

20. John Logan Allen, *Lewis and Clark and the Image of the American Northwest* (1975; reprint, New York: Dover Publications, 1991), xxvi.

by Chickasaw people. Allen argued that this second topic masked Jefferson's real agenda: to find a water route across the continent.[21]

In contrast, Jon Kukla has argued that "The project was cloaked in secrecy, but *not* for diplomatic reasons—indeed Jefferson consulted secretly the Spanish, French, and British representatives about his plans for 'a small caravan' to explore the Missouri River, and he secured foreign passports for its commanders." Rather, according to Kukla, "[T]he secrecy answered domestic political considerations: Jefferson did not believe that the Constitution authorized the outfitting of a scientific and 'literary' expedition at public expense."[22]

While both of these explanations seem reasonable enough, review of the letter suggests that there was another reason for secrecy. First Nations were becoming increasingly adamant about not ceding land, and Jefferson wrote, "[I]n order peaceably to counteract this policy of theirs, and to provide an extension of territory which the rapid increase of our numbers will call for, two measures are deemed expedient." The measures were "to encourage them to abandon hunting, to apply to the raising stock, to agriculture and domestic manufacture," and "to multiply trading houses among them & place within their reach those things which will contribute more to their domestic comfort than the possession of extensive, but uncultivated wilds."[23]

Given that the letter contained Jefferson's request for funds so that Lewis and Clark could embark on what was ostensibly a reconnaissance mission, this issue of land acquisition also made the communication confidential:

> [B]ut between the Ohio and the Yazoo, the country all belongs to the Chickasaws, the most friendly tribe within our limits, but the most decided against the alienation of lands. [T]he portion of their country most important for use is exactly that which they do not inhabit. [T]heir settlements are not on the Missisipi but in the interior country. [T]hey have lately shown a desire to become agricultural, and this leads to the desire of buying implements & comforts. [I]n the

21. Ibid., 71–72.
22. Kukla, *Wilderness*, 260.
23. Thomas Jefferson, "President Thomas Jefferson's confidential message to Congress concerning relations with the Indians," January 18, 1803 (Record Group 233, Records of the U.S. House of Representatives, HR 7A-D1; National Archives); available online http://www.ourdocuments.gov/doc.php?doc=17 (accessed November 12, 2007). The brief text describing the Web version of document makes no mention of why the document was secret.

strengthening and gratifying of these wants, I see the only prospect of planting on the Missisipi itself the means of it's own safety. Duty has required me to submit these views to the judgment of the legislature, but as their disclosure might embarras & defeat their effect, they are committed to the special confidence of the two houses.[24]

This plan to acquire land by cultivating desire for material goods and creating insurmountable debt was something that Jefferson discussed in other private communications as early as six months before the Louisiana Purchase was finalized. As Anthony F. C. Wallace has pointed out, Jefferson's "first statements of the principles to guide America's relations with the Indians were made" in a December 29, 1802, "private letter to Secretary of War Dearborn outlining in candid terms the purposes and methods of American Indian policy." Wallace continued,

> Jefferson followed his private instructions to Dearborn with a special confidential message to Congress on January 28, 1803, on the subject of "trade." The security in which he wished these communications to be kept was needed, he felt, because if the Indians, now almost universally averse to selling any more land, became aware of the real purpose of the factories and the civilization policy, they would reject both. That real purpose, for the present, was the peaceful acquisition of the Mississippi frontier, from the Yazoo north.[25]

Though Jefferson made special note in the letter to Congress that secrecy was necessary for this plan to be efficacious, later presidents who followed the same policy trail were not so concerned about public disclosure.

Most notably, in his 1830 Message to Congress, entitled "On Indian Removal," President Andrew Jackson noted that "the benevolent policy of the Government, steadily pursued for nearly thirty years, in relation to the removal of the Indians beyond the white settlements is approaching to a happy consummation."[26] That ironic turn of phrase

---

24. Ibid.; spellings are as in the original.

25. Wallace, *Jefferson*, 221, 222.

26. Andrew Jackson, "President Jackson's Message to Congress 'On Indian Removal,' December 6, 1830," Records of the U.S. Senate, 1789–1990, National Archives; available online at http://www.ourdocuments.gov/doc.php?doc=25&page=transcript (accessed November 12, 2007).

described what would occur over the next decade. In the years 1831–1838, the U.S. government implemented the displacement of the honorifically titled "Five Civilized Tribes" (Muskogee or Creek, Cherokee, Chickasaw, Choctaw, and Seminole) from their homelands. During the years 1835–1838, the majority of the Cherokee people were forcibly removed from their lands in the East to territory in Oklahoma, a process and route that would become known as *Nunahi Duna Dlo Hilu-I*, "Trail where They Cried," or the Trail of Tears.

An estimated two thousand removal advocates moved before 1838, when federal troops systematically interred the majority of the approximately sixteen thousand remaining people who opposed removal and had refused to emigrate. Cherokee people were rousted out of their homes, many of their possessions were confiscated, houses and crops were burned, and the people were confined in concentration camps. Many thousands of people, perhaps as many as a quarter or more of the estimated total population, died in the camps, in transit to Oklahoma, or soon after their arrival.[27]

The two actions, cession of land and removal of First Nations peoples, were inextricably linked in the mind of Andrew Jackson, as they had been for Thomas Jefferson. About this Jon Kukla has remarked, "Years later, when President Andrew Jackson offered the Choctaw Indians 'a country beyond the Mississippi,' he described it as one of the 'valuable objects which Mr. Jefferson promised you.' America's barely visible first steps along the Trail of Tears were taken in the White House as Thomas Jefferson pondered the implications of the Louisiana Purchase."[28]

Just as clearly, the Lewis and Clark Expedition was linked to these and other events to come in U.S. history. Hine and Faragher contended that the expedition "also set a pattern, establishing a precedent for a strong government role in the development of the American West." Noting that this was "the first American exploration mounted and pursued with government encouragement and financing," Hine and Faragher continued:

27. "Trail of Tears," in *Encyclopedia of North American Indians,* ed. Frederick E. Hoxie (New York: Houghton Mifflin, 1996), 639–40; Duane H. King, "Cherokee," in ibid., 106; Russell Thornton, with the assistance of C. Matthew Snipp and Nancy Breen, *The Cherokees: A Population History* (Lincoln: University of Nebraska Press, 1990), 63–77. See also Perdue and Green, *Cherokee Removal.*
28. Kukla, *Wilderness,* 303.

Historians have tended to overlook the basic preparations for westward expansion undertaken by the government—surveying the land, marking the routes, building the wagon roads, clearing the rivers for navigation, dredging the harbors along the coasts, planning and digging canals, subsidizing railroads, suppressing the protests of Indians, and in general standing close behind the pioneers as they elbowed their way to the Pacific.[29]

It is particularly chilling to consider that these routes over the surveyed land would expedite and facilitate certain events of the next century. The Lewis and Clark Expedition made the basic preparations necessary for westward expansion, but the expedition also made the basic preparations necessary for the subjugation, containment, and in many cases the removal and relocation of First Nations peoples.

Maps of the time reflected the developing narrative. As Richard White has noted, while sixteenth- and seventeenth-century maps showed an occupied western American landscape, "[B]y the nineteenth century all this had changed." Maps either portrayed the land as sparsely populated, or as wide open spaces, as White noted further: "[T]he map of the early republic in the companion atlas to Emma Willard's widely used nineteenth-century school text vividly portrays the West as empty land. . . . Willard has completely erased Indians."[30] In short, in this emerging narrative, wide open spaces plus no people equaled no problem.

When assessing various textbook narratives of U.S. history, both religious history and general history, two points seem clear regarding the treatment of these events: 1) the Lewis and Clark Expedition, as a result of the Louisiana Purchase, is presented separately from the Trail of Tears, another result of the Louisiana Purchase; and 2) a common narrative model presents itself time and time again. This raises the question, are the two factors related? Does the common narrative model resist presenting the relationship of such events? What are the parameters of such a model, if it even exists?

29. Hine and Faragher, *American West*, 143.
30. White, "Frederick Jackson Turner," 17.

It is my sense that many recent American religious history survey publications rely upon the historian William G. McLoughlin's *Revivals, Awakenings, and Reforms* to frame and order their narratives. Further, this book is a definitive statement of what was the prevalent narrative structure in both religious studies and history for many years prior to its publication. In it, McLoughlin codified a model of decline and revitalization in American religious history derived from the anthropologist Anthony F. C. Wallace's interpretation of Seneca religious history in "Revitalization Movements," published in *American Anthropologist* in 1956. McLoughlin also published several important works in the area of Cherokee studies, focusing primarily on the Christian missionary enterprise, in which his line of reasoning is evident.[31]

Scholars in recent years have critiqued certain aspects of his argument, but none to my knowledge have examined thoroughly the application of the McLoughlin model to American religious history. Ironically, the model may not accurately reflect historical trends in that or other Native American communities, not to mention in U.S. religious history. Nor is it the only model available to interpreters.

In the disciplines of religious studies and anthropology, the terms "revitalization" and "revitalization movement" are associated with Anthony F. C. Wallace's article, in which he offered the following definition: "A revitalization movement is defined as a deliberate, organized, conscious effort by members of a society to construct a more satisfying culture." Wallace based his theory upon data concerning the nineteenth-century religious movement initiated by the Seneca prophet Handsome Lake among nations of the Haudenosaunee confederacy, but he argued that such movements are "recurrent features in human history. . . . Christianity and Mohammedanism, and possibly Buddhism as well, originated in revitalization movements." He

---

31. William G. McLoughlin, *Revivals, Awakenings, and Reform: An Essay on Religion and Social Change in America, 1607–1977* (Chicago: University of Chicago Press, 1978). Roger Finke and Rodney Stark recently concurred: "Great Awakenings loom large in traditional histories of American religion"; see *The Churching of America, 1776–2005: Winners and Losers in Our Religious Economy* (New Brunswick, N.J.: Rutgers University Press, 2005), 3. McLoughlin's books include *The Cherokee Ghost Dance: Essays on the Southeastern Indians, 1789–1861* (Macon, Ga.: Mercer University Press, 1984); *Cherokees and Missionaries, 1789–1839* (New Haven: Yale University Press, 1984); *Cherokee Renascence in the New Republic* (Princeton: Princeton University Press, 1986); and *The Cherokees and Christianity, 1794–1870: Essays on Acculturation and Cultural Persistence,* ed. Walter H. Conser (Athens: University of Georgia Press, 1994).

divided such movements into four nonmutually exclusive categories: "nativistic, millenarian, messianic, and revivalistic." Wallace argued that "religious phenomena per se originated . . . in visions of a new way of life by individuals under extreme stress," and he interpreted such visions "by way of psychoanalytic dream theory."[32]

As noted above, in a series of articles and books, the historian William G. McLoughlin employed Wallace's notion to interpret cultural movements, first in terms of U.S. religious history and then later in his career specifically with regard to movements among Cherokee people in both North Carolina and Oklahoma. In *Revivals, Awakenings, and Reforms*, McLoughlin asserted that "beneath the recurring pattern of ideological or (theological) change lies a common core of beliefs that has provided continuity and shape to American culture." He aimed to "trace the evolutionary changes in a group of interlocking myths, hopes, and ideals that have shaped, and been reshaped by, the events of our history." He further remarked,

> This individualistic, pietistic, perfectionist, millenarian ideology has from time to time been variously defined and explained to meet changing experience and contingencies in our history, but the fundamental belief that freedom and responsibility will perfect not only the individual and the nation but the world (because they are in harmony with the supreme laws of nature—and of nature's God) has been constant. American history is thus best understood as a millenarian movement.[33]

Throughout this book, McLoughlin's narrative voice presents "what we believe," and sometimes it is difficult to separate this from "what he believes," as in the following: "As God sheds 'new' or 'further light' on our mission, we refashion our pattern of life and enculturation to enable rising generations to cope with the unfolding complexities of human redemption."[34]

While Wallace had argued that the individual vision experiences that gave rise to revitalization movements were a type of experience

---

32. Anthony F. C. Wallace, "Revitalization Movements," *American Anthropologist*, n.s., 58, no. 2 (April 1956): 264, 267, 268, 270. He defined *mazeway* as one's "mental image of the society and its culture, as well as of his own body and its behavioral regularities, in order to act in ways which reduce stress at all levels of the system" (ibid., 266).

33. McLoughlin, *Revivals*, xiv.

34. Ibid., xv.

"that our culture generally regards as pathological," McLoughlin disagreed, arguing that "[g]reat awakenings are not periods of social neurosis. . . . They are times of revitalization. They are therapeutic and cathartic, not pathological." He argued, "[T]hey eventuate in basic restructurings of our institutions and redefinitions of our social goals" as well as help "us to maintain faith in ourselves, our ideals, and our 'covenant with God' even while they compel us to reinterpret that covenant in the light of new experience."[35] The psychological and theological overtones of these statements are readily apparent, and what is more, there is an inherent teleology to the narrative.

McLoughlin argued for a series of five relevant awakenings in American history, including an initial Puritan awakening in England. He dated "the First Great Awakening (in America)" from "1730–60" and the Second Great Awakening from "1800–1830." Though such concepts appear often in both history and religious history texts, the American historian of religion Jon Butler has challenged the existence of that particular awakening; in his suggestive article he also referred to "the so-called Second Great Awakening of the early national period."[36]

Finally, McLoughlin, echoing Wallace, argued that "[r]evivals and awakenings occur in all cultures" and are "essentially folk movements," though McLoughlin stated that "[b]ecause Wallace derived his theory from studies of so-called primitive peoples (preliterate and homogeneous), it is not totally applicable to the complex, pluralistic, and highly literate people of the United States."[37] Here, then, is an important contradiction: McLoughlin stated that the model did not apply completely because of what he understood as fundamental differences of complexity and literacy between the Seneca people as a homogeneous unit and the larger population of the United States. Yet in a broader sense, this model, in whole or in part, *has been* applied to U.S. religious history, by him and other scholars. Therefore, the explanatory capacity of McLoughlin's model must be critiqued both in regard to First Nations cultures and to U.S. religious history.

35. Wallace, "Revitalization Movements," 272; McLoughlin, *Revivals*, 2.

36. McLoughlin, *Revivals*, 1; 10–11; Jon Butler, "Enthusiasm Described and Decried: The Great Awakening as Interpretive Fiction," *Journal of American History* 69, no. 2 (September 1982): 305–25, reprinted in Jon Butler and Harry S. Stout, eds., *Religion in American History: A Reader* (New York: Oxford University Press, 1998), 110–11.

37. McLoughlin, *Revivals*, 2, 10.

I argue that this framework is informed by theological assumptions, makes distinctions between social groups that most contemporary scholars see as stereotypical, outmoded, and arbitrary, forces data on individual religious systems to conform to the argument, and may not be the most useful way to talk about U.S. religious history. My goal is not to denigrate his scholarship, but simply to present it as a cogent example of a prevalent model that I think could be revised. In fact, scholars such as Russell Thornton, who have continued to invoke the model, have noted that McLoughlin himself questioned the application of the concept, at least in terms of indigenous nations, and urged scholars to "recognize the difficulty of making broad generalizations regarding ghost dance movements and revitalization and stick closely to contextual circumstances within each tribe over long periods."[38]

A fine example of one way in which the revitalization model obscures related events, of course, is what I have discussed earlier in this essay. Further, if one accepts the narrative framework outlined above, the forced removal of First Nations took place immediately following what is still commonly termed the Second Great Awakening. Again, then, why is this connection not noted in any contemporary textbooks or surveys? Beyond Boyer's comments above about the "glacial slowness" of textbook change, the nonintegration of these events in common or standard U.S. religious history narratives remains puzzling. To reiterate my statement from above, clearly these events have overt significance in terms of American religious history, particularly during the antebellum period, and however difficult they are to reconcile, I argue such reconciliation is necessary if religious historians really want to change the narratives.

McLoughlin himself recognized that the awakenings had other consequences: "The colonists, after the First Awakening, first defeated the French and Indians and then threw off the corrupt king and Parliament. The Americans, after the Second Awakening, first eliminated the Indians and Mexicans and British from the West and then attacked those who would secede from the covenant in order to uphold black slavery." He further noted that "[I]t might be more

---

38. William G. McLoughlin, "Ghost Dance Movements: Some Thoughts on Definition Based on Cherokee History," *Ethnohistory* 37 (1990): 42, quoted in Russell Thornton, "Boundary Dissolution and Revitalization Movements: The Case of the Nineteenth-Century Cherokees," *Ethnohistory* 40, no. 3 (summer 1993): 360.

accurately said that our periods of great awakening have produced wars rather than resulted from them." Nor was he alone in his assessment; the historian John A. Andrew III has argued that "[t]he Second Great Awakening had clearly transformed much of the American cultural landscape, but it had not revitalized that society to the extent of creating a new political consensus formulated from its underlying principles."[39]

As indicated by the above statements, and the earlier statements by Reverend Witherspoon and the geographer John Logan Allen, the U.S. expansion of the western North American "frontier" was informed by Christian theological concepts as well as by concepts of race. Of course scholars as well are influenced by prevalent social and religious ideas, as McLoughlin's comments display. With regard to this issue, the historian Paul Boyer made several suggestive comments about the context of the production of history, noting, "[I]n the nineteenth century, history instruction and historical writing in the United States were *steeped* in religion. Christianity—and specifically, evangelical Protestant Christianity—was treated not merely as a social phenomenon worthy of scholarly attention and pedagogical notice, but as a basic framework of meaning for interpreting the national experience, and as a font of moral guidance." He continued: "[R]eligion also pervaded nineteenth-century historiography in the form of an unabashedly patriotic, nationalistic, and quasi-theological dogma."[40]

In fact, according to the University of Chicago historian Peter Novick, in order for Woodrow Wilson to be recommended for an academic position at Bryn Mawr, Wilson had to convince the president of the college that he "'believed that the hand of Providence was in all history; that the progress of Christianity was as great a factor as the development of philosophy and the sciences.'"[41] In a similar vein, the historian of religion Grant Wacker has suggested that the historical narrative of Christianity reflects a type of "tribalism," as distinguished from "the mainline academy," which "insists upon

---

39. McLoughlin, *Revivals*, 23; John A. Andrew III, *From Revivals to Removal: Jeremiah Evarts, the Cherokee Nation, and the Search for the Soul of America* (Athens, Ga.: University of Georgia Press, 1992), 267–68.

40. Boyer, "Search," 131, 132.

41. Wilson to Ellen Louise Axson, 27 November 1884, Link, 3:490, 502, quoted in Peter Novick, *That Noble Dream: The "Objectivity Question" and the American Historical Profession* (Cambridge: Cambridge University Press, 1988), 65.

such notions as contextualism, change, disconfirmation, and so
forth." Wacker argued that in the former "framework the truly significant causes are not historical at all. They are extra-historical,
tumbling directly from heaven or, if not from heaven, at least from
some realm not open to the ken of outsiders." He continued:

> Beyond this, tribalism often entails what Sidney Mead called "histo-
> ryless history," although "kangaroo history" might be more apt, for its
> practitioners try to jump over the immediate past in order to reclaim
> a distant past, a Garden of Eden, a Day of Pentecost, or a Council of
> Trent, that they regard as normative for all times and places. Again,
> the product is the same: a line of argument that makes perfect sense
> to insiders but leaves outsiders out, deleted from the narrative and
> wondering what happened.[42]

Again, though Wacker was speaking about historical narratives of
Christianity, I think that his insightful comments can be applied to
many narratives of U.S. religious history.

Interestingly, there is more than one source for such narrative
constructions. As the historians Keith Jenkins and Alun Munslow
noted in *The Nature of History Reader*, "[n]ot so long ago in the West,
there existed an essentially religious but, in the last two hundred
years, a thoroughly secularised belief that the past, history, had in it
its own intrinsic value, its own purposeful meaning, an essence."
According to the authors, "[a]lmost invariably this perceived history,
this unfolding of meaning, was cast in a form of progressive teleology." They continued: "Like all teleologies, this particular teleology
culminated in *closure*, the substance(s) of which, in this instance, was
expressed in the idea that the point of history was to bring about
emancipated human rights communities in one or two basic forms
(with internal inflections): a bourgeois, liberal, capitalist form or a
proletarian socialist/communist one."[43]

Paul Boyer seemed to echo these sentiments when he argued that
many historians, including textbook writers, "whatever their religious

42. Grant Wacker, "Understanding the Past, Using the Past: Reflections on Two
Approaches to History," in Kuklick and Hart, *Religious Advocacy,* 172, 169–70. The
quote began, "In the Christian tradition, for example, tribalist values often lead to what
theologian Russell Spittler calls a 'sacred meteor' theory of causation."

43. Keith Jenkins and Alun Munslow, *The Nature of History Reader* (London:
Routledge, 2004), 15.

beliefs—tacitly accept the secularization paradigm when conceptualizing U.S. history." He also noted, regarding more recent historical scholarship: "[I]n a partially secularized guise, as a component of what Robert Bellah and others have called America's 'civil religion,' this view of the United States as a divinely chosen nation, or at least as a special instrument of God's unfolding plan for humanity, proved extremely tenacious even in ostensibly 'secular' historical writing, encouraging an uncritical and triumphalist tone."[44]

Boyer remarked further that "everyone concedes the importance in American history of Puritanism and the Great Awakening, the role of evangelicalism in antebellum reform, the Social Gospel's influence, and perhaps the modernist-fundamentalist controversy." However, his conclusion is more along the lines of McLoughlin's theory: "[W]hat U.S. history in fact reveals is not a straight-line 'secularization' process but a complex pattern as religious energies ebb and flow, fade, and reemerge in new forms." In this statement McLoughlin's paradigm should be clear. Boyer did recognize, on the other hand, that scholars today are "made understandably uneasy by rose-tinted versions of history in which everything unfolds for the best and in which divine intervention becomes the central causal dynamic."[45]

To repeat my statement from the first section of this chapter, whether or not the model is one of "divine history" or "secularization," the result is a bounded history that often obscures events of a place—in this case, the partition of land now known as the continental United States—and the complex history of all its inhabitants, past and present. Recognizing such a disjunction, Jenkins and Munslow have argued that "we have come to the end of history in metanarrative forms; in those Hegelianised Marxist formats; in those various linear (generally progressive) fables that believed that the end—toward which we are moving—was given in the beginning." The authors went on to say that "[a]s with all teleological thinking. . . . [I]n this act of the imagination, the end is always in the process of becoming 'nigh.'"[46] Politically or theologically constructed, it does seem that the time for such fables has come to an end, at least as thematic cores for historical narratives.

44. Boyer, "Search," 128, 133.
45. Ibid., 128, 129, 134.
46. Jenkins and Munslow, *Nature of History*, 320.

———†———

So then, what are the alternatives? In 1998, religious studies scholar Thomas Tweed edited an important collection of essays entitled *Retelling U.S. Religious History.* Providing an introductory overview of different paradigms, Tweed identified several key models of U.S. religious historiography; in addition to that volume's offerings, he noted several additional alternative models that have been proposed to the dominant Protestant paradigm. To my knowledge, none of these has been applied in a textbook or survey format. None of the contributors discussed McLoughlin's model, and though they all were cognizant of issues of metanarrative, one statement in particular, by Joel Martin, stands out: "We have not yet written narratives centered on contact or fully cognizant of colonialism and its legacies." In his conclusion, Tweed stated that "[t]here are many stories to tell, many sites from which to narrate them, and many motifs to order the plots." Noting that "some stories await telling" while "the old narratives retain some interpretive power," he concluded that these stories "can only help as we look for ways to tell more inclusive stories of America's complex religious past."[47]

Another interesting collection of viewpoints from religious studies scholars on this subject appeared in the June 2002 issue of the journal *Church History,* entitled "Forum: Is There a Center to

47. Joel Martin, "Indians, Contact, and Colonialism," in Thomas A. Tweed, ed., *Retelling U.S. Religious History* (Berkeley and Los Angeles: University of California Press, 1997), 153; Tweed, *Retelling,* 23. In a footnote, Tweed listed the following alternative models to the dominant Protestant paradigm. He began with Jon Butler's idea to use "six 'Catholic' themes to write U.S. religious history," rather than what Butler argued were motifs drawn from Puritanism. Tweed also noted Nathan O. Hatch's concept of "Methodist motifs," Tweed's own "model that derives from the history of Asian religions in America," and David Wills's offering that "race—or relations between blacks and whites—could serve as an illuminating motif." He also noted approaches that made use of more than one motif, particularly Clifton E. Olmstead's 1961 narrative in which "'adaptation,'" as well as "'diversity' and 'diversification,'" were employed along with "an image associated with the stages of growth of butterflies"; thus Olmstead stated "that the 'saga of American religion is one of metamorphosis'" (ibid., 235n23); quotations from Clifton E. Olmstead, *Religion in America: Past and Present* (Englewood Cliffs, N.J.: Prentice-Hall, 1961), 3, 160. Reflecting on the volume in a later essay, Tweed noted that it "tried to move toward new plots, even if it did not propose any single full-blown narrative." He also spoke of his plan to write a "comprehensive narrative" drawing on the themes of "mapping, meeting, and migration." Thomas A. Tweed, Grant Wacker, Jon Pahl, Valerie H. Ziegler, and William D. Dinges, "Forum: Teaching the Introductory Course in American Religion," *Religion and American Culture* 12, no. 1 (winter 2002): 3, 4.

American Religious History?"[48] Amanda Porterfield argued that "the *myth* of the Puritans as religious founders" was "a good candidate for premier topos" and a "central category for organizing multiple forms and dimensions of American religion." She offered four "ways of working with the topos of Puritanism," noting that different "perspectives on American religious history are often expressed through stories about the Puritans" and that stories about them "often carry arguments about the nature and trajectory of American religious history."[49]

In his contribution, Stephen J. Stein noted the move against "the centered historiography of American religion" and cited *Retelling U.S. Religious History* as the "most sophisticated statement in favor of the decentered history of American religion." Stein went on to list three "problems with the loss of a center" in American religious history: "decentered histories are often simply recentered histories"; they suffer "the loss of awareness of contact and negotiation between and among religious groups"; and "decentered history of either the microcentric or the isocentric variety severely handicaps any effort to understand the larger religious story." Stein suggested that centered histories ought to be "inclusive, expansive, fair, and detailed" as well as "multiple." He stated, however, that he did not "believe such a thing exists," though he argued that shouldn't deter scholars from trying to "construct useful narratives." He also suggested "the image of the marketplace as an organizing metaphor."[50]

William Vance Trollinger Jr. also referenced, as he put it, "Tweed and his merry band of decenterers"; with regard to the general problem at hand, he argued that "the various historical narratives overlap and are intertwined with one another—and in many ways it is at these points of overlap and intertwining that we may be able to make general comments about religion in the United States." Trollinger

48. "Forum: Is There a Center to American Religious History?" *Church History* 71, no. 2 (June 2002): 368–90; the papers included Amanda Porterfield, "Does American Religion Have a Center?"; Stephen J. Stein, "American Religious History: Decentered with Many Centers"; William Vance Trollinger Jr., "Is There a Center to American Religious History?"; and Peter W. Williams, "'Does American Religious History Have a Center?' Reflections." According to a prefatory note, the papers and response constituted "a panel sponsored by the American Society of Church History and held in conjunction with the annual meeting of the American Academy of Religion in Nashville, Tennessee, in November of 2000" (368).

49. Porterfield, "Does American Religion?" 369, 372, 373.

50. Stein, "American Religious History," 376, 377, 378–79.

concluded that "we will probably not come up with a fully satisfying interpretive paradigm," but that was "in keeping with the messy realities of American religion."[51]

Finally, Peter W. Williams began his response to the three papers by referencing the Japanese film *Rashomon*, in which "four differing and incompatible accounts of the same event are presented by the central characters, leaving the viewer to wonder which, if any, is the 'true' version." For Williams it seems that such a narrative model would be interesting though unsatisfactory; rather, he invoked the concept of "host culture" to argue for the possibility of an inclusive narrative that retained particularities of detail. In this way, he argued, "American religious history can thus be presented ... neither as the inexorable march of Protestant progress nor ... as just 'one damn thing after another.'"[52]

Selected further perspectives, again among many possible ones, are relevant. The first is offered by the historian Philip Deloria, who argued with regard to histories of First Nations peoples that the "best contemporary scholarship treats Indians and non-Indians in a changing world, with historical consciousnesses that are the products of that world and of those changes. Such scholarship recognizes the need to both dissolve and reassert boundaries at the same time." American Studies scholar Neil Campbell, writing from the perspective of a British academic post in *The Cultures of the American New West*, presented a valuable survey of postmodern theoretical contributions from a range of scholars whose work is relevant to this discussion. These included Mary-Louise Pratt ("contact zone"), Edward Soja ("trialectics of spatiality"), Michel de Certeau (in "previously silenced zones . . . a 'new history' finds its focus"), Walter Benjamin ("historical materialism"), and Michel Foucault ("effective history"). Campbell also cited Paul Gilroy in his text.[53]

---

51. Trollinger, "Is There a Center?" 382, 384.
52. Williams, "Does American Religious History?" 386, 390.
53. Philip J. Deloria, "Historiography," in Philip J. Deloria and Neal Salisbury, *A Companion to American Indian History* (Malden, Mass.: Blackwell Publishers, 2002), 21; Neil Campbell, *The Cultures of the American New West* (Edinburgh: Edinburgh University Press, 2000), 18, 21, 13, 12, 13. Thomas Tweed has referenced many of the same individuals, including Homi Bhaba ("third space"), though he focused his attention on the relative position of the interpreter. Thomas Tweed, "On Moving Across: Translocative Religion and the Interpreter's Position," *Journal of the American Academy of Religion* 70, no. 2 (June 2002): 253–77; 261.

Like other scholars discussed above, the historian Jerry H. Bentley also has noted that overturning the prevalent narrative model can have pitfalls. In an article entitled "World History and Grand Narrative" he critiqued "postmodern and postcolonial critics" of what he called "received Eurocentric grand narratives." Bentley argued that though they "offer some cogent critiques and make some sorely needed corrections to the Enlightenment story," "[t]hese counter-narratives basically invert the Enlightenment story: they are derivative reactions, and as such they lack the power to escape the Enlightenment's gravitational field."[54]

In his attempt "to construct more useful alternatives to the received Eurocentric grand narratives that can serve as framing devices for historical scholarship," Bentley argued for an approach that "leaves the end of history open and recognizes the capacities of human actors to organize their societies and conduct relations with others in unpredictable ways." Such an approach, he argued, differed from a "triumphalist or teleological or totalizing conception" in that "it acknowledges the roles of all peoples in the making of a world inhabited by all." Whether or not such a history can be written remains to be seen, but it is certainly an interesting counterpoint to the standard teleological narrative structure. I am reminded, however, of a statement by religious studies scholar Sam Gill, who, invoking Jean Baudrillard's use of the well-known "map-territory" metaphor to describe the process in which the map becomes the only reality," has noted that this "broad analysis of Western culture applies, to a degree not yet appreciated because it would be too damning, to the academic study of religion." According to Gill, "The implication is that we may have come to rely so deeply on our maps, on our generic ideas regarding religion, that our presentations of religion are simulations of culture and history; hyperrealities with few territorial or referential realities beyond the simulation."[55]

All of these scholars provide useful models to think about and describe this space and these interactions. How might one construct

---

54. Jerry H. Bentley, "World History and Grand Narrative," in Benedikt Stuchtey and Eckhardt Fuchs, eds., *Writing World History, 1800–2000* (London: Oxford University Press and German Historical Institute, 2003), 49.

55. Ibid., 49–50, 64, 65; Sam Gill, "Territory," in Mark C. Taylor, ed., *Critical Terms for Religious Studies* (Chicago: University of Chicago Press, 1998), 309. The three factors mentioned by Bentley are essential to his model of world history; they are what he called "three realities of global human experience" (Bentley, "World History," 51).

a narrative that would leave "the end of history open," as Bentley said, that would "recognize the need to both dissolve and reassert boundaries at the same time," as Deloria suggested, and that would be "neither . . . the inexorable march of Protestant progress nor . . . just 'one damn thing after another,'" as Williams so eloquently summarized? Perhaps Stein and Trollinger are correct in asserting that such a narrative does not and cannot exist, respectively, but I agree that continuing to try is essential. My suggestion would be to attempt a narrative along the lines of the film *Rashoman,* as described by Williams; my own model might look something like Milorad Paviæ's *Dictionary of the Khazars: A Lexicon Novel,* in that it would strive to present selected different perspectives of individuals and events. However, I understand the pitfalls of such a model that several scholars discussed above. The historian John Lewis Gaddis used the example of two works of art that depict the same subject to illustrate his related point that historians must "strike a balance"; they must recognize "a trade-off between literal and abstract representation."[56]

I have a second model, less literary than my first one but in my mind no less effective: video driving games. These games have advanced a great deal since I was a boy; the most intriguing advance is a button that one can press and achieve different views of the action: one from inside the car, one from behind the car, and one from above the car. The experience of playing the game—struggling to reach the finish line in sufficient time to achieve extended play, all the while furiously switching between perspectives to find the best view for the race—is exactly the feeling I get as I attempt to construct and then teach the narrative of American religious history anew. As suggested above, this might not be such a bad thing. I do think that the notion of switching between perspectives as one goes along is an interesting idea, akin to the use of hypertext, though it would need much refinement. In this regard, a page of the Talmud might serve as a model as it is similar to what a page of hypertext might look like if it was all printed onto a single sheet.

—+—

56. John Lewis Gaddis, *The Landscape of History: How Historians Map the Past* (New York: Oxford University Press, 2002), 12.

It remains to be seen what events will transpire in the years leading up to the Trail of Tears bicentennial. Will there be government-
sponsored commemorations, a spike in related publications, or new
approaches to the historical rendering of the events? As was the case
in 1993, when muted celebrations and counterdemonstrations to
commemorate Columbus's "discovery" replaced the grandiose spectacle of the 1893 Columbian Exposition, will there be a similar shift
away from such previous commemorative activities as the "Five
Civilized Tribes" commemorative stamp issued by the U.S. Postal
Service in 1948?

As noted above, one official governmental expression of national
memory is the creation of national historic trails. Among the many
other commemorative publications coinciding with the Lewis and
Clark bicentennial, a new map was issued by the U.S. government
that delineated the explorers' route, including the Lewis and Clark
National Historic Trail, established in 1978. The Trail of Tears
National Historic Trail was established in 1987. Why it took almost
twenty years to produce an interpretive plan is unclear; nevertheless,
according to the 2004 final report, the Cherokee event was recognized by Congress "as the most enduring feature of the tragic Indian
Removal period in American History." In addition, though, "the
Cherokee experience was recognized as a window into the experience of all tribes removed from the Southeast United States as a con-
sequence of the Indian Removal Act of 1830. . . . Whenever possible,
interpretation activities along the Trail of Tears will seek to identify
experiences and associations of other tribes who participated in the
Removal experience."[57] At Cape Girardeau, Missouri, the trails crossed
briefly, the travelers headed in two very different directions.

Of course I recognize the fact that a nation is not going to go out
of its way to commemorate its own historical blight, but museums
and commemorative activities concerning events such as the
Holocaust and slavery do exist. No doubt there are other examples

---

57. National Park Service, Trail of Tears National Historic Trail, preface to "Trail of
Tears National Historic Trail: Interpretive Plan, Final, June 14, 2004," http://
home.nps.gov/applications/parks/trte/ppdocuments/ACF1B77.pdf (accessed November 12, 2007). In November 2007, the National Historic Trail Feasibility Study
Amendment and Environmental Assessment identified additional routes of Cherokee
removal eligible for inclusion on the existing Trail of Tears National Historic Trail. This
and other relevant documents are available at http://parkplanning.nps.gov/
documentsList.cfm?parkId=448&projectI=17939d (accessed December 20, 2007).

of what I have illustrated above: textbooks and surveys that present selected events and the communities that experienced them like a group of tops: spinning in time, yet always in a separate orbit, a separate trajectory, from other events. A balance must be struck between integrating the data and forcing it to conform to an overarching framework, or continuing to isolate or ignore it.

The Trail of Tears—all of the forced removals—and the Cherokee events that have come to stand for all, were products of their time. They also were products of the national cultural narrative or national mythology—what remains the narrative today. They are representative of motivations, ideals, and resultant circumstances, as well as being historical occurrences. These events need to be integrated into the national narrative—not tacked on as anomalies, not identified with one individual's administration, but presented as constituent, necessary parts of that history. The missing links between these events create wide open spaces in the narrative of U.S. history that obscure their close relationship. The Trail of Tears needs to "stand" next to the Louisiana Purchase as well as the Second Great Awakening in the narrative. Only then can scholars begin to write a postfrontier, postcolonial, postmodern history.

Crossroads, the Cosmos, and Jazz in the Heartland
Oklahoma City's Deep Deuce and Kansas City's Vine Street

DOUGLAS HENRY DANIELS

THE ACQUISITION OF THE LOUISIANA TERRITORY AFFECTED THE nation's culture and religion for decades after the exploratory mission of Lewis and Clark. African Americans who moved into Kansas City and Oklahoma City in the late nineteenth and early twentieth centuries have been largely neglected by standard histories, even though they brought with them some of the most salient features of black culture in popular music, jazz dance, community celebrations, and age-old worship practices.

Scholars have examined African American folklore, songs, ring shouts, and hoodoo or vodun, and usually within the context of the rural South—either the plantation or small farm—but the continuation of other African, West Indian, and specific Louisiana cultural retentions within twentieth-century urban settings should cause us to reconsider both the history of religion and the culture in that huge expanse of territory. Jazz, blues, and the accompanying dances were so much a part of a diasporic religious heritage in Oklahoma City and Kansas City that it should cause us to rethink what we mean by worship and even religion. Moreover, these forms were not limited to the black community; they were of primary importance for subsequent developments in so-called mainstream music and dance culture during the remainder of the twentieth century.

West African retentions in black music culture and in the religious heritage, as well, were noted within but not limited to New Orleans's Congo Square and Louisiana. Few historical or cultural studies have focused on the music culture of North American blacks living within the Louisiana Purchase territory and outside of what became the state of Louisiana. This study of the special urban sites of black city-dwellers in Deep Deuce, as Oklahoma City's East Second Street was known, and Vine Street, black Kansas City's main stem (more specifically, 12th, 14th, and especially 18th and Vine), suggests that certain cultural features related to jazz's roots are not only deep but also widespread, and that even popular music reflects vital elements of their religious heritage.

One would be hard-pressed to identify other sites as sacred as Congo Square, but 52nd Street near Broadway ("The Street," as it was familiarly known) in Manhattan, Central Avenue around 42nd Street in Los Angeles, and W. C. Handy Park with its statue of the bandleader on Beale Street in Memphis come to mind. In the former Louisiana Territory, Deep Deuce in Oklahoma City and Vine Street in Kansas City are the closest to Congo Square in significance.[1]

Not only Kansas City but also Oklahoma City needs to be given greater prominence in the culture, religion, and history of the region. For example, the reputation and musicianship of Oklahoma City's Blue Devils has not been properly appreciated. Bandleader Count Basie considered it to be the best band he ever heard, and so did many others from the region. In his first orchestra he tried to re-create the bonhomie of his territorial years with the Devils. Then too, while the Kansas City roots of the band have been emphasized, they are more complicated than this single-city analysis indicates.[2]

1. Linda Miller, "Deep Deuce Spirit Alive, Growing," *Sunday Oklahoman* September 23, 2001, 1; Kendrick Moore, *Oklahoma City African American Discovery Guide* (Oklahoma City: Oklahoma African American Trail of Tears Tours, 2000), 38–39. Typically, works such as Frank Driggs and Harris Lewine, *Black Beauty, White Heat: A Pictorial History of Classic Jazz, 1920–1950* (New York: Da Capo Press, 1996), trace the music from New Orleans to Chicago to New York and then Kansas City—and do not mention Oklahoma City at all. For the Los Angeles jazz scene before and following World War II, see Clora Bryant et al., *Central Avenue Sounds: Jazz in Los Angeles* (Berkeley and Los Angeles: University of California Press, 1998). See also Steve Cheseborough, *Blues Traveling: The Holy Sites of Delta Blues,* 2d ed. (Oxford: University of Mississippi Press, 2004); I wish to thank Jim Masker, of Cate School, Santa Barbara, for informing me of this work. Cheseborough's sites are different from the author's, as he includes the former homes, juke joints, and graves of blues musicians. Recently I read Mircea Eliade, "Sacred Space and Making the World Sacred," in his *The Sacred and the Profane: The Nature of Religion,* trans. Willard R. Trask (New York: Harcourt, 1987), which strengthened my convictions about sacred sites and the crossroads.

2. Douglas Henry Daniels, *One O'clock Jump: The Unforgettable History of the Oklahoma City Blue Devils* (Boston: Beacon Press, 2005).

Additionally, while New Orleans music and Dixieland persists, it has not been quite as prolific, leading to new styles, as the music coming out of the aforementioned cities. New Orleans bands introduced ragtime and horns playing countermelodies alternating with the melody, and New York orchestras produced polished performances, but neither has given us the jump blues, stomps, swing, and rhythm and blues, termed rock and roll when adopted by whites, subsequent developments in jazz, such as bebop, hard bop, or progressive jazz, and even modal forms such as Miles Davis's *Kind of Blue* album, and then rock. Moreover, blues revivals have also characterized U.S. and British culture, starting in the 1960s, but nothing parallel has occurred with respect to New Orleans music, a factor that must be taken into account when assessing the significance and impact of the different cultural traditions.

No less remarkable is the fact that the fusion of swing music, dancing, and trancelike states, characteristics of Kansas City and southwestern popular music, carried over into the big band era and affected whites, especially teenagers, as much as it did African Americans. As early as 1965, Charles Keil noted the African roots in blues music and performances, including the manner in which the audience danced and participated. More recently, Dr. Robin Sylvan explored the retention of specific African music cultural characteristics—including those that I have noted—in rock concerts, particularly those of groups like the Grateful Dead. These bands and their faithful followers, he maintained, constituted veritable cults in terms of their fierce loyalty, their shared beliefs, and their behavior.[3]

Crossroads

The crossroads concept is a particularly important element of West African cosmology that is crucial to understanding the significance of certain celebrations and the sites where they took place in Oklahoma City and Kansas City. The crossroads is more than the intersection of two metaphorical (or actual) roads, as its spiritual

3. Charles Keil, *Urban Blues* (Chicago: University of Chicago Press, 1966); Robin Sylvan, *Traces of the Spirit: The Religious Dimensions of Popular Music* (New York: New York University Press, 2002); Robin Sylvan, *Trance Formation: The Spiritual and Religious Dimensions of Global Rave Culture* (New York: Routledge, 2005).

dimension is the most vital aspect. Nor is it limited to this one plane where byways cross; it also has a vertical dimension intersecting where the two roads meet. The two planes, the horizontal and the vertical, correspond to the physical and spiritual worlds with the vertical axis plunging one into the subterranean dimension where ancestors, spirits, and deities dwell.[4]

When dancers circle around the vertical axis, spirits from this netherworld often possess them. This descent into the spiritual world represents depth, or profundity, as in "Deep Deuce," or for that matter, "deep blues"—blues that are otherworldly, eerie, and profound, from "way out in the cotton patch." Maya Deren explained the importance of the concept: "[T]he cross-roads is more than a metaphysical principle. . . . It is at this point of intersection that the abstract and ancestral principles which are the *loa*—whose location is in absolute time and absolute space—become a living organism of this immediate moment and this particular place."[5] Furthermore, "as the principle enters reality it not only acts upon that reality but is, of necessity, defined, shaped, and modified by it. It is at such intersection that tradition meets contemporary need and faith becomes the *act* of ritual service and divine response." Something similar takes place during the ring shout of the plantation and rural South, but the songs, circular movement, and possession in the ring shout were strictly religious phenomena.[6]

If black residents of Oklahoma City and Kansas City danced and celebrated just anywhere (as a community and not simply as individuals), it would be different, but they seemed to prefer certain specific intersections in their respective neighborhoods—particular streets and dance halls on the East Side in each instance. Their dance temples and nightspots were centered near historic intersections, such as 18th and Vine, the site of the Cherry Blossom, or nearby on other horizontals—the Lone Star and Sunset on 12th Street, less than one block east of Vine.

---

4. Maya Deren, *Divine Horsemen: The Living Gods of Haiti* (Kingston, N.Y.: McPherson, 1983), 73, 37, 96–102.

5. Ibid., 73.

6. Ibid. Saxophonist and swing arranger Henry "Buster" Smith used the term "deep blues," and in 1982 when I asked him what he meant, his response was, "That's what I mean, it's deep." On the ring shout, see Sterling Stuckey, *Slave Culture: Nationalist Theory and the Foundations of Black America* (New York: Oxford University Press, 1987).

Congo Square

The concept of the crossroads is of vital importance in the black diaspora. In New Orleans, observers made frequent reference to Congo Square, situated across Rampart Street from the French Quarter and between St. Philip and St. Peter streets. Here African and African American slaves sang, danced, and celebrated on their day off—Sundays—from the late eighteenth and into the nineteenth centuries. This was a sacred space at a particular time on a specific day—one in which the blacks "possessed" or owned the territory.

Benjamin Henry Latrobe, perhaps the best-known of the several observers of Congo Square activities, explored the Crescent City's "back of town" area one Sunday afternoon in February 1819 and "heard in the distance an extraordinary noise." He found that, rather than horses trampling, the noise came from an assembly of five to six hundred persons in the public square who were clapping their hands, stamping their feet, and playing various percussive and banjo-like instruments. The participants were all black, as he "did not observe a dozen yellow faces."[7]

Significantly, the crowd "was not a single mass, but a series of clusters. The members of each cluster crowded around to form" a circle about ten feet in diameter. Two or three musicians sat or squatted in the middle or on the edge of each circle, and "from two to a dozen dancers moved to the rhythm of the circle's music, song, and chant." The various melodies, chants, dances, instruments, and hand clapping reflected the participants' common African heritage.[8]

Congo Square is the most famous site of its kind in the United States. In the mid-nineteenth century, Anglo-American Protestants regarded the Sunday activities of the Francophone and Catholic Creoles of color in Congo Square as blasphemous in much the same way that certain ministers viewed jazz dancing in Kansas City and Oklahoma City nightclubs with disdain. "After going to mass on

---

7. On Congo Square gatherings, see Jerah Johnson, "New Orleans's Congo Square: An Urban Setting for Early Afro-American Culture Formation," *Louisiana History* 32, no. 2 (spring 1991): 117–57.

8. Latrobe, quoted in ibid., 118–19, quotation on p. 140; and Richard Knight, *The Blues Highway: New Orleans to Chicago—Travel and Music Guide* (Surrey, U.K.: Trailblazer Publications, 2001), 42–43. Of Congo Square, Johnson observed, "No other single spot has been more often mentioned in scholarly speculations about the origins of jazz or about the relationship of pre-jazz New Orleans music to jazz itself" (Johnson, "Congo Square," 119).

Sunday morning, the Creoles made the rest of the day a festival, indulging themselves in public entertainments, going on outings and excursions, enjoying picnics, and barbeques, shopping the street markets, and, on Sunday evenings, drinking and dancing."[9] Today the former Congo Square is Louis Armstrong Park. The statue of the Crescent City's most famous native son stands here, and even more impressive is the lighted display over the park entrance at night: an illuminated rainbow-shaped arc with Armstrong's name across it.

East Second Street and Vine Street

Like Congo Square, Deep Deuce and Vine Street possessed a continuous history that can be documented because of their singular importance to local African American residents. It is particularly noteworthy that in Deep Deuce, as in New Orleans, dancing was a public institution. All three sites verged on sacred territory, and they were important for nonmusical as well as musical reasons. They embodied the history of the African American communities and reflected their social and economic successes as well as their ethnic pride. Local citizens have made efforts in recent years to revive the historic activities and celebrations in Armstrong Park and in the street carnivals and neighborhood development in Oklahoma City and Kansas City. At the same time, and paradoxically, these celebrations, dances, and sites were regarded with both levity and a surprising measure of reverence.

Indeed, we can assess the survival of West African religious heritage on Deep Deuce and on Vine Street on certain occasions. There is no reason to believe Louisianans settled in these cities in disproportionate numbers, but it is clear that certain specific street intersections were "sacred" in the sense that they possessed very specific meaning for the African American residents of the respective cities. They were the sites of rituals that gave alternative meaning and value to the lives of these city dwellers, as the racist social structure of the respective cities and the nation denied all but the most enterprising anything but menial jobs in the workaday world.

Deep Deuce and Vine Street between 12th and 18th were mainly African American neighborhoods in the nation's urban heartland.

9. Johnson, "Congo Square," 120.

Black vaudeville and movie theater owners; nightclub, restaurant, hotel, and rooming house operators; and doctors, dentists, hairdressers, barbers, bootleggers, undertakers, journalists, lawyers, and other professionals worked and lived in or near these black neighborhoods. Most importantly, different African American residents revered these sites and felt the responsibility to gather here and dance when celebrating holidays, such as the Big Labor Day stomp in the summer of 1935.

These black urban sites, located in cities with the largest African American populations in the territory (outside of St. Louis and New Orleans), were closely connected not only with the historic pioneer periods of African American settlement, but also with black music and early jazz dance in each locale. Black music in these cities revealed the deep roots of West Indian and West African cultures and religions in the new territory. In these respects, the portrait that emerges contrasts sharply with the usual depiction of the history, the emerging culture, and residents' lives in the Louisiana Territory and, also, with traditional analyses of religion that are concerned primarily with the usual organized faiths—Protestant Christianity and Judaism, with respect to whites, and Baptist and Methodist, for African Americans.[10]

Ragtime, Blues, and Jazz in the Heartland

Fans, critics, and scholars distinguish different genres of African American music, but the distinctions between ragtime, jazz, and blues are often either academic or best understood by musicologists. Furthermore, many entertainers who are now regarded as early "jazz" musicians maintained that they called it "ragtime" before it was given the new name around World War I. Little is known of Oklahoma City's contribution to ragtime, and it appears that local black pioneers possessed a preference for European semiclassical music as well as religious.[11]

10. Miller, "Deep Deuce," 1; Moore, *Oklahoma City,* 38–39. St. Louis's black residents numbered nearly 93,000 by 1930, while Oklahoma City and Kansas City housed nearly 15,000 and 39,000, respectively, that year. Fifteenth Census of U.S., Population, vol. 3 (Washington, D.C. 1932), 64–65.

11. Based upon examination of the *Oklahoma City Black Dispatch* for the years 1917–1919. For Kansas City ragtime, see Rudi Blesh and Harriet Janis, *They All Played*

The most important characteristics of the blues, of course, are blue tonality and harmony, and songs in this genre often have a specific length of twelve bars (though not necessarily), and the blues can "flavor" (to use a current term) ragtime, jazz, gospel, and other musical styles—not simply African American. For our purposes, it is important to understand that many musicians consider blues, with its emphasis on improvisation, as one of the main roots of jazz, and whereas blues differed from much of ragtime, the two also fused, as in the compositions of Jelly Roll Morton. In each instance, by the 1920s, local reporters in the two cities recognized some of the music played by local bands as jazz. Moreover, these two cities were significant in the music's development, having their own jazz bands by 1923—the year that Jelly Roll Morton, Ma Rainey, Bessie Smith, King Oliver, Louis Armstrong, and other musicians made their first recordings.[12]

Deep Deuce

African American settlers of the late nineteenth and early twentieth centuries considered themselves to be pioneer Oklahomans like their white counterparts, who also traveled on foot and horseback and in covered wagons to stake claims in what was originally designated as Indian Territory. Later they came by train or by automobile, and by the 1920s, the newcomers settled in or near the center of Oklahoma City's black community—the 300 block of East Second from Central to Stiles avenues—just a short distance north of the train tracks that paralleled East Second and that always ran by or

Ragtime (New York: Oak Publications, 1966), which details the early contributions of Kansas City to ragtime and jazz. See also Ross Russell, *Jazz Style in Kansas City and the Southwest* (Berkeley and Los Angeles: University of California Press, 1971); Daniels, *One O'clock Jump*; and Frank Driggs and Chuck Haddix, *Kansas City Jazz: From Ragtime to Bebop—A History* (New York: Oxford University Press, 2005).

12. Lawrence Gushee, *Pioneers of Jazz: The Story of the Creole Band* (New York: Oxford University Press, 2005), 233–34; Philip Pastras, *Dead Man Blues: Jelly Roll Morton Way out West* (Berkeley and Los Angeles: University of California Press, 2001); Sandra Lieb, *Mother of the Blues: A Study of Ma Rainey* (Amherst: University of Massachusetts Press, 1981); Daphne Duval Harrison, *Black Pearls: Blues Queens of the 1920s* (New Brunswick, N.J.: Rutgers University Press, 1988). The first genuine New Orleans jazz recording was made in Los Angeles by Edward "Kid" Ory's band in 1921; see Douglas Henry Daniels, "Los Angeles's Jazz Roots: The Willis H. Young Family," *California History* 82, no. 3 (2004): 48–50.

through black neighborhoods in U.S. urban settings. On Deep Deuce, African American residents of Oklahoma City as well as visitors from outlying regions gathered not simply to hear music, to dance, and to fraternize, but to eat out, to purchase new outfits, to have their hair done and their shoes shined for a night on the town, and to find accommodations with friends or in one of the lodging houses.[13]

Additionally, the 200 block to the west and the 400 block to the east (of East Second), as well as East First, were part of Deep Deuce, too, to an extent, but the 300 block was the heart of the black community from the 1920s into the 1990s.[14] Leading Deep Deuce residents exemplified the economic successes of black urbanites on the East Side and served as models for residents shut out from respectable jobs that paid well. For example, the successful businessman Percy H. James, from Louisiana, invented and bottled Jay-Kola, a soft drink, on the East Side. Another pioneer, entrepreneur Sidney Lyons, the hair oil manufacturer, was born in Oklahoma around 1865. His success permitted him to purchase a large brick home on Central just north of Second and then a new piano worth thirty-five hundred dollars in 1922. The African American hotels that also provided offices as headquarters for the fraternal lodges were in the same block on Central.[15]

Oklahoma City's black migrants were mainly descended from slaves, so they brought with them their profound and cherished music culture—profane as well as sacred forms—and this carried over into their urban life. A Creole Jazz band emerged in McAlester, Oklahoma, early in 1914, about the same time that the Original Creole Jazz Band, consisting entirely of New Orleans musicians, went on the road in Vaudeville and popularized this new music, and three years before jazz recordings became the national sensation.[16]

---

13. For a history of blacks in Oklahoma, see Jimmie Lewis Franklin, *Journey toward Hope: A History of Blacks in Oklahoma* (Norman: University of Oklahoma Press, 1982); and John Hope Franklin and John Whittington Franklin, eds., *My Life and an Era: The Autobiography of Buck Colbert Franklin* (Baton Rouge: Louisiana State University Press, 1997).

14. Miller, "Deep Deuce," 1.

15. On James, see 1930 Manuscript Census, Oklahoma City, E. D. 55–67, sheet 6B; Miller, "Deep Deuce," 1; and "Buys $3,500 Piano," *Oklahoma City Black Dispatch,* July 27, 1922, 5. Manuscript Census 1930, Oklahoma City, E. D. 55, p. 7B, indicated that he owned $50,000 in real estate. *Oklahoma City City Directory, 1929.*

16. Gushee, *Pioneers,* 299; see also his fourth appendix: "On the History of the Word 'Jazz.'"

Black pioneers and professionals regarded Deep Deuce with special affection because it possessed historical significance, also because it was where the Ideal and the Blue Devils, as well as other territorial bands, performed at the Aldridge Theater (named after the nineteenth-century black actor) and at Slaughter's Hall. These vital African American venues were located on Deep Deuce near the corner of Second and Central and at the end of the block on the northwest corner of Second and Stiles, respectively, from the early 1920s.[17]

Dr. W. H. Slaughter and four other black physicians, a dentist, and two life insurance agents maintained Slaughter Building offices, and they focused on the physical well-being of black Oklahomans. They held their regular daytime office hours, then, after sunset, nighttime dance bands promoted spiritual well-being, insofar as local and touring dance bands reigned on the building's third floor. On the rooftop on hot summer nights at the corner of East Second and Stiles, African Americans danced to the rhythms and sounds that brought great joy, exhilaration, and sometimes trance. On Deep Deuce, highly rhythmic dance music was central to the celebrations and, most importantly, it called to the ancestors to visit the participants and to bless the occasion.[18]

Old-timers frequently mentioned the Ideal and the Blue Devils as the city's earliest jazz bands. Most impressive is the fact that some of the original members of the Blue Devils ran a music school in which classical music and European languages were taught, indicating they were not musical illiterates and were not limited to African American music culture. Walter Page and Willie Lewis, two of the music school professors, and Jimmy Rushing studied music and attended college, as well. Page, Rushing, Eddie Durham, and several other

17. "Ideal Still Favorites with Dance Fans," *Oklahoma City Black Dispatch*, December 27, 1923, 5. This article pointed out that, though located currently in Tulsa, the Ideal's musicians "still call Oklahoma City their home." The first mention of jazz in this city appears to be in "Social Whirl," *Oklahoma City Black Dispatch*, December 17, 1920, 5, though from the description, one must wonder what kind of music was played by Mr. Julian Turner, who performed "jazz music which was entrancing and full of melody." Additionally, Glover's "5" Jazz Orchestra was one of the first bands in the city that played this music, or claimed to.

18. On the spiritual dimension of jazz, see Douglas Henry Daniels, "Vodun and Jazz: 'Jelly Roll' Morton and Lester 'Pres' Young: Substance and Shadow," *Journal of Haitian Studies* 9, no. 1 (spring 2003): 109–22; and Douglas Henry Daniels, *Lester Leaps In: The Life and Times of Lester 'Pres' Young* (Boston: Beacon Press, 2002). See also Neil Leonard, *Jazz: Myth and Religion* (New York: Oxford University Press, 1987).

Blue Devils subsequently joined Bennie Moten and later made up the core of Count Basie's orchestra. This is remarkable evidence of the city's rich though unexplored music heritage.[19]

The dances held in Slaughter's Hall, the three-story brick structure, took place at the intersection of the major crossroads—East Second Street and Stiles Avenue. These celebrations were singular high points, dramatic emotional climaxes, so to speak, and, of course, appropriate for the crossroads. Within individual songs, virtuoso musicians achieved similar climaxes in their solos. When a band reached this high point, dancers could not stop dancing, while excited fans clamored for encores and would not allow the band to leave the stage.

The introduction of blues after midnight was another such climax, when couples danced closely and slowly while romantic sentiments went through their heads. In his reminiscence "Remembering Jimmy," the writer Ralph Ellison, who grew up in the capital, recalled how in his youth, singer Jimmy Rushing, who was born in Oklahoma City, belted out the blues from the rooftop garden of Slaughter's Hall. The bluesman was the herald of a new order, spreading the blues ethos to city dwellers with whomever he sang—with the Oklahoma City Blue Devils, then with Kansas City's Bennie Moten, and later with the Count Basie Orchestra for nearly two decades.

> On dance nights, when you stood on the rise of the school grounds two blocks to the east, you could hear [Rushing's voice] jetting from the dance hall like a blue flame in the dark; now soaring high above the trumpets and trombones, now skimming the froth of reeds and rhythm as it called some woman's anguished name—or demanded in a high, thin, passionately lyrical line, "Baaaaay-bay, Bay-aaaay-bay! Tell me what's the matter now!"—above the shouting of the swing band.

Ellison concluded, "His voice evoked the festive spirit of the blues. Indeed, he was the natural herald of its blues-romance, his song the singing essence of its joy."[20]

The sense of community solidarity among African American residents was impressive and evident in their social life in the 1920s and 1930s. Music, musicians, and their friends dominated community

19. The band's history is discussed in greater detail in Daniels, *One O'clock Jump.*
20. Ralph Ellison, "Remembering Jimmy," in *Shadow and Act* (New York: Signet Books, 1966), 235.

life in Deep Deuce to a degree that was not true on the other side of town. For example, Hallie Richardson, a former high school football star and native Oklahoman, ran a shoe-shine stand at 308 East Second and was the friend of musicians, in particular, and black city dwellers, in general. He was a member of the musicians' clique even though he was not a musician. Edward Christian, columnist for the local *Black Dispatch* and a musician and bandleader, as well as Charlie's older brother, observed that Richardson "has been around musicians for a good many years, and the cats take him to be one."[21]

When Kansas City drummer Edward McNeil, one of the original Blue Devils, died suddenly after an Easter performance in 1935, musicians and locals prepared for his funeral. "Mr. Richardson's car was in service at 7 o'clock Friday morning, to awaken the musicians that had to work late hours the night before." On this sad day musicians cooperated with one another "in every way," and Christian believed that "this cooperation came from every musician's heart."[22]

Like their New Orleans counterparts, black residents of Oklahoma's capital also paraded on East Second Street when the Elks and the Knights of Pythias celebrated. Then too, in late winter 1942, the coffin of the famous electric guitarist Charlie Christian, who grew up in the state's capital, was borne in a procession up the hill from Deep Deuce to Calvary Baptist, on Walnut Street, for the deceased to lie in state for the thousands wishing to pay their respects. Oklahoman Eugene Jones reminisced, "when someone died, if he was a musician, they would march with the casket up the hill to the church playing. I heard they did that for Charlie."[23]

Black Oklahoma City residents created and sustained a remarkable sense of unity through their popular music culture and dance, which is not to say other organizations—churches and fraternal orders, and topics such as civil rights, for example, were not important, but the music and dance culture, and its singular impact, has been overlooked except among jazz historians. Even in these studies, however, the love of dance, any spiritual traces, and the presence of

21. Edward Christian, "Musical Low-Down," *Oklahoma City Black Dispatch*, May 2, 1935, 8. Christian died of tuberculosis, as did his brother, Charles, in 1942; see the obituary, "Edward Christian Dies," *Oklahoma City Black Dispatch*, October 16, 1948, 1–2.
22. Christian, "Musical Low-Down."
23. Peter Broadbent, *Charlie Christian: Solo Flight; The Story of the Seminal Electric Guitarist*, 2d ed. (Blaydon on Tyne, U.K.: Ashley Mark, 2003), 125; Wayne E. Goins and Craig R. McKinney, *A Biography of Charlie Christian, Jazz Guitar's King of Swing* (Lewistown, N.Y.: Edwin Mellen Press, 2005).

West African and Caribbean traditions go unexplained. Significantly, however, Leroy Parks, tenor saxophonist with Eddie Christian's Blue Devils in 1935, recalled,

> We used to play in those open air things when they roped off 2nd Street between Central and Stiles. . . . They would block the whole block off down in "deep deuce," and there would be hundreds and hundreds of people out in the street. There would be no drinks or barbecues[,] they'd just come down to enjoy the music 'n' dance. Everyone knew everyone 'cos it was like that [during] segregation 'n' we were all put in one little pot. We had some wonderful weather in those evenings.[24]

The tremendous sense of community solidarity enhanced by the music, dance, and celebrations was memorable for many black Oklahoma City dwellers: "We had a lovely time, out in the street, and we had no problems and everybody was just having a good time. We just all knew each other, 'n' people would just dress up [in] their suits 'n' dresses 'n' things and they would just have a lovely time and usually Billy Taylor and all those guys would give a little floor show." These celebrations were revived for the Charlie Christian Festival in the summer of 1991, when Deep Deuce and, a few years later, the parking lot at the top of Deep Deuce, across from Calvary Baptist Church, were roped off; bands entertained; vendors sold barbecue, cold drinks, commemorative T-shirts, and memorabilia; some celebrants boogied or did the electric slide; and everyone had a great time.[25]

Deep Deuce was the historic site where ancient rhythms and dances were maintained late into the twentieth century. The very name "Deep" suggested not only that was it at the bottom of a hill, but also that it was closer to the depths that traditionally held spiritual significance. Though very possibly unwittingly, insofar as many celebrants were exemplars of middle-class rectitude, viewing themselves as Americans, black city dwellers connected with their ancestors who danced to similar rhythms in the practice of their religion,

24. Quoted in Broadbent, *Charlie Christian*, 56–57. The author also had the opportunity to interview Mr. Parks ca. 1990.

25. Ibid. The author attended two Charlie Christian festivals in the 1990s. One of them took place in the 300 block of Second Street and the other in a parking lot across the street from Calvary Baptist Church.

thereby linking themselves with the living, the ancestors, and the chain of spirituality that tied them to the cosmos.[26] In this respect, and in ways that were not particularly apparent, they perpetuated the specific activities and values of their Haitian, other West Indian, and West African forebears. Perhaps at some time in the future, similar sites will be found elsewhere in the Louisiana Territory, in St. Louis and Minneapolis, for example.[27]

Vine Street

Having a much larger African American population than Oklahoma City, Kansas City, Missouri, was well-known for its vibrant nightlife, its devotion to dance, and its numerous trendsetting swing bands. Two Kansas City historians recently maintained, "Jazz arrived at the corner of 18th and Vine one hot, dusty afternoon in July 1917."[28] This was the Original Creole Jazz Band, which toured on various Vaudeville circuits from 1914 to 1918. They were a hit, but they did not record. (A white band, the Original Dixieland Jazz Band, recorded in 1917, and its members acquired the fame and credit the Original Creoles might have garnered.)[29]

The first black Kansas City crossroads at Vine Street can be dated from the early twentieth century, when African Americans from Missouri and the surrounding states migrated to Kansas City to reside near 12th and Vine east and south of downtown. In fact, "12th Street Rag," a popular composition by Euday Bowman, the Texas pianist who made Kansas City his home in 1897, memorialized this legendary intersection. This song was one of the biggest hits of the ragtime era. Less known are his "13th Street Rag" and "Kansas City Blues." Significantly, blues was also documented in this urban milieu before the nation's discovery of jazz. Writer Langston Hughes claimed he heard his first blues in Kansas City as a teenager around 1914.[30]

26. On African religion, see Newell S. Booth, ed., *African Religions: A Symposium* (New York: Nok Publishers, 1977); and Jacob K. Olupona, ed., *African Traditional Religions in Contemporary Society* (St. Paul, Minn.: Paragon House, 1991).

27. See Douglas Henry Daniels, "North Side Jazz: Lester 'Pres' Young in Minneapolis, the Early Years," *Minnesota History* 59, no. 3 (fall 2004): 96–109.

28. Driggs and Haddix, *Kansas City,* 3.

29. Gushee, *Pioneers,* 233–34, points out that both bands played what we would call ragtime rather than jazz.

30. Driggs and Haddix, *Kansas City,* 32–34.

As noted, the city's history was rather singular with respect to ragtime. James Scott, considered one of the three most famous of ragtime composers (with Scott Joplin and Joseph Lamb), moved from Carthage, Missouri, to Kansas City in 1920 and conducted the black theater orchestras on Vine Street. Bennie Moten, the city's most successful bandleader, led a ragtime trio that gradually increased to a full-size jazz band by the end of the 1920s. The black community of this city was literally honeycombed with dance bands—those of George and Julia Lee, Paul Banks, Dave Lewis, and later, Jasper "Jap" Allen, Thamon Hayes, Harlan Leonard, and Andy Kirk—not to mention Jay McShann and Count Basie.[31]

On Vine, between 12th and 18th, musicians, entertainers, fans, and hangers-on dressed sharply, congregated on street corners and in front of the joints, greeted friends, told jokes, laughed, drank, and danced in the clubs, rejoicing in the urban nightlife that was so legendary. Of course, Kansas City's notorious and extensive vice and political corruption made possible this nightlife and supported this music. Herman Walder, Bennie Moten's saxophonist, reminisced, "All the musicians came here because the joints were open all night. There was a club on every corner." He also noted "if you were on 18th and Vine you had to be sharp."[32]

Many nightclubs and dance halls for African Americans clustered on and near Vine. Twelfth Street featured two important after-hours spots during the Depression. Their size as well as the atmosphere brought celebrants together, promoting a very powerful sense of community cohesiveness. In the clubs, they associated with their distinctive heroes. The Sunset, at 1715 East 12th, was a deep but very narrow club about sixteen feet wide; here, bartender Joe Turner was known for regaling the patrons, "moaning the blues throughout the night." Run by Walter "Little Piney" Brown, it featured a big floor show on weekend nights and included singer Pha Terrell and Pete Johnson and his Sunset Orchestra, assisted by Oran "Hot Lips" Page and Walter Page (no relation), both former Blue Devils. The Lone

31. On the Kansas City scene, see Driggs and Haddix, *Kansas City;* and *Good Morning Blues: The Autobiography of Count Basie,* as told to Albert Murray (New York: Random House, 1985); on Scott, see Russell, *Jazz Style,* 43–44.

32. "Kansas City Revives Jazz Landmark," *New York Times,* May 2, 1985; I would like to thank Brian Horrigan for this article. On Kansas City segregation, race relations, and neighborhood development, see Sherry Lamb Schirmer, *A City Divided: The Racial Landscape of Kansas City, 1900–1960* (Columbia: University of Missouri Press, 2002).

Star Gardens was across the street at 1708, and it was even narrower—a mere twelve feet wide, a physical dimension that enhanced
the spirit and moods that were engendered by the celebrations.[33]

As African Americans moved south along Vine, the crossroads
included 14th as well as 18th streets and Vine—admittedly a varia-
tion on the idea that it encompasses only two intersecting streets. On
14th, and only two blocks from Vine on Highland, sat the large five-
story Labor Temple, where black celebrants held the many holiday
dances that typified their festive occasions. At the "Big Labor Day
Stomp," several bands performed in this temple from nine in the
evening until three in the morning at the end of every summer season. At a "Big Sunday Night Stomp" one winter night during the
Depression, Moten's band entertained at the Labor Temple; his
nephew, Ira "Buster," was on accordion and piano, and three former
Blue Devils—James Rushing, Count Basie, and "Hot Lips" Page on
trumpet—were among the stars.[34]

Black Kansas City celebrants exhibited their deeply felt devotion
to dance—a distinctive feature of their African heritage that was evident from the World War I years—in dance halls and nightclubs. In
1918, Moten teamed up with drummer Dude Langford and singer
Bailey Hancock to form B. B. and D. When they debuted at the Labor
Temple late in December of that year, a streetcar strike and bad
weather—it was snowing and cold—caused them to fear for the
worse. Nonetheless, they reluctantly went to the dance, mounted the
bandstand, and were shocked when they saw "we had twenty-three
hundred on the floor." Langford recalled, "[T]hings was on in them
days. That place was packed, you couldn't get in, the first floor and
the second. . . . I'll tell you we was blowed, knocked us out."[35]

Touring Blue Devils helped black Kansas City dancers celebrate an
autumn holiday despite the inclement weather that threatened the

33. Sanborn Fire Insurance Maps for Kansas City provided the dimensions of these
clubs. "Chicago Entertainer at East Side Musicians Sunset Club," *Kansas City Call*, May
10, 1935, 13; "East Side Musicians Sunset Club Announces Its Opening" (ad), *Kansas
City Call*, November 9, 1934, 13; Frank London Brown, "From Kansas City to
Copenhagen: Boss of the Blues," *Down Beat*, December 11, 1958, 18–19. Another 12th
Street club, at 1510, the Rhythm Rendezvous, featured Hot Lips Page late in 1935.
"Rhythm Rendezvous, New Night Club Here, Opens," *Kansas City Call*, December 6,
1935, 8.
34. "Big Labor Day Stomp" (ad), *Kansas City Call*, August 31, 1934, 13; "A Big Sunday
Night Stomp" (ad), *Kansas City Call*, January 25, 1935, 12.
35. Driggs and Haddix, *Kansas City*, 43.

success of the affair in 1928. "Kansas City opened its arms Hallo-wee'en night with a riotous welcome for Walter Page and his sizzling Blue Devil orchestra at Paseo hall." These dancers were as commit-ted as true believers could be. The fact that the dance took place "in spite of the heavy rain" may have been also because the crowd recog-nized Page as one of theirs. (He attended school and learned music in Kansas City.) In any case, "1,700 people turned out to the dance." City dwellers manipulated their identities with their outfits, and in the fashion of Mardi Gras paraders, some switched gender for the evening. Almost exactly a year before the onset of the Great Depres-sion, Kansas City celebrants wore costumes "colorful and brilliant; they ranged from Mexican outfits to Pierrot costumes, and the usual men dressed as girls and vice versa were strongly in evidence."[36]

On at least one occasion in Kansas City, Dave Dexter, the Kansas City jazz fan and promoter, reported unique behavior on the part of African American dancers that mirrored possession in "holy roller" churches, where congregants suddenly fell on the floor writhing, or spoke in tongues—another distinctive feature usually associated with African religious heritage. Dexter did not understand what he witnessed in these terms but saw it mainly as a matter of not main-taining proper decorum. That winter night when Pete Johnson and his sidemen held sway at the Sunset, the band "felt it," as Dexter put it, and Johnson played for maybe "10 to 75 consecutive choruses. . . . Occasionally the colored patrons got excited and threw themselves on the floor, completely hysterical by the rhythm and atmosphere."[37]

Kansas City nightclub dancers also received considerable atten-tion, such was the importance of dance for black celebrants in this city. Professional entertainers provided examples of how to maneu-ver bodies, limbs, and feet in ways that contrasted sharply with Euro-pean and Euro-American dance styles. Though black city dwellers performed the popular dances of the day, including the new Lindy from New York City, by early spring of 1931, occasionally some entertainers reminded nightclubbers of their historic dance heritage. For example, Mable Hill performed the rumba, a dance with Afro-Latin roots, at the Cherry Blossom, to the music of Count Basie's orchestra shortly before Christmas 1933. In spring 1935, Emma

36. "Blue Devils a Riot at Hallowe'en Dance," *Kansas City Call*, November 2, 1928, 10.
37. Quoted in Driggs and Haddix, *Kansas City*, 131.

Smith, a local citizen and former Cotton Club dancer appearing with the Harlem Nightclub troupe at the Labor Temple, "gave a sizzling exhibition of snake hips and brought down the house with her original style of dancing."[38]

Two other entertainers, Fling and Josephine, "gave the local hoofers some new ideas in duet dancing," leaving the audience yelling for more at the Labor Temple in 1935. The Edwards sisters' dancing climaxed the show. Significantly for the language used describing the dance orchestra's role that night, "The benediction was given by the celebrated Bennie Moten band." At that point, "the swinging got so good many dancers stopped in their track to listen and watch the cats work." They also stopped dancing when Jimmy Rushing sang. These were signal moments, dramatic climaxes that required their rapt attention.[39]

On special festive occasions one band alone could not satisfy the Kansas Citians' deep and abiding love of dance. In late spring of 1933, the Musicians' Ball at the Paseo Club promised "6—Crack Orchestras—6" at its "Monster Celebration and Cabaret Party." This was in effect a marathon of continuous music meant to quench the desires of the most devoted dancers. Two years later, at their "Big Dance of the Holiday Season," the Musicians' Annual Ball, black dancers ushered in the Christmas season with "6 Hours of Continuous Mirth and Music," beginning at nine in the evening, to five bands, including Andy Kirk's Twelve Clouds of Joy and Harlan Leonard's K.C. Rockets.

The very names of these two bands indicated to dancers that they would be propelled to heights suggestive of spirit possession in other black communities. The rather large amount of time—six full hours—of dance also assured that the most dedicated would attain otherworldly realms. "No one who has ever attended one of the many annual Musicians ball[s] has ever left the hall disappointed," promised the *Kansas City Call*. Black Kansas Citians willingly endured some measure of hardship to enjoy these dances, as three

38. On the Lindy, see "Dance Gossip by E. W. W.," *Kansas City Call*, March 27, 1931, 9. "Mable Hill Dancing the Rhumba," (ad), *Kansas City Call*, December 8, 1933, 11. L. H. H., "Bands Turn on the Heat at Dance at Labor Temple," *Kansas City Call*, May 24, 1935, 11; "'Night in Hollywood' Scores with Dance Patrons Here," *Kansas City Call*, November 15, 1935, 9.

39. "Bands Turn on the Heat at Labor Temple," *Kansas City Call*, May 24, 1935, 11. *Kansas City Directory, 1931.*

hundred determined dancers braved zero temperatures to celebrate at this affair.[40]

Often African American dances were held at unusual hours—as if to accommodate the larks among the dance population instead of the night owls. The Tall Timbers, a "pleasure resort and dance palace" outside of town, featured Bennie Moten's band at a "Break-O-Day" dance on July 4, 1934. A carnival and barbecue were planned for the special occasion, and beginning at five in the morning, early risers and late-night celebrants fox-trotted and Lindy hopped to Moten's band.[41]

Eighteenth and Vine

Eighteenth and Vine is one of the most celebrated intersections in blues, and it included a number of venues, including the Eblon and Roby Theaters and the Cherry Blossom, the nightclub where the bands of Bennie Moten and Count Basie entertained at the dawn of the swing era. Black Kansas City's music spilled over to Paseo, the wide boulevard one block west of Vine, where Street's Hotel was located, and where progressive political rallies for workingmen attracted large crowds. The national convention of the Brotherhood of Sleeping Car Porters held open meetings in this East Side hotel late in January 1935 after a mass meeting at Allen Chapel. A. Philip Randolph, the main organizer, from New York City, and C. L. Dellums, a railroad man from Oakland, California, were among the speakers at Street's. Despite the management's possible political sympathies, Kansas City jazz was not far distant; Street's Blue Room featured Shaw's Melody Boys, with Count Basie on piano, that winter.[42]

Some nightlife citizens were patrons of the arts or were service-oriented, like Hallie Richardson, devoted to the welfare of the community of East Side black residents. Ellis Burton, of the Yellow Front, "was the kind of guy that just liked musicians, and he had music round the clock." One of twenty-three children born to his family

40. "Monster Celebration" (ad), *Kansas City Call*, June 14, 1935, 11.
41. "Pete Woods Resort at Tall Timbers Saturday, Sunday," *Kansas City Call*, June 22, 1934, 11.
42. Ads for these events and for those at Allen Chapel and Street's, *Kansas City Call*, January 25, 1935, 12.

from Houston, Texas, he was active as an Elk and as a Mason—evidence of his abiding concern for the community's welfare. He went into the restaurant and nightclub business and was also a rather colorful bootlegger. One night some men were bothering pianist Sam Price, and Burton told them, "If you interfere with Sammy Price anymore, forget those favors I used to do for you." Price's problems went away.[43]

Walter "Piney" Brown (earlier known as "Little Piney"), an associate of Felix Payne, a newspaper editor and businessman who ran gambling operations, and Burton "were like godfathers actually for most musicians." Count Basie considered Piney Brown to be "sort of a gentleman about town" who "was good to all musicians." Brown was a minister's son, and Bennie Moten reedman Eddie Barefield recalled, "Piney was like a patron saint to all musicians," and "if you came there as a musician, it never cost you anything." Barefield figured that the way Brown took care of musicians, he could not have made any money at the Subway.[44] Such patrons were not formally educated and were populist rather than elitist, but they were alternatives to ministers, lawyers, and upstanding members of the community for those needing help. Their influences in the community were considerable.[45]

In these after-hours spots, musicians met and enjoyed themselves when their jobs at the Cherry Blossom and the Paseo were done. As night people, they lived differently from others in the city. Eddie Durham, a composer, arranger, trombonist, and electric guitarist who was a Blue Devil before he joined the Moten and Basie bands along with Basie and Rushing, recalled, "Kansas City bands come off the stage at 8:00 and 9:00 in the morning for people to go to work. And that's the way it was all night long, because they had liquor stores that stayed open 24 hours in Kansas City." Then, "after all the jobs was over, all the musicians would meet right on 18th and Vine, and the meeting place was right in the . . . street."[46]

43. Nathan W. Pearson Jr., *Goin' to Kansas City* (Urbana: University of Illinois Press, 1987), 99–100.

44. Quoted in Driggs and Haddix, *Kansas City,* 131. "Mother of Piney Brown Buried Here," *Kansas City Call,* July 19, 1935, sect. 2, p. 1; Walter "Little Piney" Brown took the name from his older brother, Thomas ("Big Piney"), who died in the early 1930s. "Funeral for Ellis Burton This Morning," *Kansas City Call,* May 29, 1936, 1.

45. Pearson, *Goin' to Kansas City,* 97.

46. Eddie Durham, Jazz Oral History Project, Reel 3–4, pp. 43–44, Institute of Jazz Studies, Rutgers University, Newark, N.J.

Durham also mentioned the fact that people never discussed this custom—perhaps because like dance, it was more easily lived or demonstrated than articulated verbally. Also, the sources of many such customs are unknown by those who practice them. Most likely many residents did not understand that this street intersection was the crossroads that is so significant in African, Afro-Caribbean, and Southern religion and folklore.

Significantly the musicians, heralds of the blues/jazz order, met at the crossroads and, furthermore, at the time between times—liminal time, so to speak. They completed their nocturnal duties and would eventually retire—but many did not go home immediately, as they needed this time and space to themselves at 18th and Vine. In their conversations and social exchanges, they revitalized themselves. Then, too, this time—nine or so in the morning—was precisely when the daytime professionals and others showed up at work. So the musicians assembled at the end of their work night and at the beginning of others' routine, behavior enhancing their in-betweenness, their occupying a very special time as well as special space.

Contributing Factors

In addition to the crossroad sites in these cities, there were certain noteworthy facts that were intriguing with respect to Haitian heritage. While residents of Haitian descent were seemingly nonexistent or rare, other references to this island nation cropped up in the 1930s. For example, in the spring of 1935, the fraternity Alpha Phi Alpha played its signature song, "Voodoo Chant," over radio station W9XBY during its "Magic Stick" broadcasts in Kansas City.[47]

Kansas City's black celebrants took "voodoo" seriously enough, after twenty years of the United States' controversial and brutal occupation of that nation, to use the term for their festivities in the 1930s. They perhaps mocked the Haitian themes on the stage during the Depression, as well as the superstition about Friday the thirteenth, on that day and date in September 1935 in Kansas City. The Wayne Miner Post 149 of the American Legion promised a "Voodoo Jamboree" where Andy Kirk and Twelve Clouds of Joy performed at

---

47. "'Magic Stick' Broadcasts Return to Air over W9XBY," *Kansas City Call*, May 10, 1935, 13.

Paseo Hall, and a floor show and various novelties and acts were staged, and the post's drum and bugle corps was also featured.[48]

Even more significantly, dances in Kansas City and elsewhere were often referred to as "stomps," and numerous compositions included this word in their title. Euro-Americans, it should be noted, did not use the term. For African Americans, stomps (songs and dances) were what it was all about; they were "the real thing," times when the dance community achieved a singular solidarity. On the other hand, this analysis is complicated by the fact that if there were street dances in Kansas City, they were not mentioned in the local newspapers or in interviews.

Stomps—community dances—were vital to the residents' spiritual health insofar as they were a means of communicating with the ancestors and spirits of antiquity. The sounds of thousands of feet pounding the floor, synchronized by the rhythm, constituted drumming, and this was the traditional way of communicating with their forebears and calling the spirits to emerge from the netherworld at the crossroads. The stomp represented one vital motif in African American music culture, while to "jump" (often used in the titles of songs) or soar constituted another—the attempt to enter new realms of consciousness or paradisiacal sites. Nonetheless, these were not group dances like the European quadrille or most white American dances, or even like ring shouts, but collections of individuals, many of whom were relatives or friends—somewhat like in Congo Square. Unlike the Congo Square and traditional African dance practices, however, these were couple dances.[49]

Then, too, the personification of blues, for which Kansas City, in particular, was known, reminds one of the *loa* or deities in Haitian and West African religions. Blues singer Wynonie Harris was known as "Mr. Blues," but even more significant, Oklahoma City's Jimmy Rushing caught the spirit, singing "Good mornin' blues / blues, how

48. "Voodoo Jamboree" (ad), *Kansas City Call*, August 30, 1935, 8. Occasionally, ironic references to African heritage were reflected in the name of a band, such as the Jungle Rhythm Boys from Omaha, who covered all the bases; they promised they would "sing, dance and clown." "Jungle Rhythm Boys Landed for Cherry Blossom Club," *Kansas City Call*, July 21, 1933, 2B. In St. Louis, in the spring of 1934, the film *Drums o' Voodoo* was advertised as "At Last! A Real COLORED Folks Play," based upon "the sensational stage play *Louisiana* by J. Augustus Smith." Of course, the movie sensationalized "the horror of the voodoo curse" like many other popular entertainments of the time that focused on Haiti; see *St. Louis Argus*, May 11, 1934, 4.

49. I discussed this in Daniels, "Vodun and Jazz."

do you do?" as if "blues" had awakened him or was sitting by the side of his bed. In the song "My Friend Mr. Blues," Rushing indeed sings of the latter scenario, with "Mr. Blues" appearing in the morning "beside his bed," announcing, "How ya doin, / I'm here to worry you."[50] Here, the blues is so familiar to Rushing that it has become a friend, and perhaps this is a way of reversing bad fortune. These are certainly not the only time blues is personified in song, but until we analyze these personifications more closely, it is difficult to make comparisons with other spiritual phenomena in the diaspora.

Once we expand our areas of research to include calypso and reggae in addition to jazz and blues, such comparisons can be made more confidently. Like Mardi Gras, carnival, and jonkanoo in other nations, these street dances helped to revitalize celebrants and connect them in a meaningful way with a heritage that they demonstrated more readily than they articulated and discussed. This aspect of cultural life and traces of religious heritage in the states constituting the Louisiana Purchase has gone unexamined.

The Legacy

Black Oklahoma City residents appreciated and revived the historic tradition of celebrating in the streets in the mid-twentieth century and in subsequent decades, which is ample evidence of the vitality and relevance of this tradition. The practice could be compared to religious revivals in which they once again celebrated the respective crossroads' unique heritage. The *Black Dispatch* announced in late summer 1950 that "A revival of the 'Street Dance,' which actually means dancing in the street, will be presented, ladies and gentlemen, for your enjoyment Labor Day, September 4." This event was held "in honor of the laboring people of our community, all of us."[51] The *Dispatch* recognized that they were primarily a working people and

50. "My Friend Mr. Blues," *The Essential Jimmy Rushing*, Vanguard VCD 65/66. Lee Morris and Rose Marie McCoy wrote this song.

51. "Local 703 Big Band to Play Free Street Dance Labor Day," *Oklahoma City Black Dispatch*, September 2, 1950, 9. This event was similar to one in 1939 when the 300 block was closed for dancing; "3,000 Attend Street Dance," *Oklahoma City Black Dispatch*, August 19, 1939, 12. This happened about the time Charlie Christian left town; see the famous photograph of Charlie and Edward Christian and friends just before the guitarist boarded the train to join Benny Goodman's band in Los Angeles; *Oklahoma City Black Dispatch*, August 19, 1939, 12.

lacked an affluent and idle contingent or upper class that lived off its wealth and investments. Furthermore, such people were worthy of being honored by the public institution of community dancing.

Sponsors of the dance included John C. Parker, manager of Parker's News on Deep Deuce, and the Eastside Federation of Musicians (Local 708). A twenty-piece band provided music for the occasion. This band performed at Washington Park a few weeks earlier "and was prompted by the warm reception and enthusiasm of that audience plus rehearsal listeners to become an 'institution' of Oklahoma City." Indeed, it became "a fixture, dedicated to serving the community."[52] It was apparent that music and community service were respected and highly valued among Oklahoma City's East Side residents at midcentury.

After the Charlie Christian Festivals of the 1990s, however, Deep Deuce was transformed. Several of its buildings remained unoccupied for years—mute testimony to the vitality of the community from the 1920s. An attempt to establish a historical museum in one of the buildings on East Second failed. Following the death of a Deep Deuce property owner, and while the details are not altogether clear, a developer bought up several lots from the person who inherited them and built modern condominiums on the north side of East Second within the past few years. The degree to which this changes Deep Deuce remains to be seen, but at least one old-timer expressed severe disappointment at this outcome.

The music history of the black district in Kansas City has been preserved in urban renovation and educational programs. In the past decade, Vine Street has been rehabilitated by preservationists as the 18th and Vine Historic District, and residents created the American Jazz Museum, renovated the Gem Theater across the street, opened a working jazz club at the corner of 18th and Vine, and constructed an apartment building at 18th and Vine. The Jazz Museum is part of a complex that includes the Negro Leagues Baseball Museum that pays tribute to the Kansas City Monarchs and other black teams, and the Blue Room, which presents live Kansas City jazz. The Gem Theatre's 1912 facade was restored and the

---

52. "Local 703 Big Band to Play," 9. The next year a rodeo parade was led by the Community Band of Mrs. Zelia N. Breaux; "Oklahoma City Community Band Sparks Drumright Rodeo in Saturday Evening Parade," *Oklahoma City Black Dispatch*, August 24, 1951, 6.

interior renovated, and it became a performing arts center seating five hundred, where annual jazz concerts are held.

The Charlie Parker Memorial stands one block from the museums and behind the apartment complex. A seventeen-foot bronze statue commemorating the great saxophonist and composer, who was born and raised—and learned to play jazz—in Kansas City, was completed in 1999 by the accomplished California-based sculptor Robert Graham. The skyscrapers of downtown Kansas City arise behind the sculpture, whose pedestal is inscribed, simply, with "Bird Lives." This phrase originally appeared as graffiti on buildings and subway walls in New York City shortly after Parker's death in 1955.

The Jazz Museum's events contribute to the cultural revival, bringing together residents to listen to and to appreciate Kansas City historical and musical traditions as well as national heritage. For example, the museum events in the autumn of 2005 featured "Jammin' at the Gem," including a tribute to Billie Holiday on what would have been her ninetieth birthday, and also National Endowment for the Arts Masters Wayne Shorter, Dave Brubeck, and Ron Carter in subsequent presentations. In late August 1997 the museum scheduled a free Charlie Parker Celebration at the Blue Room. Jazz storytelling by musicians for preschool age children were held in the museum's "Wee Bop Room," while poetry jams, "curricula that use jazz as a vehicle to teach youth about our nation's history and cultural diversity," and other colloquia were also included in the museum's program.[53]

Additionally, the Education Department of the Jazz Museum catered to senior citizens with a new program that encouraged them "to reminisce and move to the beat of Kansas City jazz." This program, called "Swing Time," was the idea of Dr. Robert Groene of the University of Missouri–Kansas City and was held exclusively in local nursing homes. Local jazz artists participated in live performances. Seniors were "encouraged to discuss what memories specific songs evoke as well as to dance and move." Nursing home staff reported that the results were "therapeutic," which is exactly how dance and musical performances functioned in dance halls as well as churches, in the Louisiana Territory and in West Africa and the Caribbean.[54]

---

53. Fall 2005 and Summer 2007 Calendars of American Jazz Museum; American Jazz Museum Membership brochure in author's possession.
54. Fall 2005 Calendar of the American Jazz Museum.

The Missouri city has revived and celebrated its unique heritage in other ways. "Kansas City," the blues classic written by Jerry Leiber and Mike Stoller and recorded in 1952 by Little Willie Littlefield, became the official song of the Kansas City Parks and Recreation Department in summer 2004. Furthermore, a *Kansas City Star* reporter campaigned to have this song adopted by the City Council as the city's official song, and citizens dedicated a new park at this intersection named Goin' to Kansas City Plaza. Parking was to be provided for tour buses, and tourists and residents would read about the area's contributions to music history on a thirty-one-foot-long plaque.

The early development of jazz and blues in Kansas City and Oklahoma City at about the time when it emerged in Chicago suggests that the history of the music must be rethought and that its relationship to ancient religious heritage needs consideration. This new music was more widespread than has been conceived by many scholars, and this should enhance our understanding of the importance and significance of black culture in the Louisiana Territory and outside of New Orleans. In the same way that the Original Creole Jazz Band had its imitators, so did the black dance bands in the heartland, as well. Perhaps someday the African roots of the swing phenomenon, with its avid jitterbugs, will be examined in light of African and American heritage and religious survivals.

If not for the Louisiana Purchase, these kinds of connections would not have existed and could not be made. Moreover, who would ever think that the Haitian revolution and Napoléon's bargain with Jefferson would give us not only new expressions and forms of blues, jazz, and swing, from the nation's heartland, but also rock and roll and rock concerts, and that scholars would find African cultural roots and religious traces among even the white practitioners of this song and dance.

The Shifting Nature of Reform Envisioned on the Mississippi Steamer

Exchanges, Masks, and Charities in Herman Melville's *The Confidence-Man*

CAROLE LYNN STEWART

Introduction

It was through the Mississippi River that the French first gained their entry into the lower part of North America from Canada. Its control in the hands of foreign powers, first the French and then the Spanish, threatened the communications, internal trade, and geographical integrity of the lands of the United States east of the Mississippi. Jefferson's purchase of Louisiana in 1803 and thus gaining control of the Mississippi eliminated the foreign threats. American civil society, in its formation and its meaning, moved toward an intense confrontation with the unsettled issues of the American Revolution, of slavery, of the place and situation of the aboriginal populations, and of the fundamental destiny of the nation-state. The Louisiana Purchase—at least from the point of view of the geographical acquisition of territory—constituted a new beginning, of sorts. The debates, discourses, and policies set in motion by the event of the Louisiana Purchase can be seen as a form of American civil religion, and it is in terms of this civil religion that the meanings of American civil society and its future find expressions.

In Herman Melville's *The Confidence-Man*, the issues that constitute the debates and discussions about the nature of "free" exchanges in this era extend backwards to the founding of the nation and develop into the present, as the Mississippi steamboat, the setting of the novel, floats to its New Orleans destination. Melville's multiple dialogues and duplicitous characters, through their lack of "trust," question any possible future for the territory of the country during the antebellum period. Because of its difficulty, *The Confidence-Man* is rarely discussed as a key text on these issues, but it is in this book that Melville set forth and outlined an analogue to the problems Mark Twain portrayed in his later writings. This can be seen, of course, in Melville's title, but also in the popularity of the phrase taken from this book, which Melville titled "The Metaphysic of Indian Hating." Clearly Melville touched on a dynamic that was deeply ingrained in the American psyche and cultural consciousness, since it has been discussed by critics of American thought, culture, and politics for some time. Two uses of the frame that resonate or are used in critical studies on nation building can be found in Roy Harvey Pearce's *Savagism and Civilization* and Richard Drinnon's *Facing West*.[1]

The Confidence-Man was, however, a book that was said to have been Melville's farewell to narrative and to more discursive modes of literature, a "problem novel." It was ironically first published on April 1, 1857,[2] and it continues an investigation of the metaphysical "ambiguities" that Melville raised in other works, especially in the book that immediately followed *Moby-Dick:* Melville's *Pierre; or, the Ambiguities.* During Melville's time, it signaled for most readers and reviewers a breach with sanity and an entrance into obscurity for the author. The ambiguities he raised, however, were also ones of freedom, race, and religious meaning in the construction of an "American" identity and the dominant civil faith or religion. The backdrop for both novels is a series of compromises that come in the wake of the Louisiana Purchase: The Missouri Compromise and the Fugitive Slave Act, and the Dred Scott decision, which was first filed in 1847 but was finally decided by the Supreme Court in 1857. These actions reflect territorial and regional tensions around the issue of slavery, creating the political crisis that led to the Civil War. *The Confidence-Man* explores these tensions, deceptions, duplicities, and ambiguities as expressed in the estranged polyglot group of passengers on a

---

1. Roy Harvey Pearce, *Savagism and Civilization: A Study of the Indian and the American Mind* (Berkeley and Los Angeles: University of California Press, 1988); Richard Drinnon, *Facing West: The Metaphysics of Indian Hating and Empire Building* (New York: Meridian Books, 1980).

2. See the notation found in Oxford World's Classics, Herman Melville, *The Confidence-Man,* with an introduction by Tony Tanner and explanatory notes by John Dugdale (New York: Oxford University Press, 1989), xxxviii.

Mississippi steamboat as it departs from St. Louis to the "never-arrived-at-port" of New Orleans. Melville's unfinished journey to "Mecca—New Orleans" suggests a critique of the merchant port of New Orleans. The possession of New Orleans had been the initial goal that led to the purchase of the entire Louisiana territory.

Ironically and perhaps hopefully, Melville's satire ends with the line, "Something more may follow this masquerade,"[3] but we never arrive at a point of satisfaction—a point where satisfying, authentic exchange occurs between various Americans in the country at large or among the pilgrims aboard the metonymical steamer of the expanding continent. It will be the burden of this essay to explore the various levels and meanings involved in what I am referring to as "authentic exchanges" as they are expressed in the novel.

Even the most casual reader of Melville's corpus cannot fail to observe the decided locale of geographical waters; *Typee* and *Omoo* evoke the waters of the Pacific Ocean while *Moby-Dick*, *Benito Cereno*, and *Billy Budd* take place on the high seas of the world. This novel, *The Confidence-Man*, also takes place on the waters—the great inland waterway of the Mississippi River. One might assume this novel would represent a kind of "domesticated water," as opposed to the turbulent waters of the great oceans of the world.

Such "domestication" applied to the Mississippi, however, is deceptive, since the river presents its own forms of "wildness" and turbulence. Beginning as a small stream flowing from Lake Itasca in Minnesota, it meanders through the heartland of America for 2,350 miles, emptying into the Gulf of Mexico through New Orleans. The river, through its long course, conceals hidden eddies, sandbars, abrupt changes of depth, and acute changes of direction. It is a treacherous river; even at its mouth, the levees are unstable, never submitting to the human agencies of engineering for any length of time. And so it is upon the inland waterway of the Mississippi that Melville's domestic tale of America's destiny takes place.

The Form of the Novel

Some find all of Melville's novels rather strange. While this may be true, few would deny that this is a rather odd novel. In his novel *Pierre*,

3. Herman Melville, *The Confidence-Man: His Masquerade*, ed. Hershel Parker (Norton: New York, 1971), 217. Subsequent references will appear in parentheses in the text.

Melville characterized the problematical situation of American culture at this time with the term *ambiguities;* in *The Confidence-Man,* the subtitle is *His Masquerade.* The notion of the confidence man is taken from an article published in the *New York Herald* in 1849.[4] This article describes the incidence of a "confidence man" who stole a man's watch by appearing to be an honest and respectable gentleman. Though Melville makes use of the singular pronoun "his," the confidence man is not one but several, appearing at one time or another in most of the passengers on the steamboat. The notions of "masquerading" and "masking" form the thread that runs through all of the manifestations of the confidence man. Thus, *The Confidence-Man,* like the Mississippi, is ubiquitous, a floating and fluid phenomenon. The novel does not relate any significant human actions—it is composed of forty-five interrelated conversations woven together in a dialectical and dialogical style. The only real movement in the novel is the movement of the steamboat down the Mississippi from St. Louis to New Orleans—stopping in Cairo—and the changes from day to night during the two days recounted. The dynamic between free and slave territory is implied throughout the novel, particularly in having this brief stopping point as the shift to the second half.

Two intertwined structures emerge; one structure is defined by the various characters and their conversations. These conversations are subtly drawn, and one must read them carefully to discern who is being conned and how the person being conned may at the same time be creating a "sting" for his interlocutor. The second structure is that these conversations are punctuated by notions and ideas that reveal the larger context upon which the novel is refracted. Melville examines how the dominant Northern "enlightened" ideologies of charity and philanthropy in their confrontations with racial "others" cohere through a form of rugged individualism, Protestant work ethic, and abstracted exchanges that then further devolves into its own style of civil religion: the confidence game. For my purposes in outlining the problems that Melville saw as reflected in the acquisition of the territories and the subsequent attempts to homogenize, the two most important segments of the novel are the ambiguous exchanges that are unleashed in the opening chapters

---

4. This source appears in the Norton edition of *Confidence-Man,* 227. To be sure, critics have noted the wider range of "confidence" men, from Benjamin Franklin to P. T. Barnum and, in another vein, Ralph Waldo Emerson.

with a beggar named Black Guinea and in the famous discussions on "The Metaphysics of Indian Hating."

The movement west and the expansion of America into the areas inhabited by Native, Spanish, French and even Canadian is a thematic concern. A diverse group of passengers—"pilgrims"—enter and exit the steamer at each port, never establishing long-term connections with one another. The pilgrims consist of "natives of all sorts and foreigners," hunters of all kinds—"farm-hunters and fame-hunters, gold-hunters, buffalo-hunters"—and of course, because the quest expresses a furtherance of the promises of "American" freedom, they are all "happiness hunters." Passengers from all religions are assembled, including "quakers," "Jews, Mormons and Papists," races of all kinds and admixtures, including "Mississippi cotton-planters," and "slaves, black, mulatto, quadroon; modish young Spanish Creoles, and old-fashioned French . . . grinning Negroes and Sioux chiefs." The narrator ironically remarks that here is "a piebald parliament, an Anarcharsis Cloots congress of all kinds of that multiform pilgrim species, man" (6).[5] Deception, mistrust, and the growing Northern market orientation would come to dominate and obscure the diverse nature of what it means to be American in the mid-nineteenth century.

Distrust was a logical outcome of the Purchase; in Donald Meinig's words: "Louisiana was an imperial colony of alien people—this all American leaders recognized, though they differed as to how comfortable they were with that fact and what means should be taken to 'Americanize' this sudden addition." Certainly, all aboard the steamer remain "strangers," with no connection to one another or to the land. On the steamer, all passengers are equally "strangers," a word that John Bryant notes occurs more than fifty times in the novel.[6] The strangeness is, however, not only a result of the epistemological

---

5. Anarcharsis Cloots, a radical universalist, was famously described by Carlyle in *The French Revolution*. De Clootz was a Prussian noble who in 1790 brought a diverse delegation from different countries to the National Assembly (Dugdale, in Oxford edition of *Confidence-Man*, 340n9). Melville alludes to Anarcharsis Cloots in *Moby-Dick*, and as with most of Melville's writing, he is directing the reader to the anarchical events of Revolution and the ambiguities, or, in this case, masquerades, that slavery and expansion inhere in the American democratic faith.

6. Donald W. Meinig, *The Shaping of America: A Geographical Perspective on 500 Years of History*, vol. 2, *Continental America, 1800–1867* (New Haven: Yale University Press, 1993), 15; Bryant quoted in Gustaaf Van Cromphout, "'The Confidence-Man': Melville and the Problem of Others," *Studies in American Fiction* 21, no. 1 (1993): 37ff, 2.

problem of knowing that occurs, but also because of the setting of
the novel. Melville's narrator notes the aleatory quality of human
contact and exchange on the steamboat, the *Fidele,* which, "though
always full of strangers, she continually, in some degree, adds to, or
replaces them with strangers still more strange; like Rio Janeiro
fountain, fed from the Corcovado mountains, which is ever over-
flowing with strange waters, but never with the same strange parti-
cles in every part" (5). The distance from any intimate relationship
to each other was something that Unionists feared would occur with
the Purchase and the movement west. Criticizing Jefferson's purchase, in 1803 Senator Samuel White of Delaware proclaimed that
"our citizens will be removed to the immense distance of two or
three thousand miles from the capital of the Union, where they will
scarcely ever feel the rays of the General Government; their affec-
tions will become alienated; they will gradually begin to view us as
strangers; they will form other commercial connexions, and our
interests will become distinct."[7] The crowd aboard the *Fidele,* or what
Melville presents as a new world order, "Anarcharsis Cloots congress,"
rather than bringing about a revolution with these diverse passengers, seems to confirm White's fears.

Expansion, Exchanges, and the Problematics of Inherent Value

Though not voiced by Senator White, the Louisiana Purchase
raised deeper fears for Native Americans and for enslaved Africans.
Would the aboriginal inhabitants of these lands be decimated? And
what would happen to the institution of chattel slavery, now that
there was space that could allow for "free territory" or for a wider
extension of the unfreedom of slavery? Working out the nature and
distribution of the exchanges of goods and values formed the backdrop of all issues of this kind.

Within this context, Melville comments on the dilemmas facing an
ever-expanding "federation" based on mistrust and a distrust that is
enacted around descendants of Africans and Indian tribes during the
expansion and the ambiguous transition from slave territory to "free."
Early in the novel, in St. Louis, we meet a handicapped beggar dubbed

7. Quoted in Meinig, *Shaping of America,* 2:13.

"Black Guinea." It should be noted that along this stretch of the Mississippi, one side is slave territory (Missouri), and the other side is free territory (Illinois). Most of the novel—except for a flicker of the ubiquitous area of Cairo, the only sign of freedom—is set in slave territory, although not all the passengers are slave owners or Southerners.

Critics have turned their attention to the debate on the authenticity and the ambiguous identity of Black Guinea. This character is suspected by many passengers, particularly the misanthropic customs officer, to be a white in blackface. To be sure, the suspicion is warranted, given that we are in a slave state and one would not think that a slave's begging was encouraged. At the beginning of this chapter "a drover"—slave driver—asks "Black Guinea" who his master is, to which the latter explains that nobody would "want to own" him because he is "cripple[d]" (7). Oddly, this seems explanation enough for the drover. I write "oddly," because St. Louis was one of the largest slave markets, and the hunt for fugitives and the laws for loitering during the decade preceding the Civil War in this area were quite severe.[8] Perhaps Black Guinea's handicapped state implies that he is a runaway, his legs having been damaged in the process or as punishment. Indeed, the passengers press him for some papers, "any documentary proof," to "attest . . . that his case was not a spurious one" (10), which he does not have. He is quite eager to "shuffle" (8) away from the drover, who keeps questioning him about his living circumstances, and he seems all too eager to "shuffle" (14) away from the crowd once he receives a coin from a Northern merchant. Dominique Marçais argues that "Black Guinea's peculiar 'shuffling' (10, 11) may also hide a reference to the double-shuffle performed at Pinkster." Drawing on Sterling Stuckey's explications of Melville's acquaintance with Ashanti customs in the New World, she locates the subversion of minstrel stereotypes in *The Confidence-Man* by attending to Melville's allusions to West African dance and structures of orality that double the stereotypical and offer an "indictment of slavery."[9] Melville furthermore suggests the ubiquity of Guinea's identity in

---

8. William Wells Brown, a former slave of St. Louis, commented on the rigor of patrollers in St. Louis; see *The Narrative of William W. Brown, an American Slave, Written by Himself,* online at http://docsouth.unc.edu/fpn/brownw/brown.html (accessed November 12, 2007); this site also contains some information on the Slave Codes.

9. Dominique Marçais, "The Presence of Africa in Melville's *The Confidence-Man: His Masquerade*," in *Holding Their Own: Perspectives on the Multi-ethnic Literatures of the United States* (Tübingen, Germany: Stauffenburg, 2000), 182, 188.

noting that "it is human weakness to take pleasure in sitting in judgment upon one in a box" (9). The reference to "box" refers to the scaffold or the witness box, but perhaps also the "box" that was a famous
method of escape for slaves, Henry Box Brown being the exemplar.

The "charity game," and the "hermeneutics of suspicion" however,
with which the Northerners are involved, implies that the understanding of Northern antebellum structures of exchange cohere
around the spectacle of "blackness." The passengers who actually
believe that "Guinea" is black or authentically in need are limited to
a "young Episcopal clergyman," a "Methodist minister" who is "a
Tennessean by birth, who in the Mexican war had been volunteer
chaplain to a volunteer rifle-regiment" (10), and a northern "merchant" (13), who is the first to give "guinea" a coin. The Methodist,
after an impassioned speech on confidence, begins to mistrust
Guinea, and the only two left who have confidence are the Episcopal
clergyman and the merchant from Philadelphia. This stands to reason, because they are the Northerners in the crowd and would be
more accustomed to black begging than would be the Southerners,
who would suspect Black Guinea to be either white or a runaway,
especially since he has no papers. After all, even a handicapped slave
could be put to work in some capacity, as was often the case; his
hands are not crippled, for instance, for he is playing a tambourine.
The pro-slavery argument that the South had no beggars was a long
counterpoint to Northern ideals of freedom. Although Melville does
not champion slavery, the point that Northerners seem oblivious to
the codes and various circumstances of slavery brings us to Melville's
critique of Northern liberalism.[10] "Free" persons of African descent
did not possess the legitimacy of citizens in the North. Apropos of
Guinea's desire for an individualistic form of freedom, we are told by
the narrator that he is, like every other "would be pilgrim" searching
for a rootless "happiness" "stump[ing] out of sight, probably on

10. James Duban analyzes Melville's critique of liberal Protestantism at length and
Unitarianism in particular in his book *Melville's Major Fiction: Politics, Theology, and
Imagination* (De Kalb: Northern Illinois University Press, 1983). While Duban argues
that Melville criticizes the demand for "'moral certainty,' in which sensory experience
was thought to offer degrees of confidence" (197), I think that this desire crystallized
around race and natural hierarchies, especially after Dred Scott, which emphasized the
uncertainties of racial purity with the widespread phenomenon of "passing" as white.
There was the need to restabilize some form of "American" faith when racial categories
were on the verge of no longer defining the "free" self.

much the same errand as the rest" (14). Thus, whether "Guinea" is a white con man or a subversive West African trickster, Melville's point seems to be that none of these subversions, though fast becoming performances of civil religious freedom, can serve as the basis for a radically democratic faith that would be accompanied by a social revolution and relative redistribution of the wealth. Black Guinea is not "owned" by anyone and is not property. Nonetheless, much like the other would-be pilgrims, neither does he have a god who would both limit and enhance, thus binding one to a community to which he is attached and that would provide a structure of interdependence, rather than dependence or independence, ownership or unbridled and detached liberty.

Melville begins by having the drover ask Black Guinea, "who is your master?" and I want to keep this question at the forefront. Melville begins the novel with a motley group of pilgrims on an "errand," and he references Chaucer's *Canterbury Tales* throughout: "As among Chaucer's Canterbury pilgrims, or those crowding the red Sea towards Mecca in the festival month, there was not lack of variety" (6). The allusion to pilgrimages and the constitution of *communitas* recurs. The reference to Chaucer carries with it Chaucer's critique of the mendicant orders and corrupt representatives of the Catholic Church; this refers to a period of church history that marked a transitional period when the church began to experience problems with the institution of charity. Problematical as it may be, the traditional institution of charity encouraged the relative redistribution of wealth because individuals gave as part of their faith and thus served as the companion of the doctrine of good works. Protestant reformers focused on the corrupt institution of good works, the buying of one's salvation, and thus the corrupt nature of the mendicant orders and pardons for the dead.[11] We should recall that Chaucer's tales are, on one level, about the loss of an efficacious meaning of charity and poverty on the part of the manipulative representatives and priests of the Roman Catholic tradition. It seems there are two senses of charity for Melville—one is Christian charity that arises from having acknowledged one's sinful nature and becoming less judgmental and more selfless. This first sense of charity connects back to earlier, medieval forms of charity and piety evoked

11. See Lee Palmer Wandel, "Social Welfare," in *The Oxford Dictionary of the Reformation*, ed. Hans Hillerbrand (Cambridge: Oxford University Press, 1996), 4:77–83.

by allusions to Chaucer. In this form, the poor are honored and appear as revelations of God. Toward the end of the fourteenth century, as Lee Palmer Wandel notes, there appeared in Europe a new kind of beggar, "the sturdy beggar"—one who chose to beg, not out of need or service to God but for other, sometimes sinister, reasons. These "sturdy beggars" began to taint the genuine beggars and the institution of charity itself. Wandel comments that although "sturdy beggars" presented problems for Catholics, the institution retained its association with St. Francis of Assisi. Begging was a "gesture that fully captured each person's relation to God." Giving alms allowed one to extend *caritas* and also to acknowledge humility and dependency on the grace of God: "Alms became an essential system in a complex web of dependency and reciprocity: donors and poor depended on one another to make visible and articulate a vision of the interrelationship of God and humankind."[12]

In Melville's novel as well, the reference to "sturdy beggars" surfaces in a conversation over the "Christian injunction to give." Egbert, who many critics argue is a parody of Thoreau, argues that, while he may loan money with interest, he cannot give to a "friend," but only to a stranger. He says to Frank Goodman (the main confidence man in the second half of the novel, who is also a failed confidence man): "Take off your hat, bow over to the ground, and supplicate an alms of me in the way of London streets, and you shall not be a sturdy beggar in vain. But no man drops pennies into the hat of a friend, let me tell you. If you turn beggar, then, for the honor of noble friendship, I turn stranger" (192).[13] We witness the shift in the meaning of charity with the advent of Calvinism. Michael Paul Rogin contends that this philosophy resonates with the one described by Benjamin Nelson in his book *The Idea of Usury: From Tribal Brotherhood to Universal Otherhood;* Nelson describes charity as part of a system of capitalist exchange that is without "brotherly" attachments, friendships, or reciprocities. Rogin makes use of Nelson to note that "the modern doctrine of usury . . . eliminates the special, tribal obligations."[14] Yet while there is a sense of

12. Wandel, "Social Welfare," 80.

13. Also noted by Brian Higgins in his paper on Emerson, Thoreau, and Melville, "Mark Winsome and Egbert: 'In the Friendly Spirit,'" in the Norton edition of *Confidence-Man,* 341.

14. Michael Paul Rogin, *Subversive Genealogy: The Politics and Art of Herman Melville* (New York: Alfred A. Knopf, 1983), 248.

"universal otherhood" on the steamboat, there is equally a sense of individualism and self-reliance when it concerns the formation of "friends" or "brothers." In theory, loans may promise a veneer of reciprocity as quid pro quo (although in the novel we witness the poverty and ruin caused by loans as well). Nonetheless, charity makes reciprocity impossible when it is detached from the institution of good works as encompassed within a community. This is, I suspect, why the issue of race frames the novel, with Black Guinea (a spectacle of property without the agency to exchange), with the confidence man (John Ringman, who poses as a charitable agent for the Seminole Widow and Orphan Asylum), and later, with the *benevolent* "Indian Hater." The objects of charity, as in the case of Native Americans, are entirely outside of the form of interest-bearing friendships for Euro-Americans who are self-reliant others and yet transcendental "friends."

The modern Protestant-derived sense of charity is "charity as a business." This form of charity feeds into the giver's self-aggrandizement, but it must remain unattached to the object of benevolence, because it cannot understand exchange outside of a structure of usury and rationalized equivalence. In contrast to charity for the glory of and obligation to God and his community, the meaning of charity as a business rests on the ambiguity of individualism, man's natural benevolence, and the goodness of the self's appearance. The dilemma of charity emerges in relation to the black beggar over the question of his authenticity, in part because, with the impending demise of the slave system, as Susan M. Ryan notes, race was becoming a dominant criterion for charity—which in turn is an estranged exchange: "The portrayal of [the] black beggar raises questions that most conventional charity texts approached only obliquely: how were benevolent hierarchies and racial hierarchies mutually constitutive in US culture?" The question is incisive and characterizes the philanthropic need for the poor, black body to bolster its benevolent and salvific purposes. Ryan also notes that following the Fugitive Slave Act, public suspicions increased that African Americans might be duping the white population, that blacks might be passing for white, and that the truly needy might be suspect and conning. Carolyn L. Karcher also argues that Guinea's appearance and his transformation into various guises of the con man represents the return of the repressed and the apocalyptical force of slavery; this certainly affects the long-term possibility for "trust" between races.[15] (The words *trust, charity,* and *no trust* recur throughout the novel.)

But the question of how to constitute value in the midst of cross-cultural contact arose much earlier, becoming increasingly opaque in the transition from Roman Catholicism to Protestant forms of iconoclasm, and in Melville's time resurfacing to foment a new religion of the trickster qua confidence man. "Who is your master?" asks the drover to Guinea, who is otherwise referred to as "der dog widout massa" (7). The question resonates with early encounters between primarily Roman Catholic missionaries and conquerors, who would ask the aboriginal populations they encountered something like "Who is your God?" However, with a secularized work ethic and the rise of rugged individualism, the question implies that either another human being—a master as in the master-slave relationship—is the owner, or that there is no master, no God. This question will recur when the herb doctor, one of the confidence men, asks a Missourian, Pitch, if it is true that "though living in a slave state," the Missourian is presumably "without slave sentiments." The Missourian replies "Aye, but are you? Is not that air of yours, so spiritlessly enduring and yielding, the very air of a slave? Who is your master, pray; or are you owned by a company?" (97). In one sense, Melville poses a debate that would chime with Southern apologists for slavery such as George Fitzhugh, who composed *Cannibals All! or, Slaves without Masters* in the very same year. The threat of a loss of natural race hierarchy also, for later opponents of the Fifteenth Amendment, according to Michael O'Malley, led many to search for a gold standard or an intrinsic value to money, leading to a desire for the continued objectification of the black body or "specie." As he writes, "The search for intrinsic value—for a gold that always stays valuable—paralleled the search for racial purity and stable difference."[16] It is equally ironic that the search for the inherent value of specie—of coin—was taking place in a context that had denied the inherent value of the human species through the institution of chattel slavery.

15. Susan M. Ryan, "The Misgivings: Melville, Race, and the Ambiguities of Benevolence," *American Literary History* 12, no. 4 (2000): 686–87; Carolyn L. Karcher, *Shadow over the Promised Land: Slavery, Race, and Violence in Melville's America* (Baton Rouge: Louisiana State University Press, 1980).

16. Michael O'Malley, "Specie and Species," *American Historical Review* 99, no. 2 (April 1994), 382.

Melville highlights the point that slaves have difficulty entering the system of exchange, or even charity, because they have only been considered as property, and more specifically, as fetishes in relation to the European-derived exchange system. It is doubly ironic that the beggar is referred to as "Black Guinea"; although Guinea refers to the coast of West Africa, it also refers to a coin. Melville plays with the word in order to highlight the point that the primary guarantee of benevolence and philanthropy, in this ambivalent transition from slave to free, will depend upon the restabilization of white hierarchies and abstracted exchanges. "Guinea" black, with *Guinea* used as an adjective, rather than black "guinea," with the word as a noun, seems to be the norm; making it a noun has the effect of highlighting the increase in monetary abstraction itself in association with the African slave trade. Moreover, the use of *Guinea* as epithet, as in "Guinea black," stresses an owned "black" as primary, while "Black Guinea" accentuates an almost fetishistic quality to *Guinea*, perhaps to suggest the origins for this problematic understanding of exchange that coalesced with the slave trade and the rise of capitalism and instrumental matter.

By referring to the problem of the "fetish," I am thinking of Charles H. Long's application of the cultural historian William Pietz's tracing of the emergence of the fetish to a theory of "religion" in the modern world. The confusion over racial hierarchies and stability of the benevolent self in the wake of the question of slave freedom parallels, in a secularized framework, the "language of fetishism [that] emerges out of the contact of the Portuguese with the traders along the coast of West Africa." Long shows how this problem of materiality for the Portuguese, who, in the sixteenth century, along the coast of Guinea, confronted a "polyglot Creole society" of "disinherited Africans" who presented a new notion of matter to the traders. When they asked, "who is your master?" the inhabitants of the west coast said that it was the gold worn around their neck. The traders were surprised that these societies were willing to trade their gods. Here, Long points out, a new notion of matter emerged in contact with the Creole societies; because the Portuguese were also in an alien environment, detached from the familiar structures of exchange and prior concepts of materiality as idols, the discussions of the fetish clarify the fascination with a new relation to matter understood as the god within the gold. In the Enlightenment, particularly with the advent of a structure of "otherhood," suspicions

about the god within the gold or any inherent value to matter—
which was primarily understood as idolatry or personalized matter—the Cartesian doubt fed into new notions of materiality and
abstracted exchanges that placed materiality within the commodity
structure, girded in natural hierarchies, progressive ideologies, and
instrumentalist ideas about matter.[17]

Melville had traveled widely, confronting numerous cultures and
races; he had also, as Stuckey shows, read many books on West Africa,
including Mungo Park's *Travels in the Interior Districts of Africa*
(1799) and T. Edwards Bowditch's *Mission from Cape Castle to Ashantee*
(1819).[18] While "Guinea" as a problem of the nature of the American
self and its relation to others comes to the fore in *The Confidence-
Man*, with Black Guinea as trickster and con man, the reader of
Moby-Dick will recall that Guinea appeared, with Ahab lamenting
his loneliness and solitariness after "forty years" of "guinea-coast
slavery of solitary command!" Further, in *Moby-Dick* a gold coin, the
"Doubloon" of the "purest, virgin gold" from Ecuador served as a
symbol to bind the polyglot crew to Ahab's quest to destroy the
whale; the whale is at least symbolic of a form of materiality that falls
outside of the mercantile system and has a nonhuman inherent
value. The Doubloon is a promise to restore, control, and rationalize
the nonhuman nature of that matter. In a discussion related to the
fetish and "Guinea" coin, William Pietz notes that *Guinea* had a double meaning—one representing "black Africa" and the other the
"first coin immune to debasement by clipping and shaving around
the edges." The coin "helped bring about Europe's unprecedented
monetary stability after 1726." The word itself connotes a scene of
cross-cultural contact, and in its application to all sorts of commodities—as in "Guinea fowl," "Guinea hens," "Guinea corn," and so
forth—came to represent "any far-off land, not just black Africa. For
instance, 'guinea pigs' are from South America."[19]

17. See Charles H. Long, "Indigenous People, Materialities, and Religion: Outline for
a New Orientation to Religious Meaning," in *Religion and Global Culture*, ed. Jennifer I. M.
Reid (New York: Lexington Books, 2003), 172–75.

18. Marçais, "Presence of Africa," 181. See also Sterling Stuckey, "The Tambourine in
Glory: African Culture and Melville's Art," in *The Cambridge Companion to Herman
Melville* (Cambridge: Cambridge University Press, 1998), 337–64.

19. Herman Melville, *Moby-Dick; or, The Whale* (London: Penguin Books, 1986),
651, 540; William Pietz, "The Problem of the Fetish, III: Bosman's Guinea and the
Enlightenment Theory of Fetishism," *Res* 16 (autumn 1988): 105n3. The meaning of
Guinea is also ubiquitous in documents on the transatlantic slave trade. *Guinea* was not

The Guinea gold coin had a figure of an elephant on it because it was first used by "the Company of Royal Adventurers of England trading with Africa."[20] This could be why Melville describes the beggar as "throwing up his head and opening his mouth like an elephant for tossed apples at a menagerie" in the "game of charity." While he is opening his mouth to catch the pennies, in a "pitch penny" game, he is said to be able to swallow his indignation even as he "retain[s] each copper this side of the œsophagus" (8). When he finally receives charity from the merchant, his "face glow[s] like a polished copper saucepan," resembling the penny (14). Melville implies that the black body is a commodified marker for exchange in general, blackness being a quality that can most easily mark a ubiquitous and expanding system of exchange based upon an abstract human relation: The suspicion around Black Guinea's crippled body, abstracted as a coin, comes to represent a crisis and possibility in the field of exchange as the country attempts to bring to birth a national identity without the existence of slavery. In light of this notion of free blacks and of an end to a slave system, how do whites configure their relation to the appearance of this masterless object and former property? How do they construct their own identity as their former property has to be configured as human, given that the formation of the modern American self depends so heavily on defining itself in relation to abstracted and instrumental matter? Black Guinea, read as a fetish object, brings to light the continuity with problems that early conquerors faced in their understanding of the material world. Combined with a nation of "others," with nothing but the ideology of a benevolent self as the basis for value, Melville captures the problems that Americans have in the expansion of the West in

---

only the appellation for the majority of slaves shipped from Greater Senegambia, which is the more precise area of "Guinea." As Gwendolyn Mildo Hall points out, "There is still credible evidence that as late as 1811 'Guinea' or the 'Coast of Guinea' still referred to Africans from Sierra Leone." The majority of Africans shipped as "cargo" during the French slave trade to Louisiana seemed to originate from "Senegambia narrowly defined." Hall clarifies, "the African coastal origin of Louisiana slaves during the Spanish period was much more varied than Atlantic slave voyages indicate." Moreover, "the database defines the African coast recorded in documents as 'Guinea,' or the 'Rivers of Guinea' as an unknown African coastal origin, writing the mistake into cybernetic stone." *Slavery and African Ethnicities in the Americas: Restoring the Links* (Chapel Hill: University of North Carolina Press, 2005), 82, 95.

20. This description of the guinea is taken from OED. The guinea originally received the popular name because it was used in "guinea trade." *Oxford English Dictionary Online* (Oxford University Press, 2003).

understanding of materiality—especially as matter was expressed in former property, or slaves—that falls outside of the instrumental notions characteristic of the work ethic and variants of antebellum Protestantism and Enlightenment natural hierarchies.

While the figure of Guinea unleashes the structure of the confidence game, one confidence man preceded him: Melville tells us that on April Fool's day, "there appeared, suddenly as Manco Capac at the lake Titicaca, a man in cream colors, at the water-side in the city of St. Louis" (1). With "neither carpet-bag, nor parcel," and "unaccompanied by friends," this man is a "stranger," without human connections. According to Eric Wertheimer, the stranger is "an original American" and a "metaphor involving the founding of the Inca Empire, invoked in the first sentence." This is also "a bubble blown into the everyday life of a now ahistorical continent." Cut off from speech, a "mute," the first confidence man captures the image of founding myths and abstractions used to romanticize the Anglo-Americans' form of colonization, or to demonize the Spanish "Black Legend" of destroying the noble Inca. The first appearance of a founding myth of conquest is followed by Black Guinea, and the issue of originality deepens around those associated with racial identities. In reading Melville, we are confronted with a question that Long poses about the obsession with "originality" in the creation of the modern West. "Why," he asks, "in the modern period of the West has so much concern and attention on the scholarly as well as the popular level been related to cultures and peoples who have been classified as archaic, primal, or indigenous?" Long notes that the classifications did not "originate with the people designated by them."[21]

This desire for a pure, benevolent, and founding myth of the American republic seems to cohere around the obsession with an Original American.[22] In antebellum America, a passionate effort to heal the sense of estrangement and mistrust in the union arose with benevolent societies and reform movements. Melville mocks their purpose, given that the predominant mode of healing stems from an alienated sense of individualism, one that has little sense of material exchanges that would tie communities together but rather appeals to

---

21. Eric Wertheimer, *Imagined Empires: Incas, Aztecs, and the New World of American Literature, 1771–1876* (New York: Cambridge University Press, 1999), 147; Long, "Indigenous People," 168.

22. R. W. B. Lewis, *The American Adam* (Chicago: University of Chicago Press, 1955), is one of the most cogent discussions of this theme in American literature and culture.

the original "goodness of the inner heart," as opposed to the "Original Sin." The confidence man will ask that his would-be dupes believe in the "genuine me," the original self. Antebellum civil religious modes were based in Yankee ideals, numerous "hunters," either of the market, with its appeal to "confidence," secrets, and risk taking, or of its philanthropic charities, in pursuit of benevolence, "happiness," and purity. The former exploit the land and dispossess people; the latter perversely work as a Band-Aid, bolstering the Northern sense of self-satisfaction, benevolence, and goodness that becomes so problematic in the novel.

The Metaphysics of Indian Hating: Unity, Expansion, and the Fear of Contact

Melville has already adumbrated the meaning of Original American when he alluded to Manco Capac, the cultural hero of the Inca Empire. He has skillfully played this meaning of the Original American with that of the notion of Original Sin, then, in his discourse on Indian hating, he brings to fruition the American amalgam of these meanings expressed through the tradition of a nation of pilgrims who remain strangers. He bases his portrait of the Indian hater on a character, Moredock, drawn from two of Judge James Hall's books, *Sketches of History, Life, and Manners in the West* and *Wilderness and the Warpath,* told by the cosmopolitan Charlie Noble.[23]

Around this character of an "Indian hater," Moredock, an interwoven, dialectical, and ironic conversation takes places between Pitch, Noble, and Goodman (the names themselves are suggestive, given the nature of the conversation). It is revealed that Moredock became an Indian hater and hunter because Indians had killed his whole family. While the metaphysical and physical violence may be reprehensible, it is understandable as an act of revenge. The conversation about Moredock, however, centers not so much around an act of revenge or even the hypocrisy of having a loving heart while bent on hate and killing; the conversation rather revolves around the

---

23. The first source from Judge Hall is provided by the Norton edition of *Confidence-Man;* the second source was brought to my attention by Tom Quirk, "A Pragmatic Defense of Source Study: Melville's 'Borrowings' from Judge James Hall," *Mosaic: A Journal for the Interdisciplinary Study of Literature* 26, no. 4 (fall 1993): 21–35.

necessity and desirability of holding these antithetical traits together as the sine qua non of the civilizing mission. Moredock moves from being a reprehensible, hypocritical character into a "civilizing hero," in the same spirit as Alexander the Great. He is "to America what Alexander was to Asia—captain in the vanguard of conquering civilization" (126). The sense of holding two antithetical traits together returns the reader to the motley crew on board who smugly con each other and recognize what Gary Lindberg calls the "sacramental nature" of the confidence game, while desperately longing for some form of authority. According to Lindberg:

> The work of settling a new country has advanced far enough so that the characters are not only smug about their comparative safety . . . , but nostalgically titillated by stories of earlier violence and audacity. If they have little to fear, they also have little to bind them together. This gathering is significantly not a community but a "public" and its underlying malaise is apparent in its yearning for even that minimal authority proclaimed by a wanted poster into this unnervingly fluid world.[24]

That submerged desire for authority must not resolve ambivalent feelings toward the nature that the sometimes "merciless savage[s]" and other times "noble savages" represent. These "savages," at a formative level, have a religion that considers reciprocal exchange with the land, a land that is hollow for most of the passengers being duped or who are playing the con game themselves. Indian hating moves from the description or explanation of a singular act to a "metaphysics," that is, an originary and sustaining structure of culture, anticipating Frederick Jackson Turner's "Frontier Thesis." On the metaphysical level, it evokes a meaning of purity, though such purity never escapes the rhetoric of brotherhood. The paranoia toward French and Catholics emerges when the confidence men confront these precise issues of charity and attachment, especially around Native Americans and the land; Catholics, without completely hollowing out religious ceremony, could remain brothers while being charitable, since they were giving out of duty to God and not out of self-oriented philanthropy. The Know-Nothing party had

24. Gary Lindberg, *The Confidence Man in American Literature* (New York: Oxford University Press, 1982), 46–47.

arisen in 1850, but assuagement of guilt through allegorical tales of pagans and papists, was, of course, long established, strengthened too by the founding Protestant tenets, the fears of popish plots, the French and Indian War, and the Monroe Doctrine. In the first half of the novel, one auditor to the confidence man notes that he could be an "original genius"; later, another suspects him to be "one of those Jesuit emissaries prowling all over our country" (79). As Meinig points out, "in Anglo-American eyes, the French were tainted by their tendency to mix and socialize too freely with other races."[25] The connection with Catholicism worked for both stereotypes of the French and the Spanish; Melville's Indian hater is described in such terms as "a Spaniard turned monk" (130). But the characterizations are all left at levels of analogy for the fate of the skeptical "misanthrope" who does not believe in the goodness of man. This diluted Indian hater, "after some months' lonely scoutings [and much solitude,] . . . is suddenly seized with a sort of calenture; hurries openly towards the first smoke, though he knows it is an Indian's, announces himself as a lost hunter, gives the savage his rifle, throws himself upon his charity, embraces him with much affection, imploring the privilege of living a while in his sweet companionship" (135). Although this is a diluted version, the ambivalent feelings expressed allow us to understand the violent desire for authenticity that accompanies the rationalized world of modern America.

In the Indian hater are consequences of a world that has distanced itself from attachments. We are told that "The backwoodsman is a lonely man. He is a thoughtful man. He is a man strong and unsophisticated. Impulsive, he is what some might call unprincipled. At any rate, he is self-willed." This Indian hater possesses "self-reliance," and he "stands the trial" of "[s]olitude" (125). As a corollary to his desire for solitude, the backwoodsman is in fact a benevolent, good-hearted type of fellow. Later, we are informed that "nearly all Indian-haters have at bottom loving hearts; at any rate, hearts, if anything, more generous than the average" (134). Indeed, there is said to be a type of religion inherent in this backwoodsman, given that, according to Charlie Noble, "to be a consistent Indian-hater involved the renunciation of ambition, with its objects—the pomp and glories of the world; and since religion, pronouncing such things vanities, accounts it merit to renounce them, therefore, so far as this goes,

25. Meinig, *Shaping of America*, 2:189.

Indian-hating, whatever may be thought of it in other respects, may
be regarded as not wholly without the efficacy of a devout sentiment" (135). This type of religion parallels the modern American
definition of religion, by William James and Alfred Whitehead, as a
solitary act of belief.[26] The type of religion stems from the benevolent and Enlightenment belief in the lack of an inherent value to the
material objects of the world, a "renunciation of ambition, with its
objects—the pomp and glory of the world." The discussion seems
girded in Protestant forms of iconoclasm and with the lack of "tribal
bond" or "brotherliness" that arose in the Reformation and in the
development of a mercantile system. The lack of any community
(associated with priestly hierarchy) or of any sacramental objects
(associated with idolatry and then fetishism) combines with ideals of
self-reliance, unbridled liberty, and an intense hatred for the other it
has created.

And, above all, the Indian hater has a heart. Melville's critique of
liberal Protestantism revolves around this observation. We may also
turn to Hannah Arendt, who in a different context considers the violent effects behind a notion of human goodness and compassion
when it enters the realm of public affairs and human society: "the
heart, moreover . . . keeps its resources alive through a constant
struggle that goes on in its darkness and because of its darkness.
When we say that nobody but God can see (and perhaps bear to see)
the nakedness of a human heart, 'nobody' includes one's own self—
if only because our sense of unequivocal reality is so bound up with
the presence of others that we can never be sure of anything that
only we ourselves know and no one else."[27] The vacillations of the
Indian hater depend upon a dominant mode of "religion" that has
divested itself from human objects, meaning, people, and the objects
they have made, and looked instead to nature for an inherent value
of benevolence—a value that they themselves impute to it.

Melville leaves us reflecting not so much on a lost form of authentic exchange or charity that could be recovered, or on a lack of
"inwardness" that could counter the increasing focus on outward
appearances and masks that plagues the steamer, an allegorical new

26. See William James, *The Varieties of Religious Experience* (New York: Random
House, 1902), 31–32; and Alfred North Whitehead, *Religion in the Making: Lowell
Lectures, 1926* (New York: Fordham University Press, 1996).
27. Hannah Arendt, *On Revolution* (New York: Viking Press, 1963), 96.

republic of the Purchase. Indeed, he shows us how the extreme inward and outward are bound together with the Indian hater, Colonel Moredock, a great war hero who was so popular that he was "pressed to become candidate for governor" of Illinois; he declined because of his commitment to true Indian hating, leaving the show of love, "friendly treaties," and benevolence to officials, the "paternal chief-magistra[tes]" (135). He does not want to expose the violence that is the other side of the benevolent coin—neither he nor they want to admit in public the necessity of killing Indians in order for them to prosper. While Black Guinea brings us to the extremely hollow nature of exchange, with the exchange of human persons as human specie and specie as money, the confidence game itself has become the new religion of the West, a structure that persists in the culture and language of the United States.

Mixed-Race Ecstasy across a Single Line

The Deep South Roots of Pentecostal Tongue Speaking

ELAINE J. LAWLESS

Most people acquainted with the scholarship on Pentecostalism—including the work of Robert Anderson, Harvey Cox, Dickson Bruce, Martin Marty, Vinson Synon, W. J. Hollenweger, Ann Taves, and others—will know that there are several different accounts of the birth of this twentieth-century ecstatic religion. Tracking down the origin of religious behavior is not an easy task. Certainly, ecstatic religious experiences in America had been reported long before the turn of the twentieth century, and various movements swept across the country exhibiting various charismatic religious attributes, such as shouting and dancing in the spirit.[1] And the enthusiastic worshipping styles that characterize Pentecostal religious services today are reminiscent of early-nineteenth-century Methodist revivals and camp meetings.[2] Even with these early

1. Robert Mapes Anderson, *Vision of the Disinherited: The Making of American Pentecostalism* (New York: Oxford University Press, 1979); Harvey Cox, *Fire from Heaven: The Rise of Pentecostal Spirituality and the Reshaping of Religion in the 21st Century* (Reading, Mass.: Addison-Wesley, 1995); Vinson Synan, *The Holiness-Pentecostal Movement in the United States* (Grand Rapids, Mich.: Eerdmans, 1971); William J. Hollenweger, *The Pentecostals* (Minneapolis: Augsberg Press, 1972). My own work, *God's Peculiar People: Women's Voices and Tradition in a Pentecostal Church* (Lexington: University Press of Kentucky, 1988), includes a lengthy discussion of the early camp meeting revival meetings and the holiness movement (24–34).

2. For more information on these movements, see Dickson D. Bruce Jr., *And They All Sang Hallelujah: Plain-Folk Camp-Meeting Religion, 1800–1845* (Knoxville: University of Tennessee Press, 1974); Charles Johnson, *The Frontier Camp Meeting* (Dallas: Southern Methodist University Press, 1955); William Warren Sweet, *Religion on the American Frontier* (New York: Henry Holt, 1931); Bernard Weisberger, *They Gathered at*

precursors, the accumulation of several ecstatic behaviors connected with a particular Pentecostal "experience," according to some accounts, began in Topeka, Kansas, in 1901 during an "upper room" experience of a prayer group led by Charles Parham, a white preacher who advocated religious enthusiasm much like that documented in both the first and second great religious awakenings, both in the United States and abroad.

Many will also know that this origin narrative of Pentecostalism has a counterpart story that claims a nearly simultaneous outbreak of tongue speaking that occurred in 1906 or 1907 (the dates vary) on Azusa Street in Los Angeles, California, at a black church led by Charles Seymour, a black minister who was inclined toward ecstatic and enthusiastic religious practice. It is interesting to note that some records suggest that Seymour had been a student and close colleague of Parham's before he moved to California, and, as far as I am able to discern, both of them had moved from the South—from Kentucky and Mississippi.[3]

This paper was originally an invited talk delivered at the University of Missouri in 2004 at a conference devoted to new understandings of the influence that the Louisiana Purchase, and subsequent travels of cultural forms along the Lewis and Clark trail, had on early religion. In light of that focus, I set out to question these received narratives of the beginnings of Pentecostalism and the heightened importance of tongue speaking as it began to acquire new religious authority and develop increased status as proof of salvation. My research took me to accounts from New Orleans that offered a different, and quite exciting, origin narrative for Pentecostalism, one that began in the Deep South, moved up the Louisiana Purchase with slaves, newly freed black men, and white traveling evangelists who worshiped alongside these new African visitors. As an ethnographer of religious behavior, I am more interested in trying to discern what was actually going on in the religious encounters in the Deep South prior to the popularity of both of the more accepted "origin" narratives about Pentecostalism than I am

---

the River (Chicago: Quandrangle Books, 1958); and Ann Taves, *Fits, Trances, and Visions* (Princeton: Princeton University Press, 1999).

3. There are several different accounts of both the Kansas "outbreak" and the one in California in Nils Block-Hoell, *The Pentecostal Movement* (Oslo, Norway: Universitetsforlaget, 1964); John Nicol, *Pentecostalism* (New York: Harper and Row, 1966); and Synan, *Holiness-Pentecostal Movement*.

about parsing these separate narratives. In this article, I want to trace these religious experiences back further than either of the contested origin stories.[4]

By reading historical and personal accounts of the religious contexts in the Deep South, I find clear ethnographic evidence that blacks and whites in the South worshipped together on a regular basis in biracial churches, secluded brush arbors, and camp meeting tents and outdoor "tabernacles." By most accounts, camp meeting revival religion was marked by the participation of middle- and lower-class whites, black slaves, and freedmen. Certainly, by the early 1800s the elite whites were congregating in more "mainstream" churches, such as the Presbyterian Church, where the wild enthusiasm of the camp meeting revival tradition and the ecstasy of the Second Great Awakening were avoided and largely discredited, while southern Baptist groups and some Methodists continued to seek out and embrace the more "enthusiastic" gatherings, where they worshipped alongside blacks who were largely Haitians, African blacks brought as slaves, and newly freed blacks still residing in the South.

Accounts of slave religion stress that blacks were discouraged from gathering on the plantations for exclusive religious services. It was clear to the plantation owners and their overlords that Voudou and other Haitian and African-based religious practices prevailed, even as they implemented cruel punishments for the slaves to desist in these religious traditions. Slaves were "encouraged" to convert to Christianity and practice religion alongside Southern whites. There is also evidence in the records that when plantation owners, or their paid employees, suspected that their slaves were continuing with African-based religious practices, they visited the slave religious

---

4. As a folklorist and an ethnographer, I conducted fieldwork in a wide variety of midwestern Pentecostal churches from 1980 until the late 1990s in regions from Indiana to Missouri. This work resulted in the publication of two books and many articles on the oral, performative charismatic experiences of the religious groups I had the privilege to research. In 1981, I also coproduced a documentary video, *Joy Unspeakable*, with my colleague Elizabeth Peterson. This video is still available through Indiana University Radio and Television Video Library, and although it is over twenty years old, the video still accurately depicts Pentecostal beliefs and practices that are alive and well in the midwestern counties where I live. I add this information in order to clarify that I am not a religious historian, nor do I claim to be in this article. However, having read various journals, diaries, and firsthand historical accounts of the charismatic religious services in the Deep South, as whites and new black immigrants mixed their religious fervors, I certainly hear echoes of the same language about the "language of God that takes over the tongue" that I have heard nearly every day in my own field research.

gatherings to make certain they were actually "religious" in nature, not subversive and revolutionary, or practicing what they feared was "black magic" against the owners and their kin. Many stayed to watch, and some admitted they could not resist being drawn to the worshipping styles of the enthusiastic believers.

Some of these firsthand accounts have been used by historians to paint a picture of what slave religion was like. As the plantation owners became more adamant in their determination to erase African-based religious practices on southern American soil, it should come as no surprise that the slaves found the enthusiastic Baptist and Methodist gatherings more to their liking than the more formalized mainstream churches. More than that, however, was the reality that blacks were more welcome at the gatherings of poor whites than in the churches of the elite. Brush-arbor gatherings and the large, mostly open-air camp meeting revivals that lasted well into the night and sometimes all night long were places where poor whites, slaves, and black freedmen gathered to worship together. This is, in fact, the premise of the 1988 collection of articles edited by John Boles, *Masters and Slaves in the House of the Lord: Race and Religion in the American South, 1740–1870.*[5] As with so many other histories, Boles's collection is mostly concerned with the "Christian mission to the slaves" by Southern whites, but the collection also looks at Presbyterian, Baptist, and Methodist biracial services of mostly plain-folk whites and slaves.

Accounts abound of journals and diaries that mention with disdain that in these religious meetings of both races there was "much noise into the night."[6] Camp meeting revivals hit their heyday around 1730. This tradition took form in the southern colonies often in brush-arbor gatherings where the emotional outpourings, the "moving and the shaking," could be experienced without rebuke by the official churches or watchful plantation owners. Randy J. Sparks claims that at the turn of the nineteenth century, thousands of new immigrants settled the area of Amite County, in southwest Mississippi near Natchez, in what was then referred to as the "Mississippi Territory." These groups, including both blacks and

5. John Boles, ed., *Masters and Slaves in the House of the Lord: Race and Religion in the American South, 1740–1870* (Lexington: University Press of Kentucky, 1988).
6. Alan Galley, "Planters and Slaves in the Great Awakening," in Boles, *Masters and Slaves,* 26.

whites, arrived from South Carolina, Georgia, North Carolina, and Virginia. Sparks talks of the "pioneer efforts of religion in this wilderness." In the early 1800s, the Great Revival moved from Kentucky into the Mississippi Territory, and "soon the region was on fire with religious enthusiasm" among immigrants who were cold, poor, and brokenhearted by this unfortunate move into wilderness, poverty, and unrelenting mortality figures. "The camp meetings became regularized, institutionalized, and vital to church growth."[7] Apparently, the plantation owners were more likely to allow their slaves to gather in these settings rather than in the more secluded sites in the woods where they could not be so easily monitored.

In 1823 an estimated four to six thousand people attended a meeting at Bethel Camp Ground, near the Amite-Wilkinson county line—with both black and white participants. According to Randy Sparks, "Black attendance at services was probably larger than the membership [records] might suggest." Sparks continues with a quote from a William Winans, who wrote in 1823 that he "met the Black [people] at the M[eeting] house and held a love feast. This was quite a refreshing season. Many of these poor people appeared happier than kings (unless the king [k]new the love of Jesus) and some whites that were present were very happy also." Little did the plantation owners know that poor whites (mostly Baptists) were often strongly opposed to slavery and did not preach the "obey your master" sermons that were so prevalent in the formal churches that had both black and white congregations. The laws were very strict against black preachers, however, and Sparks concludes, "Many black preachers must have been forced to meet secretly with the faithful."[8]

Sparks relies on social psychologist George Herbert Mead in identifying a biracial religious community in terms of the "use of the same significant symbols." In Mead's view, "A person learns a new language and, as we say, gets a new soul. He puts himself into the attitude of those that make use of that language. . . . You cannot convey a language as a pure abstraction; you inevitably in some degree convey also the life that lies behind it." Mead was not actually talking about a "new language," but, according to Sparks, he lays the foundation for us to understand this newly developing religious

---

7. Randy J. Sparks, "Religion in Amite County, Mississippi, 1800–1861," in Boles, *Masters and Slaves*, 27.
8. Sparks, "Religion in Amite County," 63, 66.

community as sharing a kind of religious language that consisted of forms of address such as "Brother" and "Sister," baptism, communion, foot washing, and "shouting out" in services.[9] To these performative religious practices, I would add tongue speaking and how ecstatic religious behavior was interpreted in religious settings in the southern colonies—as blacks and whites gathered to worship together. Even if the white congregations were not totally cognizant of the influences of African-based religions on their religious meetings that included slaves and newly freed men and women, they did recognize the benefit of the slave religious enthusiasm.

Robert Hall notes that white preachers who longed for more fervor and shouting in the camp meeting revivals in the 1850s put it this way: "The way [Peter] Richardson [a Methodist preacher] fulfilled his determination 'to have some shouting' suggests that he perceived blacks as a kind of human kindling for the fires of faith. He undertook to ignite a separate black congregation with his preaching 'and have them shouting, then bring them up to the white church.'" Richardson had written that "The galleries for the Negroes were full," so "[we] went up into the gallery" and "turned them loose, and we had a stormy time until a late hour."[10]

While many religious histories focus more on the influence of Christian religion on the slave population in this country, I am more interested in taking the opposite perspective in terms of examining why the received narratives of the "birth of Pentecostalism" have settled on the California and Kansas moments rather than on Louisiana, the southern colonies, and the move up the Mississippi River into what we identify as the Louisiana Purchase territory. Along with this geographical thrust, my own field research in southern Indiana, southern Illinois, and southern Missouri suggests (as we might expect) that the religious traditions that were crystallized in the Deep South as blacks and whites worshipped together not only dispersed on the western side of the Mississippi but also similarly converged with the southernmost areas of the adjoining states of Indiana, Illinois, Kentucky, and Tennessee—which makes sense if we are aware of the plain-folk religious traditions that Dickson Bruce and others have followed in these areas, rich now in Pentecostal traditions.

9. Mead, quoted in ibid., 78.
10. Robert Hall, "Black and White Christians in Florida," in Boles, *Masters and Slaves,* 91.

As Alan Gallay and others point out, with Reconstruction, the biracial nature of plain-folk and black southern religion dissolved as blacks moved to black-only congregations. Katharine Dvorak has difficulties marking just exactly why black congregations broke so quickly from white congregations following the emancipation. She argues this move was initiated by blacks who had kept a "secret" tradition of meeting in brush arbors all along, and with the war over, they moved quickly into their own churches. She tries to discount the possibility that the white churches were also eager to have the blacks out of their congregations once they could no longer be slaves and subordinate, yet she admits this may also have been the case. At any rate, we can be fairly certain that after the late 1860s there was much less biracial religious activity than there had been before. White Christians, Dvorak posits, may have felt the guilt involved with this move as evidence of the "mighty arm of God's judgment"—and may have opted to remove themselves as far as possible from the blacks, who were moving as quickly as they could from the white-dominated world and into their own "promise land."[11] In the split, however, both black and white arenas retained characteristics that had been nourished in the years of shared worship—hence the Topeka and the Azusa Street situations shared components of the origin narratives. But the true birthplace of tongue speaking as a critical aspect of the Pentecostal experience—and evidence of the infilling of the "Holy Ghost" as proof of salvation—was in Louisiana at that tip of the Louisiana Purchase where whites and blacks worshipped together and shared their performative religious traditions.

According to the scholars in Boles's book, a look at the multiracial religious worship practices of blacks and whites in pre–Civil War southern states—mentioned are Louisiana, Mississippi, South Carolina, Virginia, Georgia, and Maryland, Tennessee, and Kentucky, and eventually Missouri—clearly maps religion in the South at the intersection of white enthusiastic religious practices that moved southward into the southern colonies and those that came in through southern Louisiana with the slave trade. Specifically, I am concerned with the charismatic practices of evangelical Christianity from the First Great Awakening through the Second as they intersected in the Deep South with Haitian and African-based religious practices of

---

11. Katharine Dvorak, "After Apocalypse, Moses," in Boles, *Masters and Slaves,* 191.

slaves and freed black men and women as they worshipped together in biracial religious gatherings. Anyone who has read or seen an account of the possession of a Loa in Haitian or African-based Voudun will recognize the nearly identical language and experience as recounted by the Pentecostal conversion narratives from the early 1900s. These possession practices of the blacks in this region syncretized easily with the enthusiasm of the evangelistic and holiness traditions that were primed through religious enthusiasm, swooning, and other charismatic practices to seek "possession" of the Holy Ghost through trance states.

Descriptions of the multiracial religious practices in the South during the eighteenth and nineteenth centuries are actually quite detailed, although nearly every religious historian who writes about these gatherings laments the lack of "official reports" because the events were oral, spontaneous, and not documented in systematic ways. Primarily, we have first-person accounts of these events, often from white visitors who were there largely to observe and document these rather rowdy Christian religious behaviors that continued to make elite whites nervous. Other accounts are from plantation owners, who correctly assumed that the religious practices of their slaves and other blacks would, and could, have an effect on white religious charismatic behaviors. Accounts also indicate plantation owners had other concerns about slave gatherings and religious activities at the revivals: There was serious concern that blacks who worshipped all night fasting, singing, dancing, going into trance states, falling out, jerking, and speaking in "different languages" were not able to work effectively the next day, and sometimes these revivals lasted for weeks and months at a time with services each night.

The more detailed descriptions of these events are the evidence for my contention about the influence of African- and Haitian-based religious practices—that is, the performative aspect of these biracial religious events—upon white participants rather than the more traditional scholarly stance that is interested in how slaves were Christianized once they embarked on American soil. Certainly, "segregation" was the rule, although this "segregation" tended to break down as the services became more enthusiastic, moving as they did into the late hours of the night with ecstatic behaviors becoming more and more enthusiastic.

By most accounts, segregation was administered largely by designated seating for blacks and whites. Apparently, slaves and other blacks were often relegated to the "upper gallery" in actual buildings or in the back or side of the open-air "tabernacles"—at least at the beginning of the services. Other accounts state that blacks and whites all sat in hewn wooden "pews" alongside each other, divided only by a single rope. But as the singing and dancing became more enthusiastic and the religious began to move about the space, the races undoubtedly mixed as they danced around the perimeter and moved toward the altar space to "fall out" in religious ecstasy, lie in trance states, and seek the evidence of sanctification through the "infilling of the Holy Ghost," and, from an African perspective, to "be possessed by the spirits."

Larry M. James also found evidence of separate standing places for black worshippers, in lofts and in "sheds" built onto the main building but open to the sanctuary. He also notes that all-black gatherings were illegal and required some white participation in order to monitor black religious activities—thus whites were often present in otherwise all-black gatherings as these activities became more popular, and in some cases the whites began to participate willingly in the gatherings as well. At any rate, James similarly asserts that blacks were relegated to separate pews, the "black pews," or were kept in the "loft or balcony" in a space built especially for blacks. He does suggest, however, that black preachers were at times allowed to preach after the white preachers finished, and that blacks could stand and testify (though his evidence for this seems more shaky). According to James, white Baptists were aware of (and perhaps condoned) "the desire of their black members to 'exercise' their spiritual gifts."[12] Certainly, in the accounts provided by James (and those of other contributors to Boles's volume) describing the popular and largely unsanctioned "brush arbor" meetings held "deep in the woods" away from the formal churches and the eyes of plantation owners, blacks and whites were more likely to interact freely in the service. They were separated only by the various seating spaces in the area, which typically became dispersed toward the end of the enthusiastic services when everyone had left their respective seats to gather in the center to sing, dance, and shout.

Historian Ann Taves, in her well-received work *Fits, Trances, and Visions*, writes about the interracial quality of the camp meeting

---

12. Larry M. James, "Biracial Fellowship in Antebellum Baptist Churches," in Boles, *Masters and Slaves*, 55.

revivals, as well, where "the tradition of 'shouting' was developed and passed on by means of embodied performances" that are difficult to imagine in any "systematic fashion." Yet Taves goes on to say that it was in the camp meetings that the "call-and-response style of worship, the spirituals, and the ring shout" began and eventually led to the "interracial Holiness and Pentecostal movements." By the late 1780s, Taves claims, nearly half the population of Virginia was of African descent. She develops the argument that the interracial quality of the camp meeting revivals came to sacralize different kinds of religious experiences. She contends that much of the move toward song, dance, shouting, preaching in syncopated styles, clapping, falling out "slain in the spirit," and chanting had been contributed by the African members of the Methodist congregations. Taves does not return to the connection between shouting and the "holiness movement" and the roots of Pentecostalism until nearly a hundred pages later. Interestingly, her account most noticeably focuses on how the radical wing of "old fashioned Methodists" (often referred to by the "church" Methodists as schismatic, fanatical, and disloyal) formed the "National Camp Meeting Association for the Promotion of Holiness" in 1867 to promote sanctification, holiness, and clear evidence of God's spirit in the camp meeting arenas (which they found sorely lacking in the Methodist churches that had become, in their words, "cold and stolid"). Evidence of God's presence became recognized, rather, as the sanctified experience of holiness, largely recognized through intensive trance states and the "infilling" of the Holy Ghost or Holy Spirit, and generally followed by tongue speaking.[13]

Even more interesting, perhaps, is Taves's recognition of the importance during this time of Phoebe Palmer, a white traveling itinerant preacher who brought the holiness message and taught people how to create "holiness bands." Taves documents the importance of this woman and her "altar services," where believers lined up to lie down upon the altar as a "living sacrifice, and waited for the fire of heaven to fall, consume, and purify them." Although Taves suggests that Palmer did not yet at this time encourage tongue speaking as a *requirement* of sanctification, she clearly was a pivotal leader in this transition between camp meeting, revival-shouting religion (recognized as Methodist) and the emergence of a connection between sanctification, holiness, trance states, and an early

13. Taves, *Fits*, 76, 77.

recognition that tongue speaking was *the evidence of the infilling of the Holy Spirit.* Apparently, Palmers's influence was augmented by the presence of another woman on the scene, holiness evangelist Maria Woodworth, dubbed the "trance evangelist," who insisted on even more "old-fashioned" Holy Spirit encounters. Of Woodworth's influence, Wayne Warner (who wrote a book on her) quoted from a firsthand encounter with her evangelism, wherein the observer stated he had not "witnessed the like since I attended the meetings of the poor black slaves in Kentucky, thirty years ago."[14]

It is not surprising to learn that, given this movement into spirit trances and tongue speaking, Woodworth's evangelism was linked to hypnotism, hysteria, and "magnetic phenomenon."[15] Reminiscent of blacks' accounts of being "ridden by the Loa," Woodworth often claimed that when the spirit filled her, she "floated away" and "left the area" for some considerable time, rarely remembering exactly where she went or what she did there (although she had some memories of visiting heaven or encountering particular people, both living and dead). While Woodworth enjoyed some short-lived positive notoriety in the South, when her evangelism brought her up the Mississippi River to St. Louis, critics in the local newspapers complained about the "healing, visions, [and] trance-like behaviors" evidenced by her and her followers as early as 1890. The accusations of her questionable powers over her followers, her "dubious" healings, and her own sanity eventually led to her arrest and trial as a charlatan. She was eventually released, but the damage to her reputation had been done. This may have been the reason why the accounts of tongue speaking by Charles Parham's group, which occurred in their "upper room" setting in Kansas, held more sway and caused less public concern than Woodworth's public enthusiasms. Certainly, Parham's declarations following the group experiences were met with skepticism and worry about "cultish" activities, but the male "Reverend" had more credibility than the female traveling evangelist could ever muster.

In her account, Taves relies primarily on the Kansas Parham version of the "birth of Pentecostalism," although she begins with an account of Woodworth and Palmer and the southern camp meeting revival tradition that was moving northward up the Mississippi. She

14. Ibid., 240, 417; Warner's quotation on 417n152.
15. Ibid., 417.

notes the connection of this tradition to black slave and freedmen's ecstatic tradition that included the "possession of the spirits"— which had obviously been embraced by these female evangelists and incorporated into their conception of "full sanctification" as the remarkably similar "infilling of the Holy Spirit." However, Taves rests her discussion of the birth of Pentecostalism with the Parham account, probably because he connected his group's collective tongue speaking experience with the biblical account of the "Pentecost"—hence the naming of this charismatic religion as "Pentecostalism."[16]

As Taves continues her historical account of the birth of Pentecostalism, she also notes the "other" most popular explanation of the origin of this religion by including Seymour and the California movement in this manner:

> If Charles Parham, preoccupied with counterfeits, was (loosely speaking) the Jonathan Edwards of Pentecostalism, then William J. Seymour was Pentecostalism's John Wesley. Seymour had been a student at Parham's Bible School for a short while in the early 1900s. By 1906, he was a recognized minister in Parham's Apostolic Faith Movement and the founder of the Azusa Street Mission in Los Angeles, the fastest growing and most publicized of the Pentecostal revivals. Although the "Pentecostal fire" fell on Los Angeles in April 1906, Parham did not visit until the following October. . . . Many came to view Azusa Street as the birthplace of Pentecostalism, but Seymour explained that the Pentecostal work had begun "five years ago . . . when a company of people under the leadership of Charles Parham . . . tarried for Pentecost in Topeka, Kansas."[17]

Interestingly, Taves and other scholars note that when Parham visited Azusa Street and encountered Seymour and a mixed-race

---

16. It is worth noting that most Pentecostals I have interviewed over the past twenty years in the American Midwest generally make a distinction between the "Pentecostal experience" and "Pentecostalism" as a denomination. Many prefer the first (the "experience") rather than the link to a formal denomination, claiming that the tongue speaking as evidence of the infilling of the Holy Ghost, sanctification, and salvation is an experience, *not* a denomination. Of course, as modern denominations began to vie for larger numbers in their tallies and in their efforts to gain both national and international recognition, several Pentecostal sects have gained prominence, including the United Pentecostal Church, the Assemblies of God, and a wide variety of "Holiness" and "Tabernacle" smaller sects that populate the Midwest and the South.

17. Taves, *Fits*, 329.

congregation shouting, jerking, falling out, going into trance states, and speaking in tongues, he quickly disavowed his connections with that group, went home, and claimed only the Kansas experiences were "authentic." In an aside, Taves notes that one of Parham's primary followers, a woman named Faye Carothers, thought Parham hasty and misguided by his rejection of the authenticity of the Azusa Street revival. Most interestingly, Parham discerned that the "tongues" he heard at Azusa Street were not proper "tongues." That is, he clung fast to the notion that true, spirit-filled tongue speaking would be "xenoglossia," or tongues that were identifiable as other, identifiable languages that could be understood by natives from those cultures. This claim is, of course, based purely on the semantic quality of the tongues in Parham's experience and would, in fact, discount any African-based trance induced "tongue speaking" that did not sound linguistically similar to what Parham had previously encountered. While I do not know for certain where Seymour was born and raised before he found Parham, it is probable that he was a southern black who brought Phoebe Palmer and Maria Woodworth's message up the Mississippi River, along with all the combined black and white traditions that had been birthed in the Deep South in those camp meeting revivals where the performances of the blacks were in clear evidence to the whites who worshipped right alongside them—rope or no rope. Without question, religious experiences are a direct result of shared religious performances in religious contexts.

Obviously, the "transmutation" of religious experiences, beliefs, behaviors, and "performances" worked both ways. Christian religion certainly helped to shape New World religions of recent immigrants in the South, but the evidence of African and Haitian influences on traditions of "possession" *upon* the evangelical experience of energetic, emotional religious fervor links the African performance of "possession" with a new Protestant insistence upon this religious performative practice as a conversion ritual. African-based religious practices included exactly the same embodied performances as those just described: Believers fast, sometimes for days; they sing, dance, jerk, "fall out," and go into trance states that are recognized as the possession of the person's body by one of the Loa, the spirits of the Voudou pantheon, such as the god Gede. The accounts given by Haitian and African believers in this tradition give accounts of the trance and possession experiences that are nearly identical to those given by the practitioners of the early camp meeting revivals—and certainly those given by practicing Pentecostals in the early twentieth century that I have personally interviewed. Interestingly, modern believers are quick to note that their religion is not a "cult," and the "infilling of the Holy Ghost" is not to be confused with "possession" practices.

Zora Neale Hurston, folklorist and writer about Voudou in the South in the 1930s, was more specific, and her firsthand accounts are far more sympathetic than most of the scandalous reports by wide-eyed nonbelievers. She writes, "There can be little doubt that shouting is a survival of the African 'possession' by the Gods. In Africa it is sacred to the priesthood or acolytes, in America it has become generalized. The implication is the same, however, it is a sign of special favor from the spirit that it chooses to drive out the individual consciousness temporarily and use the body for its expression. In every case the person claims ignorance of his actions during the possession." Hurston describes at least twelve distinctive types of identifiable "shouting," most characterized by screaming, crying, twitching, seizures, falling out, stiffened limbs, limp collapse, struggling violent maneuvers, twirling, and turning. Similarly, she reports: "The rise of the various groups of 'saints' in America in the last twenty years is not the appearance of a new religion as has been reported. It is in fact the older forms of Negro religious expression asserting themselves against the new."[18]

In her descriptions of southern black religion, Hurston asserts that southern blacks have not been as "Christianized" as historians would like to claim. She tells us the chant is the congregation's effort to "bear up the speaker," while the sermon is "loose and formless and is in reality merely a framework upon which to hang more songs." Hurston put her finger on it: "The Saints, or the Sanctified church, is a revitalizing element in Negro music and religion. It is putting back into Negro religion those elements which were brought over from Africa and grafted onto Christianity as soon as the Negro came in contact with it."[19]

For an ethnographer like Hurston, and for someone such as myself who continues to do field research in Pentecostal churches,

18. Zora Neale Hurston, *The Sanctified Church* (1930; reprint, New York: Marlowe, 1981), 90, 91–94, 103.

19. Ibid., 105.

the evidence that all this free-flowing, enthusiastic religious fervor was performed in a religious space occupied both by blacks, only recently arrived from Haiti and Africa, and by whites who had already embraced the "awakenings" of spiritual religion and enthusiasm, *divided only by a single rope,* is convincing. The performances of the blacks had just as much influence on the whites as the whites had on the blacks—perhaps more. Many whites had been searching for years for religious enthusiasm that broke the bounds of formalized religion. They were seeking personal experiences with an immanent God, through encounters of the "infilling of the Holy Ghost." The black religious practitioners in their midst were clearly on the same page, performing nearly identical religious enthusiasms, sharing the love for repeated choruses that brought the services into a fevered pitch, and providing the open space and time for the freedom to dance, jerk, and actually seek the possession of the Loa within a "Christian" context must have been intoxicating indeed. When blacks were possessed by the Loa, they often spoke in tongues that were not familiar to the whites in their midst. In fact, accounts of these revivals say the blacks often spoke in "tongues" that were not recognized. No doubt, African blacks and Haitians were speaking the languages of their homelands as well as the trance-induced languages of the Loa, "tongues" that would be totally unrecognizable to the whites. Yet in this context, whites referred to them as the "languages of God."

The ecstasy that traveled across that thin, single line was translated in both directions. One account, provided in Taves's volume, of "possession of the Holy Spirit" at Azusa Street deserves a full quotation here. A visiting believer, William Durham, had gone to Azusa Street specifically to seek the sanctification and the possession of the body by the Holy Ghost. His account describes how, on a Friday evening, the power came over him, and he "'jerked and quaked under it for about three hours.' That night, He [God/Holy Spirit] worked my whole body, one section at a time, first my arms, then my limbs, then my body, then my head, then my face, then my chin, and finally at 1 a.m. Saturday, Mar. 2, after being under the power three hours, He finished the work on my vocal organs, and spoke through me in unknown tongues." This experience left Durham with a conscious sense of having been *possessed:* "I was conscious that a living Person had come into me, and that He possessed even my physical being, in a literal sense, in so much that He could at His will take hold of my vocal organs, and speak any language He chose through me."[20]

The language of possession is still prevalent in this account that happened many miles from the shores of Louisiana. But Durham's experience, as he described it then, came to be modified as Charles Parham, and others, ultimately rejected the references to possession and trance states that had emerged in the Deep South and were accepted at the Azusa Street church, preferring to "lose" the term *possession* and rely on other language such as the "infilling of the holy spirit," or the descriptions of the way the "Holy Ghost" entered their body and took over the tongue. The differences are subtle, but even in modern field situations, I still hear echoes of these concerns. Pentecostals do not want to be perceived as religious "cults" even as they cling to the salvation-based belief that "speaking in tongues" is proof of salvation. Here, too, is evidence of a very *thin line of ecstasy.* For modern Pentecostals, the tongue speaking is acknowledged as "God's language."

This examination of religious transmutations between various racial groups in the South during the emergence of Pentecostalism as a new American religion may raise as many new questions as it answers others. But one thing it certainly can do is to raise our awareness of how vested religious origin narratives can be, even when they appear to be quite benign. Charles Parham really has no more claim on the origin narrative of Pentecostalism than does Charles Seymour. More likely we can credit the men and women who worshipped on the shores of Louisiana and brought their new religious experiences up the Mississippi, into the Midwest, and eventually to the most western borders of our country. We need to embrace the connections that make the world smaller and recognize the truth in Hurston's claims that "riding the Loa" and seeking the "infilling of the Holy Spirit" are not all that different, in any language.

20. Taves, *Fits*, 55.

Vodou Purchase

The Louisiana Purchase in the Caribbean World

PAUL CHRISTOPHER JOHNSON

Introduction

Nation-states do not come into existence simply through the acquisition of territories, battles of conquest, the writing of constitutions, or the founding of institutions. They require nation-building stories about those events that sufficiently excite the imaginations of individuals such that they begin to experience themselves as "a people." The stories told in the United States about the Louisiana Purchase often take the form of this kind of nation-building tale. They are narratives whose retellings serve not to express sentiments of an already-existing national history and destiny, but to build and fortify such sentiments of belonging, such that the nation can be imagined as extending indefinitely into the future. It is the partially shared sentiment of belonging to this collectivity (a people) and the ability to imagine that collectivity's extension into the past and future that makes "America" exist in a cultural and not merely an institutional sense.

Like all such stories, the nation-building tales of the Louisiana Purchase are woven from the fragments of documents both written and orally transmitted; from the technologies of storing, and "storying," memories. But they are, in part, instrumental memories, recollections edited by what Paul Ricoeur called "happy forgetting," to serve a purpose. Their appearance of long-standing wholeness and integrity is a carefully made effect; in fact they are assembled from

146

fragments of partial remembering, strategic forgetting, and narrative structuring around selected tropes.[1]

For example, the features of the Louisiana Purchase most often stressed in the United States are triumphal ones that link the rugged ingenuity of the explorers Lewis and Clark to the inevitable Manifest Destiny of U.S. expansion and greatness. But this preferred version is only one possible tale. As we return to examine the Purchase in the wake of the bicentennial occasion, we should aim not merely to tell the narratives again, but rather to tell them anew. We should "brush history against the grain,"[2] using the event to uncover and salvage aspects of the story previously repressed, obscured, or buried by this nation's happy forgetting. To do so will require reducing the confusion caused by three common fallacies that have affected storytelling about the Louisiana Purchase: national ideology, idealism, and erasure. Let's briefly consider each in turn.

IDEOLOGY AND STORYTELLING

The contemporary moment in which the story is retold can have important consequences on historical narrative's construction. Some things are likely to be left out, depending on current political ramifications. Consider the example of Sacagawea, the Shoshone woman who helped guide Lewis and Clark. Her felicitous recuperation by being emblazoned on a silver dollar is unlikely to be matched anytime soon by a quarter for Charbonneau, an equally important guide of the expedition and Sacagawea's husband. For it is one thing to invite an indigenous figure into a key nation-building narrative,

1. Paul Ricoeur, *Memory, History, Forgetting* (Chicago: University of Chicago Press, 2004), 412. See also Pierre Bourdieu, *Outline of a Theory of Practice* (Cambridge: Cambridge University Press, 1977); Bourdieu, *Pascalian Meditations* (Stanford: Stanford University Press, 2000); Michael Herzfeld, *Anthropology: Theoretical Practice in Culture and Society* (Oxford: Blackwell, 2001); George Lipsitz, *Time Passages: Collective Memory and American Popular Culture* (Minneapolis: University of Minnesota Press, 1990); Marshall Sahlins, *Islands of History* (Chicago: University of Chicago Press, 1985); Marshall Sahlins, *How "Natives" Think: About Captain Cook, for Example* (Chicago: University of Chicago Press, 1995); William H. Sewell Jr., "The Concept(s) of Culture," in *Beyond the Cultural Turn*, ed. Victoria E. Bonnell and Lynn Hunt (Berkeley and Los Angeles: University of California Press, 1999), 35–61; and Hayden White, *Tropics of Discourse* (Baltimore: Johns Hopkins University Press, 1978).

2. Walter Benjamin, *Illuminations: Essays and Reflections* (New York: Schocken Books, 1968), 257.

and quite another to publicly declare that colonial North America was French and Spanish before it was British.[3] Insofar as the French are permitted to join the narrative of the Purchase at all in a moment of heightened U.S.-French tensions, it is Napoléon who is the preferred character. He provides a perfect cipher of exaggerated Gaullist arrogance and ambition carried on a diminutive physique. We are confronted in the Purchase, then, with both the story and the ideology of storytelling, formed in part out of contemporary "needs" in relation to which the narrative is drawn to the surface.

THE IDEALIST FALLACY

Even when Napoléon is marshaled to the Louisiana Purchase narrative, that narrative suffers under another burden, this time one not of ideology but of idealism. The idealist version is highly cinematic, depicting great individuals choosing actions freely and without constraint. It is composed of statesmen signing treaties, of the diplomatic parries between Napoléon and Jefferson, of the intellectual sparring of the wily Bishop Talleyrand, the French minister of foreign relations and, for the United States, the stalwart Robert Livingston and James Monroe. This is a neatly manicured history with no dirty nails. But to accept it as sufficient is to forget that most crucial Marxian dictum, "Men make their own history, but they do not make it just as they please."[4] Just as "histories" only exist as sets and sequences of individual acts, individual historical actors' agency only can be formed out of preexisting structures of action that form the boundaries of what

3. The fact is especially disruptive in the singular historiographic moment during which the Louisiana Purchase story is being retold, with its bicentennial conjoined to the ongoing war of the United States against Iraq that was initiated in the spring of 2003. France, of course, provided the most important international opposition to the war, resulting in popular manifestations in the United States like the renaming of french fries as "freedom fries," and the large-scale dumping of French wine by certain conspicuous restaurant owners.

4. The citation is from the opening page of Marx's essay "The Eighteenth Brumaire of Louis Bonaparte," first published in 1852. The passage continues, "they do not make it [history] under circumstances directly found, given and transmitted from the past. The tradition of all the dead generations weigh like a nightmare on the brain of the living." That the citation is from *The Eighteenth Brumaire*, referring to the French Revolutionary calendar date for November 9, 1799, is fitting, for reasons that will become evident as we proceed. This was the day Napoléon Bonaparte concentrated his power. Karl Marx, *The Karl Marx Library* (New York: McGraw-Hill, 1972), 1:245.

was thinkable and possible.[5] It is therefore important to show how the spectacular agency of larger-than-life historical actors "making their moves" was radically circumscribed by the available repertoire of action, the limits set by their time, place, resources, needs, and possible narratives. Such will be the modest goal of this essay: to describe the actions of key individuals—especially the Haitian Revolutionary leader Toussaint-Louverture—in terms both of individual agency and of its limits.

ERASURE OF THE CARIBBEAN

Along with the ideology and the idealism of the narrative, there is a third historiographic consideration to raise. It is unsurprising, though regrettable, that in our selective remembering and forgetting of the events of the Louisiana Purchase, and in our idealist editing of it, the Caribbean is typically erased. The favored American narrative is of the pioneer pushing from eastern seaboard to western frontier, of Atlantic colonists penetrating an immense wilderness. This is a mistake in interpreting the Purchase, a mistake whose rectification requires that we shift our mental maps to the south. The error lies in the fact that the Purchase's primary meaning for both France and the United States, at the end of the eighteenth century and the beginning of the nineteenth, lay in its contiguity with the Caribbean basin. This was most obviously the case for France, as we will see. Yet even in early 1803, President Jefferson and Secretary of State James Madison were prepared to leave the immense interior lands of the Purchase to France in exchange for merely New Orleans—and with it the Mississippi Delta crucial to controlling trade—and the useful harbors and river mouths of the Floridas, east and west.[6]

My goal, therefore, is to tell a story rarely told, of the Louisiana of the Caribbean world, a Louisiana occupying the northern edge

---

5. See Jean Comaroff, *Body of Power, Spirit of Resistance: The Culture and History of a South African People* (Chicago: University of Chicago Press, 1985); Jean Comaroff and John Comaroff, *Of Revelation and Revolution*, vol. 1 (Chicago: University of Chicago Press, 1991); Michel de Certeau, *The Practice of Everyday Life* (Berkeley and Los Angeles: University of California Press, 1984); Sewell, "Concepts"; and Marshall Sahlins, *Culture and Practical Reason* (Chicago: University of Chicago Press, 1976).

6. James Madison, cited in Jon Kukla, *A Wilderness So Immense: The Louisiana Purchase and the Destiny of America* (New York: Alfred A. Knopf, 2003), 244.

of this revised mental map. There is, after all, no essential reason why Louisiana must be "mapped" in its northern context rather than with the Caribbean basin. New Orleans is far nearer to Havana than to, say, Washington, D.C., and it was socially and politically much closer to that Cuban city for a good portion of its history as well.[7] Still, though "map" is not "territory," as J. Z. Smith quipped, "maps are all we possess."[8] We cannot simply do away with maps, but we can shift their boundaries and the terrain they place into visual contiguity and implicit relationship. To accomplish the proposed shift in our thinking about the Louisiana Purchase, in what follows I offer a new map, by juxtaposing the correlated stories of Haiti and Louisiana.

The final contract that ceded Louisiana to the United States arrived in Jefferson's hands in late December 1803; the U.S. flag was first raised over New Orleans on the twentieth. Less than two weeks later, on January 1, 1804, Saint-Domingue was proclaimed by General Dessalines to be Haiti (Ayti), the indigenous (Taino) title denoting "mountainous lands." The events are directly linked, for the remaking of Saint-Domingue as an independent Haiti provides a key to the Purchase story. It was, after all, the Haitian Revolution (1791–1803) that motivated Napoléon's sudden willingness to part with Louisiana. The shifting meanings of Saint-Domingue/Haiti will be scrutinized in the next section. Moreover, we cannot effectively interpret the relationship of Jefferson and Napoléon without drawing in a third figure, in the third section, to unbalance the dyad: Toussaint-Louverture, Toussaint "of the opening" (L'ouverture), according to his self-stylization in early 1794, after dropping his plantation surname of Bréda with the French Revolutionary emancipation of slaves in August 1793.[9]

---

7. After Quebec fell to British general James Wolfe in 1759, France quickly transferred Louisiana to Spain, simultaneous with the accession to the throne of Carlos III. At least until Carlos's death in 1788, virtually all news and trade goods arriving from Europe to New Orleans passed first through Havana. Moreover, in 1803, New Orleans consisted of 3,300 French-speaking Creoles, 2,800 slaves, and 1,300 free people of color, plus scattered Spanish officials and troops and growing numbers of refugees from Saint-Domingue. See Kukla, *Wilderness*, 325; and Eric Williams, *From Columbus to Castro: The History of the Caribbean* (New York: Vintage, 1984).

8. Jonathan Z. Smith, *Map Is Not Territory* (1978; reprint, Chicago: University of Chicago Press, 1993), 309.

9. Isaac Louverture, Toussaint-Louverture's son, attributed the name "the opening" to a comment made by the French commissioner in Haiti, Étienne Polverel, to the effect

By retelling the story of the Purchase within different narrative and spatial frames than it usually is told in North America, I hope not only to pull the Caribbean into the purview of the United States' historical frame, but also to pull the United States into the Caribbean story. The Louisiana Purchase, as will become clear, is less the story of a land deal followed by unidirectional human traverse than a complex confluence of contingencies, ideas, and bodies. To take a term first applied by Fernando Ortiz to Cuba in 1940 and extend it to the north, we might thereby come to view the Louisiana territory as part and parcel of the Caribbean world. It was, and is, a *transcultured* and transculturing place of shifting and fluid groups and meanings, rather than a static or monolithic place.[10]

"Transculturation," as first used by Fernando Ortiz, connoted the idea that the assimilation of a new culture is always partial and fragmentary, as older African, European, and Amerindian cultural forms took seed in new ground. This is relevant for the case at hand in thinking about what "revolution," or "liberté, égalité, fraternité," meant in 1789 Paris compared with those same phrases' reimplementation in Cap Français and Port-au-Prince in Saint-Domingue of 1791.[11] Sugar in Louisiana did not imply exactly the same thing as

that the general seemed able to "make an opening anywhere." Perhaps not incidentally, it was in the same month (August) that Léger-Félicité Sonthonax, civil commissioner of the colony, declared a general amnesty of slaves. See Laurent Dubois, *Avengers of the New World: The Story of the Haitian Revolution* (Cambridge: Belknap Press of Harvard University Press, 2004), 172; David Nicholls, *From Dessalines to Duvalier: Race, Colour, and National Independence in Haiti* (Cambridge: Cambridge University Press, 1979), 29; David Patrick Geggus, *Haitian Revolutionary Studies* (Bloomington: Indiana University Press, 2002).

10. The neologism *transculturation* was an intellectual product of the Caribbean, appearing in Fernando Ortiz, *Contrapunteo cubano del tabaco y el azúcar (Cuban Counterpoint: Tobacco and Sugar)* (Durham: Duke University Press, 1995). The word was superior to *acculturation* (a term associated with Melville Herskovits), Ortiz proposed, because it did not imply a unilineal process of adopting a new culture, the idea that the former slate is completely erased before the new one is written. Rather, it suggested the nuances of culture-loss or "deracination," as such losses, and the responses to them, continue to inform the experience of the new situation. It also connoted the only partial and fragmentary assimilation of a new culture, as well as the completely novel creations that were bound to arise in what Ortiz called *neoculturation*. More important than this semantic dexterity was the way Ortiz wrote about "culture" in the history of Cuba as the process of human interaction with, and thinking through, the material resources at hand. Transculturation gained new contemporary currency in Mary Louise Pratt's *Imperial Eyes: Travel Writing and History* (New York: Routledge, 1992), and in a major new section of the second edition of the *Encyclopedia of Religion* (New York: Macmillan, 2005).

11. So, for example, Philip D. Curtin suggests that the tripartite chorus was split to

in Saint-Domingue; revolution did not mean the same thing in Saint-Domingue as in France; and Louisiana, as we shall see, did not look the same in the gazes of Napoléon and Jefferson.

The neologism of transculturation is therefore useful in understanding Louisiana for two reasons. First, it attempts to describe human mixture and exchange in a constant process of uprooting, hybridizing, and rerooting. Second, it attempts to describe how the meanings of human exchange are inevitably filtered through the particular territorial resources at hand, which govern the ruling social templates. In the case of the Caribbean, the guiding template since 1492 was that Europeans ruled over slaves, whose labor produced sugar, the source of wealth that built the palaces of Antwerp and Versailles and fomented the industrial revolution of England. This should remind us that the Caribbean world, including Louisiana, was not a sleepy, primitive backwater or frontier—which in any case presupposes a specifically North American mental map—but rather the laboratory of the first industrialized labor in the world, and the seedbed of the first global economic order.[12]

Louisiana and Saint-Domingue in Tandem

The purpose of Louisiana for France was as a future supply house for the Caribbean. Louisiana was not itself particularly lucrative or productive, compared with the massively profitable sugar colonies of Guadeloupe, Martinique, and above all Saint-Domingue, "the pearl of the Antilles." In 1789, Saint-Domingue had some eight thousand plantations making sugar for export, accounting for 40 percent of France's overseas trade, a level of colonial dependency only matched

---

address distinct political factions in the colony: For land-owning whites *(grands blancs)*, "liberty" was accentuated; for non-land-owning whites *(petits blancs)* and some mulattos *(gens de couleurs)*, it was "fraternity" that was especially stressed, in the sense of continued union with France; and for black slaves, "equality" of political rights was the rallying cry. This means that the cry of "liberté, égalité, fraternité" may have been a source of union in resistance in France, but an exacerbation of conflicts in the colony. Curtin, *The Rise and Fall of the Plantation Complex: Essays in Atlantic History,* 2d ed. (Cambridge: Cambridge University Press, 1998), 163.

12. Eric Williams, *Capitalism and Slavery* (1944; reprint, Chapel Hill: University of North Carolina Press, 1994); Sidney W. Mintz, *Sweetness and Power: The Place of Sugar in Modern History* (New York: Penguin, 1985); Stephan Palmié, *Wizards and Scientists: Explorations in Afro-Cuban Modernity and Tradition* (Durham: Duke University Press, 2002).

or exceeded by Spain, which derived half of its revenues from its Mexican silver mines during the same period.[13] As Jon Kukla described, "When the Bastille fell in Paris, trade with St. Domingue engaged seven hundred fifty French ships, employed twenty-four thousand sailors, and was valued at £11 million a year. France consumed one third of the island's exports, and the rest were processed in France and shipped abroad by a workforce estimated at several million Frenchmen." The sugar of Saint-Domingue drove a healthy portion of the French economy, concurrently with the radical acceleration of the European taste for sugar, above all in Great Britain. Sidney Mintz, to wit, considered that "the popularization of sucrose, barely begun in 1650, brought some of it into the hands of even the very poor within a century; then between 1750 and 1850, it ceased to be a luxury and became a necessity."[14] It was sugar that drove much of eighteenth-century European expansion, and it was sugar that was to rebuild postrevolutionary Napoleonic France.

What was to be Louisiana's niche in the plan? Its role was secondary but crucial: It was to be the supplier of raw materials, above all wood and food that would keep the hands working and boilers burning in Saint-Domingue. François Barbé-Marbois, the former French consulate's secretary of the treasury, wrote, "Louisiana had been destined to supply the other colony with provisions, cattle, and wood, and as St. Domingo was lost to France, the importance of Louisiana was also diminished." It was also envisioned as a source of free land to reward thousands of tired soldiers who had served in the Caribbean, thereby accomplishing a gradual colonization of the territory.[15]

Settlers' perspectives of Louisiana during the same period were often just as sugar-coated, though in a direct rather than supplementary way. While attempts to institute sugarcane production there flopped in 1725 and 1762 due to early frosts, by 1794 a Louisiana planter, Etienne de Bore, instituted large-scale production, and by 1805 there were no fewer than eighty-one plantations in motion.[16]

13. Geggus, *Haitian Revolutionary Studies*, 5.

14. Kukla, *Wilderness*, 147; Mintz, *Sweetness*, 161.

15. Quoted in Kukla, *Wilderness*, 215. Louisiana, officially Spanish after 1759, was transferred back to France in the secret Treaty of San Ildefonso, of 1800, when Napoléon was already master of much of continental Europe, and Spain was attempting to delay his inevitable march to the Iberian peninsula. When the march came, the Spanish crown fell in 1808.

16. Williams, *From Columbus*, 134, 243.

The need for an independent source of sugar was a problem constantly under discussion by leaders of the young republic. Jefferson,
for one, hoped that maple sugar processing might one day augment
Louisiana's cane fields to meet domestic demands through indigenous production. Other nations, meanwhile, raced to develop beet-
based sugar production as well as Asian cane-planting sites to sate
the growing dietary rage. In the narrative of the Louisiana Purchase,
sugar was key to the drama that would unfold.

Napoléon's grand plan for the use of Louisiana never came to
fruition for two related reasons: the sale of the Louisiana territory,
and the Haitian Revolution. The point can hardly be made too deci-
sively. When Saint-Domingue ceased to be viable as a colony,
Louisiana was rendered dispensable and irrelevant to Bonaparte's
scheme. Saint-Domingue became unviable, moreover, when its revolution of 1791–1803 could not be suppressed. Louisiana therefore
had already become "American," in its fate if not yet in realized form,
by January 1803. It was then that Napoléon learned of the death of
his brother-in-law General Charles Victor Emmanuel Leclerc.
Leclerc was commander of the massive French military expedition
sent to Saint-Domingue to repress the revolution and regain the
colony for France, upon which he uttered the curse (as reported by
his director general of public education): "Damn sugar, damn coffee,
damn colonies!"[17] Leclerc's death presented a forceful, and familial,
reminder to Napoléon of the loss of some sixty thousand French soldiers left dead, dying, or diseased over a decade of fighting in Saint-
Domingue. With them, Napoléon lost the dream of a robustly
French Louisiana territory and his foothold in North America. Thus,
as Laurent Dubois writes, "The victory of the black troops of Saint-
Domingue paved the way for the Louisiana Purchase."[18]

SEEDS OF REVOLUTION

Saint-Domingue, with an area the size of Maryland, produced
half the sugar and coffee circulating in the 1780s world trade. The

17. Roederer, in Kukla, *Wilderness*, 249. Leclerc had in fact died of yellow fever on
November 2, 1802, though the news did not arrive in France until two months thereafter.

18. Dubois, *Avengers*, 304.

population consisted of 500,000 slaves, 40,000 whites, and 30,000 free persons of color—three very separate factions.[19] It should come as little surprise, then, that the revolution of Saint-Domingue was brewing long before 1791. This had to do with, on one hand, worsening conditions for slaves under the demands of the accelerating sugar market, and on the other hand, a rapidly expanding caste of free *(affranchis)* persons of color *(gens de couleur libres)* but who were deprived of civic rights by the Code Noir until May 1791.[20] Alongside these worsening conditions, and ideologically problematizing them, were the Enlightenment and republican ideas that circulated throughout the Caribbean world. Beginning with Martinique's rebellion of 1789 and ending with Bahia, Brazil's uprising of 1835, this was a four-decade-long hothouse of rebellion in the Caribbean world, as well as in the United States.[21]

Some of the energy stoking the flames of rebellion came from abroad. Gens de couleur libres in Saint-Domingue had sent representatives to France since 1784, and the actions of an abolitionist group in Paris, the Société des Amis des Noirs, were closely followed in the colony. Moreover, many of the gens de couleur in Saint-Domingue who later acted as early revolutionary leaders had fought in Georgia during the American Revolutionary War. These included not a few who became central figures in the politics of Haiti's independence movement—André Rigaud, Jean-Baptiste Chavannes, J. B. Villatte, and Henri Christophe. Others, like Vincent Ogé, spent extensive time in France, were active in the Société des Amis as well as other groups, and interacted closely with Enlightenment freethinkers like Condorcet. In some cases such influences from abroad arrived only via long detours: When Ogé left Paris in disgust because

19. By contrast, the Spanish colony of Santo Domingo comprised two-thirds of the same island and had but 15,000 slaves at the same time; see Nicholls, *From Dessalines,* 30. This illustrates the hyperdevelopment of plantation society that had already emerged on the western third of Hispaniola.

20. Nicholls, *From Dessalines,* 30; Curtin, *Rise and Fall,* 165.

21. Consider, among others, the foiled Pointe Coupée plot in Louisiana in 1795, after which approximately twenty-five alleged conspirators were hung; the 1800 slave plot to kill all the whites of Richmond; the 1822 Charleston rebellion led by Denmark Vesey; the 1831 rebellion led by Nat Turner in Southampton County, Virginia; not to mention Victor Hugues's raising of the slaves in rebellion in the name of revolutionary France against the British invasion of 1794 in Guadeloupe, the 1808 and 1823 revolts in British Guiana, the 1816 rebellion in Barbados, and the 1831 insurrections in Antigua and Jamaica, just to mention a few markers during what can be called a period of constant democratic revolutionary fervor from 1780 to 1830.

of the National Assembly's failure to grant full political rights to mulattoes in 1790, he passed through both London and the United States to purchase arms and ammunition for the coming fight for those rights, which he now convened on the soil of Saint-Domingue.[22] Even earlier, in 1777, the Police de Noires laws in Saint-Domingue warned that Caribbean slaves returning from France bring with them the "spirit of independence" and "indocility."[23]

Though external influences, above all that of the French Revolution, unleashed far-reaching consequences in the Caribbean, many of the conditions leading to the revolution were generated internally, in Saint-Domingue itself. As sugar became increasingly lucrative during the 1700s, work conditions worsened as slaves went from agricultural chattel to industrial capital in what was among the first sites of industrialized labor in the world. So advanced was European dependency on sugar that when the supply was shut off in the 1790s during the war for Saint-Domingue, the result was street riots in France, and consumption and dependency in England were much worse.[24]

With the arrival of word of the Declaration of the Rights of Man, the fall of the Bastille, and the creation of the National Assembly in France in 1789, ideas of liberty, equality, and fraternity were no longer merely aloft in the Caribbean breeze but were very much on the ground. Mobs of non-land-owning whites *(petits blancs)* donned the tricolor cockades, and elected assemblies were formed in every province. When affranchised gens de couleur perceived their potential exclusion from the republican reforms, they rioted, led by Ogé and Chavannes, both of whom had fought in the American Revolution. Ogé and Chavannes were executed brutally, "on the wheel."[25] Only then did the shocked National Assembly in Paris grant gens de couleur born of free parents political rights equal to those of whites, in a compromise gesture sealed on May 15, 1791. When the governor of Saint-Domingue and white elites *(grands blancs)* refused to implement this, the gens de couleur began to mount armies. All of this was, in a sense, predictable: royalist grands

---

22. C. L. R. James, *The Black Jacobins*, 2d ed. (1963; reprint, New York: Vintage, 1989), 68, 73.
23. Geggus, *Haitian Revolutionary Studies*, 80–81.
24. Mintz, *Sweetness*, passim; Kukla, *Wilderness*, passim.
25. Geggus, *Haitian Revolutionary Studies*, 11.

blancs whites, republican petits blancs whites, and free persons of color were stirred to contest for as-yet-unknown new benefits. No one, however, had anything like the general emancipation of slaves in mind. Remember in this context that even free persons of color were themselves often slave owners. This is where the story turns to the key revolutionary leader of the ex-slaves, Toussaint-Louverture.

The point, to reiterate, is straightforward but often lost or muddled: no Haitian Revolution, no Louisiana Purchase. The links between the events were forged not only by the historical conditions recounted above, but also by key figures acting in relation and response to one another. The record on Jefferson and his cohort is amply presented elsewhere; indeed, nearly everywhere. Yet Napoléon's sale of the Louisiana Purchase to Jefferson is incomprehensible without seeing him in relation to a third figure, one the United States should be celebrating as a civic saint and eulogizing in the temples of the big screen, Toussaint-Louverture. To this end, let us now turn to the related lives of Napoléon and Toussaint-Louverture and "try them on" as a bifocal for seeing the import of the Haitian Revolution for the Louisiana Purchase, and the possible role of the religion of Vodou in those events.

PARALLEL LIVES

Napoléon's and Toussaint-Louverture's careers followed strangely parallel trajectories. Both had something to prove: Napoléon as a Corsican resentful of French imperial dominance over the place of his birth, Toussaint-Louverture as a black Creole, son of a Dahomean chief, who rose to power in a slave society. Both Napoléon and Toussaint-Louverture achieved meteoric ascents to power, moving from margin to center, and both initiated changes in their names as a mark of the transition. Napoléon was born Nabolione Buonaparte, son of a Corsican patriot; his name was translated into French with his move as an adolescent to study at the royal military college at Brienne, France.[26] Toussaint carried as his surname the title of the plantation on which he labored, Bréda, until late 1793, when a general emancipation was passed by the French

---

26. Kukla, *Wilderness*, 185.

National Assembly and when he began to lead the former-slave troops of Saint-Domingue in the name of revolutionary France instead of against the old France.

Through the hands of both passed Abbé Raynal's 1770 *History of the Two Indies*, and its eloquent call to liberation: "these are so many indications of the impending storm, and the Negroes only want a chief, sufficiently courageous, to lead them on to vengeance and slaughter. Where is this great man, whom nature owes to her afflicted, oppressed and tormented children?"[27] At around the same time that Napoléon returned from his victories in Austria to disband the directorate ruling France, on the eighteenth of Brumaire, year 8 (November 9, the "month of fog," 1799), soon after declaring himself consul for life in 1801, Toussaint-Louverture was consolidating his power over his rival André Rigaud, declaring himself governor for life by 1800. Both were hailed but also sometimes hated by their people; both held republican ideals ultimately deformed by hubris or, more particularly, by the need for constant resources to support massive standing armies that could guarantee their power. And both bit off more than they could chew. For Napoléon this occurred later, in Russia; for Toussaint-Louverture it transpired in 1800 when he annexed the eastern two-thirds of the island, Santo Domingo, to his domain without asking permission from France to do so. With this he directly defied Bonaparte and implicitly declared his independence, if not from France then at least from metropolitan authority, in March 1801.

Both moved easily in multiple worlds: Napoléon was as comfortable speaking about Montaigne and Rousseau as he was in the language of soldiers. Toussaint-Louverture spoke Creole French as well as at least a reasonable metropolitan French, cited Machiavelli, was a high-degree Freemason, and was robustly Catholic; he spoke even better Fon-Evhe, the language of his father, was skilled in the use of herbs, and was at least once declared to have been present at the Vodou ceremony the night before the onset of the revolution at or near the plantation of Lenormand de Mézy in August 1791.[28] "The Opening" was a mediator of disparate worlds: once a slave owner

27. James, *Black Jacobins*, 171, 250; Raynal quoted in Joan Dayan, *Haiti, History, and the Gods* (Berkeley and Los Angeles: University of California Press, 1995), 217.

28. According to the version recorded by General François Kerverseau, in Geggus, *Haitian Revolutionary Studies*, 82.

himself, after 1793 he became the great defender of équality, *égalité*. The two leaders were even in frequent, relatively direct contact. Toussaint-Louverture's sons, Isaac and Placide, studied in France, and after personally interviewing them, Napoléon returned them home with a letter of high though perhaps disingenuous praise, as passengers of the fleet that was to reconquer Saint-Domingue under Leclerc. The sons had dined often at the home of Josephine, Bonaparte's wife, even as Toussaint-Louverture had looked after Josephine's inherited assets in Saint-Domingue.[29] Bonaparte flattered Toussaint-Louverture at least through March 1801, since the former was constantly embattled with the British, and because he had aspirations in the east—first in Egypt, then in India—that precluded his dedicated attention to the Caribbean.

But there were key differences that divided the generals as well. Though both supported the need for some form of forced labor to return Saint-Domingue to its former wealth, they differed notably on the ultimate meaning, and importance, of the issue of race.[30] In their epistolary intercourse, Toussaint-Louverture wrote to Napoléon as "the first of blacks to the first of whites," while Napoléon declared to an interlocutor, Colonel Vincent, a desire to "rip the epaulettes from the shoulders of the 'gilded Africans' of St. Domingue."[31] Napoléon justified his view quite simply: "I am for the whites because I am white. I have no other reason, and that one is good." He presented the expedition of reconquest as "a crusade of civilized people of the West against the black barbarism that was on the rise in America" and planned to deport all black generals.[32] Though Bonaparte seems to have not been clear in his intentions for Saint-Domingue until 1802, France's reinstatement of slavery in

29. James, *Black Jacobins*, 262.

30. The level of which the revolutionary return to sugar production resembled the former slave society is debated. James wrote, "No doubt the poor sweated and were backward so that the new ruling class might thrive. But at least they too were better off than they had been. While on the one hand the authority, social ease and culture of those who, a dozen years before, had been slaves, amazed all observers, the success of Toussaint's administration can be judged by the fact that in a year and a half he had restored cultivation to two-thirds of what it had been in the most flourishing days of the old régime" (*Black Jacobins*, 248).

31. Dayan, *Haiti*, 149. He expressed this sentiment at least after the subsiding of hostilities with Great Britain, who he viewed as his only true rival; prior to this Napoléon could not afford to antagonize Toussaint-Louverture or gens de couleur directly.

32. Dubois, *Avengers*, 261, 254–56.

Martinique and Guadeloupe announced loudly enough that the institution was again considered necessary to colonial production in the Caribbean. That sentiment was nearly Jeffersonian, one might say, though more abrasively expressed than a Virginian would recommend. It was, however, auspicious for the United States' territorial ambitions for Louisiana.

In October 1801, Leclerc was named commander of the largest expeditionary army ever to sail from France, a fleet of fifty ships carrying 22,000 troops and 20,000 sailors, with 20,000 more soon to follow, commissioned to sail on to Louisiana once Saint-Domingue was put down.[33] Meanwhile, Toussaint-Louverture's Saint-Domingue was well on its way to recuperating its productivity. It was only in 1802, when word reached Saint-Domingue that full slavery had been restored in the colony of Guadeloupe, that blacks and gens de couleur ceased their mutual antagonism to fight as one force against France. By then, Toussaint-Louverture had been captured through trickery and deported back to France, leaving the insurrection divided between generals Dessalines, Henri Christophe, and the mulatto André Rigaud, all of whom briefly defected to the French side as its victory appeared imminent. Yet when the true intent of reinstating slavery became apparent, they returned to the fight against the French with a vengeance.

With the deportation of Toussaint-Louverture, a key crossroads was passed. Had Napoléon been able to tolerate the notion of a black governor presiding over a colony with a system of indentured labor rather than slavery as such—Toussaint-Louverture's plan for the colony's economic rebuilding—and had Napoléon not revealed this inability so clearly on Guadeloupe, the "Louisiana Purchase" might never have happened. Imagine that, during an interlude of peace with England in 1802, instead of sacrificing 60,000 soldiers in Saint-Domingue, those same soldiers had been sent to occupy the Louisiana Territory. Bonaparte acknowledged as much later in life (September 4, 1817): "One of the greatest follies I ever was guilty of was sending that army out to St. Domingo. . . . I committed a great oversight and fault in not having declared St. Domingo free, acknowledged the black government, and, before the peace of Amiens, sent some French officers to assist them. Had I done this, it would have been more consonant with the principles under which I

33. Ibid., 251.

was acting."[34] The fact that Napoléon could not envision that other possible outcome was in part related to his view of race and governance. His was a view commonly held in Europe. To leave the pearl of the Antilles to gilded Africans, even under the status of a colony ruled by an indigenous regent, was simply unthinkable. "Bonaparte hated black people," wrote C. L. R. James simply in his masterpiece.[35] Though his recognition of the needs of the colony almost mitigated that antipathy, it was not enough.

Now let us retrace our steps to earlier in the story.

Vodou and the Slaves' Revolution

As was stated previously, with the arrival of news in Saint-Domingue of the French Revolution, multiple factions began to convene assemblies to protect or advance particular interests submerged in the cry, "liberté, égalité, fraternité": grands blancs favored liberté (economic, that is), petits blancs and mulatto gens de couleur favored fraternité (with France, not with slaves), and slaves, of course, favored égalité. Yet no one foresaw direct action being taken by slaves themselves. Apparently out of nowhere, then, in August 1791, the slaves revolted. Not, moreover, in the name of republican ideals, but rather in the name of the king, and wearing white rather than red-white-and-blue cockades! Slaves said that the tricolor represented only the emancipation of whites, that the king himself had already declared them free, but that whites were withholding that news. Given the horrific physical conditions of intensifying sugar plantations as described above, we still must ask the question of what activated and galvanized resistance at this particular moment. Where did the rebels come from?

In Haitian oral tradition, in French colonial reports, and in twentieth-century American exoticized novels about Haiti, the slaves' rebellion was inspired by the religion called Vodou. From the Haitian side this is because—since Jean Price-Mars *Thus Spoke the Uncle*

---

34. In Kukla, *Wilderness*, 216. The Peace of Amiens was a treaty signed with the British on October 24, 1801, that temporarily suppressed naval hostilities between France and England. This was the moment Napoléon sent the invasion to retake Saint-Domingue.

35. James, *Black Jacobins*, 268.

(1928) and the work of his student (and later dictator) François Duvalier—Vodou has been taken as the very source of deep Haitianness. Just as the American narratives of the Louisiana Purchase require the visionary genius Jefferson, and the simultaneous "can do-ism" and piety of Lewis and Clark, Haitian national narratives of the revolution require its onset in a ceremony of that authentically black and national religion, Vodou. The idea that Vodou started the revolution is virtually required of the genre "national history."[36]

From the side of colonial literary production, Vodou is the source of all evil, including revolutionary "evil," a posture repeated during the U.S. Marines' occupation of Haiti from 1915 to 1934. For these authors, describing the revolution as derived from Vodou served the purpose of delegitimating any possible real grievances of slaves.

Given the complex nationalist and colonial framings of the story of the revolution's onset in Vodou, can we ever really know what happened? Most scholars hold that the legendary Vodou ceremony at Bois Caiman, the Alligator Woods, occurred sometime around August 14, 1791. The main sources are two, the best being Antoine Dalma's *History of the Revolution,* published in 1814, but supposedly written in 1793–1794, and an oral report from a mulatto woman named Cécile Fatiman, a Vodou priestess *(manbo)* who was at the event, who recited the story to her grandson, who then passed it on to Etienne Charlier, who published it.[37] David Geggus reads the Dalma source to posit that there were two meetings, one on Sunday night of the fourteenth, another the following Sunday, the twenty-first, with the revolution beginning the day following.[38] The meeting

36. François Duvalier, *Oeuvres essentielles I: Eléments d'une doctrine* (Port-au-Prince: n.p., 1966). To follow Duvalier's own words, Vodou is the "prise de conscience nationale et raciale" (167), "suprême facteur de l'unité haïtienne," and "autentique de la race" (177). Duvalier here followed the historical template of General Dessalines, the founding revolutionary. "Papa" Dessalines, as he was later called by Vodouists, came to be remembered as the paramount *indigène,* the one who had fused race to land, who had first named "Haitians," regardless of actual skin tone, as "black" *by nation.*

Duvalier's production was in part an indigenist response to the U.S. occupation that legitimated itself with the demonization of Vodou as the source of Haiti's "backwardness," later manifested in bestselling novels like William Seabrook's *The Magic Island* (1929), Faustin Wirkus's *The White King of Gonave* (1931), John Huston Craige's *Black Bagdad* (1933), and movies like *White Zombie* (1932) and Jacques Tourniers's *I Walked with a Zombie* (1941).

37. Carolyn E. Fick, *The Making of Haiti: The Saint Domingue Revolution from Below* (Knoxville: University of Tennessee Press, 1990).

38. Geggus, *Haitian Revolutionary Studies,* 82. The revolution was probably supposed

was run by one Boukman, a coachman from the Mézy plantation—
and indeed, most of the organizers were such elite Creole slaves who
had at least the limited ability to circulate freely. Toussaint-Louverture
may have been present. He too had served as coachman, spoke the
African tongues, and was from the region. The reports are likewise
consistent in descriptions of the presence of a female priestess, who
sacrificed a black pig. The blood was apparently used as an oath-
taking event; according to the Fatiman source, hairs of the pig were
taken and used as amulets in the fighting to come.

Was the Revolution an outcome of the ritual, or was the ritual a
mere consecration of what was already planned? Were Creole elite
slaves using Vodou to mobilize the plantation masses, as an ideological tool? None of this can be stated with any certainty. Was the ritual composed of elements more like what is now known as the
"Rada," or West African form (from the city of Allada), or the
emerging Petwo/Creole form of revering the *lwa*, or gods, specifically born out of enslavement? Again, we cannot know, although
oral tradition says the sacrifice was to Ezuli Danto, a fierce female
lwa and a fighter associated with the "hot" Petwo deities. Despite the
murky opacity of the role of Vodou in the slave uprising that turned
the revolution, and more importantly its narratives, into a widespread and national event rather than a local and class-bound one,
it is clear that Vodou ritual was closely related in the organizers'
minds with what was to come in the next days. If there is no causal
relation, there is at least a correlative one. Perhaps we can say with
some confidence that the ritual evoked, performed, rendered present, and then controlled terror, both the terror lived and the terror
to come. By rendering it present in material form, a science of the
concrete used in and with and for *making history,* that terror
became legible and workable. "Counter-aesthetics," Suzanne Blier
has called such ritualization; "thinking through terror," in the words
of Michael Taussig. The fearsome binding, piercing, and imagery of
death so grossly fantasized were an everyday reality under the slave
regime. The Vodou ritual served to translate what was already
occurring into a symbolic form where it could be contemplated and

---

to have been initiated on Wednesday, August 24, to correspond with a scheduled meeting of the Colonial Assembly in Le Cap on the following day. That it began prematurely
was probably due to a lack of absolute coordination among slaves from different plantations, or a leak of the plan to whites. See Dubois, *Avengers,* 98–99.

even transfigured into a new kind of historical enactment, the over-throw of terror.[39]

The surprise of the slaves' uprising in the revolution occurred a day after the Bois Caiman ceremony. Jean Price-Mars said that Haiti's independence in 1804 was because of Vodou. Was he right? Perhaps not literally, yet insofar as the ceremony became an integral component of national mythology, it "made Haiti" no less than sugar, the colonial crucible, and the revolution itself. It became a crucial nation-building story for Haiti.

With the entrance of slaves into the revolution, there were four groups at arms: royalist whites, republican whites, free persons of color, and slaves. Reinforcements arrived from France to quell the chaos but were weakened quickly by disease. In April 1792, with Saint-Domingue in flames and both Spain and England about to invade and take Saint-Domingue for themselves—Spain from Santo Domingo, England from the sea—France bestowed full citizenship on all free persons, uniting the armies of free persons of color and white republicans. After 1793, the gens de couleur libres faction became dominant, and ten thousand royalist whites, together with as many of their slaves as possible, set sail for North America, many of them to New Orleans. Even so, Spain and England remained imma-nent threats. Many former slaves, including Toussaint-Louverture, allied themselves with one or the other power in order to gain weapons and funds. The question for all factions—the mulatto General André Rigaud in the south, Spain in parts of the north, England in parts of the west, the republican civil commissioners in Port au Prince—was this: Who could mobilize and control the black masses? Republican France, through its agent Léger-Félicité Sonthonax, liberated all slaves on August 29, 1793. Shortly thereafter, in early 1794, Toussaint Bréda, until then fighting for Spain, per-formed his so-called about-face, *volte-face*. Switching to the French republican side, he changed his name to Toussaint-Louverture.

Rallying troops in the mountains around the northern city of Cap Français, he turned the tide. Spain withdrew by 1795, turning its own sugar aspirations back to Cuba. England eventually lost 15,000 out of 25,000 soldiers to battle and yellow fever and withdrew by

---

39. Suzanne Preston Blier, *African Vodun: Art, Psychology, and Power* (Chicago: University of Chicago Press, 1995); Michael Taussig, *Shamanism: A Study in Colonialism, Terror, and the Wild Man* (Chicago: University of Chicago Press, 1987).

1798. With the new colonial threats at bay, tensions between mulattoes and blacks returned in force, Rigaud in the south, Toussaint-Louverture in the north. By 1800 Rigaud had fled to France, though his successor Alexandre Pétion remained the supreme military commander in the south. For the time being at least, Toussaint-Louverture's power, at the head of an army of between twenty and thirty thousand, was complete, however precarious. To maintain such a force would take resources; resources would be gained by putting peasants back to work; putting peasants back to work would create new resentment.

Here we arrive again where we began the historical narrative, with Napoléon flattering Toussaint-Louverture and promising continued emancipation, even as Bonaparte's brother-in-law General Leclerc was sailing to take that "gilded African" down. Toussaint-Louverture watched the massive convoy from a mountain as it arrived, and he is reported to have said, "Friends, we are doomed. All of France has come. Let us at least show ourselves worthy of our freedom."[40] Showing themselves "worthy," however, took time. Leclerc's French army was greeted with joy by many who were angry at Toussaint-Louverture, the liberator now turned overlord. The good fortune of these royalists, however, did not last. As Toussaint-Louverture's forces marched to war singing "La Marseillaise," announcing themselves as the real French—those remaining true to the republic's principles—Leclerc's troops died of yellow fever at a rate of 250 a day. The French buried the dead at night to hide their losses.[41]

Toussaint-Louverture's two main generals serving under him were Henri Christophe and Dessalines. Leclerc managed a brief diplomatic victory by enticing both to switch sides. Thereafter, Leclerc sued for peace with Toussaint-Louverture, and he achieved it by guaranteeing freedom for all blacks. With the war temporarily ceased, Leclerc took Toussaint-Louverture captive by treachery, summoning him from his farm to a meeting, taking him prisoner, and deporting him to Europe. He died at the age of fifty-three, on the night of April 8, 1803, in an unheated dungeon in the Jura Mountains above Geneva. The generals Dessalines and Christophe eventually perceived Leclerc's treachery and returned to war. Leclerc himself finally succumbed to yellow fever on November 2, 1802.

40. In Kukla, *Wilderness*, 220.
41. Dayan, *Haiti*.

Many of his troops defected, among them Poles who gave to Vodou the image of Our Lady of Czestochowa, the Catholic face of the lwa Ezuli Danto.[42] Dessalines, meanwhile, chased Leclerc's vicious underling Rochambeaut into the sea and the waiting English fleets. On January 1, 1804, Dessalines declared the independence of "Haiti."

Two nation-building stories thereby converged. For Haitians, Saint-Domingue became Haiti through the revolution that began in Vodou. For Americans, the Louisiana Territory became the Louisiana Purchase through Jefferson's masterly vision and the intrepid voyage of Lewis and Clark. But as I have tried to demonstrate, these nation-building stories are not freestanding; they lean against each other. The Haitian Revolution was deeply affected by the United States: President John Adams initially supported Toussaint-Louverture's bid against France, many of the rebels' arms arrived from the United States, some of the rebel leaders had fought in the American Revolutionary War, and the first draft of General Dessalines's Declaration of Independence from France was influenced by its U.S. counterpart.[43] But far more important was the influence of the Haitian Revolution on the United States. The territory of those precariously united states to the north was doubled, as Louisiana was opened to Jefferson, Lewis, and Clark—because of Toussaint-Louverture, he of "the opening," and because of Haiti.

Denouement

Slavery was abolished in Haiti, but as a result it was accelerated in Brazil, Cuba, and Louisiana, where rivals rushed to fill the vacuum in the booming sugar market. Still, Haiti's revolution-inspired change served as an example to enslaved peoples everywhere in the Americas. The very existence of an independent black nation in the Americas gave hope to blacks in the United States even as their own enslavement dragged on for another sixty years. When Simón Bolívar needed to restart his anticolonial campaign against Spain in South America in 1815, President Alexandre Pétion of Haiti granted

---

42. One imagines this was also the origin of the last name "Lovinski," used by the renowned Vodou priestess of Brooklyn, Mama Lola. See Karen McCarthy Brown, *Mama Lola: A Vodou Priestess in Brooklyn,* 2d ed. (Berkeley and Los Angeles: University of California Press, 2001), 401.

43. Dubois, *Avengers,* 225, 298.

him use of Haitian land in exchange for abolishing slavery in Spanish South America. This Bolívar did. In the meantime, Thomas Jefferson negotiated with Haitian president Pétion during the 1820s on the issue of deporting all blacks from the United States to Haiti, especially children. Blacks were viewed as blights on Jefferson's vision of a single homogeneous people from sea to shining sea. Naturally it would be cruel to the deported children, wrote Jefferson, yet to balk at the prospect for merely humanitarian reasons would be "straining at a gnat, and swallowing a camel."[44] The United States never recognized Haiti as a sovereign nation until 1862, when it stood on the brink of finally confronting its own national identity as a slave society.[45]

And what of Vodou? It changed, incorporating new symbols as it always does: General Dessalines as a fierce deity (lwa), the Polish black Madonna as the Catholic face of the Vodou god Ezuli Danto, symbols of French Freemasons, and new historical terrors it confronted after independence. Vodou was carried to New Orleans, with the exodus from Haiti of ten thousand planters and their slaves. It became an "American religion" early in the nineteenth century, as the Louisiana Purchase dramatically transcultured the religious field of North America. Though it joined the nation's religious repertoire at the same time as many other religious traditions of Louisiana did, it came via another route, namely the exodus from Haiti during that land's epochal revolution. The continuing presence of Vodou in New Orleans, New York, and elsewhere in the United States should serve as an ongoing reminder to us of the enormous role played by Haiti, and Haitians, in the remaking of the United States in the Louisiana Purchase.

For it was in at least one sense Haiti, and black Haitians, who opened the way.

44. Dayan, *Haiti,* 188–89, 193. Given our new knowledge of Jefferson's sexual proclivities, one wonders whether this interest in the deportation of black and mixed-race children was viewed by him as holding multiple possible benefits, among others the erasure of his own biological legacy.

45. Dubois, *Avengers,* 303.

Spirituality and Resistance among African-Creoles

JOHN STEWART

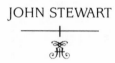

ONE EFFECT OF THE LOUISIANA PURCHASE WAS THE ERECTION OF A political boundary that separated the Louisiana Gulf Coast from the Latin-Antillean culture zone into which it had been integrated since the 1690s. In the wake of that political partitioning, what Jordan-Bychov typifies as "Romano-Caribbean culture" has gone into decline and survives now in fragmentary remains.[1] Among these fragmentary remains, Voudou and the Mardi Gras Indian masquerade are two African-Creole forms for accessing and interacting with the spirit world. An examination of the origins and functions of these forms reveals the capacity of subaltern numina to transcend not only geographical but also sociocultural boundaries.

It is often the case that when we consider the powerful influence of religious beliefs and practices in the formation of early European settlements in what is now the United States of America, our thoughts center immediately on the Puritan and other Protestant communities of early-seventeenth-century New England. This is in keeping with the dominance of a national narrative that privileges the spread of Anglo-American rule and culture from the northeastern Atlantic seaboard westward across the continent. It is worthwhile, nevertheless, to note that for years before the *Mayflower* anchored at Cape Cod, French and Spanish Catholics had been vigorously engaged in

1. Terry G. Jordan-Bychov, "The Creole Coast: Homeland to Substrate," in Richard L. Nostrand and Lawrence E. Estaville, eds., *Homelands: A Geography of Culture and Place across America* (Baltimore: Johns Hopkins University Press, 2001).

developing their own North American colonies: the Spanish in Florida, and the French in New France—a vast territory that included the Mississippi valley all the way to the Gulf Coast. As these European powers established themselves in the Western Hemisphere, the Catholic Church was empowered as a foremost agency responsible for the civilizing mission that—along with expanding the domain and increasing the wealth of the European kingdoms—served as rationale for extending imperial domination over new lands and peoples.

Catholic priests and missionaries came west across the Atlantic shoulder to shoulder with conquistadores and colonists, charged with sustaining the practice of Catholicism among Europeans in the new colonies and with establishing it as the core of a civilized culture among the newly conquered and colonized peoples. From the Bull of Pope Alexander VI (1493) and into the eighteenth century, colonizing Catholics were charged not only with building empires based on material wealth, but also on building a spiritual empire, to be carried out through the conversion of non-Christian souls to the system of Catholic belief and worship. This practice took early form in the Antilles where Spanish Catholics established their first New World colony, then had its greatest development with them in the territory now known as Latin America. French Catholics, who alternately fought against or joined with the Spanish in their colonial ventures, were neither as vigorous nor as successful in carrying out this practice, but the "mission civilisatrice" (the urge to implant Roman Catholicism and French culture) woven into the project of their overseas empire had borne substantial fruit in the area of New Orleans by the time of the Louisiana Purchase. The coastal region in which the city dominated was part of what cultural geographers typify as a Creole Coast "homeland," the lowland area along the Atlantic seaboard and around the Gulf of Mexico where early colonial culture shared fundamental elements with the older Creole culture developed in the Antilles.

In their recent work on "lesser homelands" within the continental United States, the cultural geographers Richard Nostrand and Lawrence Estaville identify fourteen such territories. They are careful to distinguish "homeland" from "cultural area," although the two might be interrelated. Homelands are politically constructed spaces where ethnic groups bond with place over a long period of time. On the other hand, culture areas map the reach and boundaries of heritages and traditions. Culture area and homeland may be interrelated where ethnic territory that has been marked off politically remains culturally linked to geographical regions beyond the political boundaries. Such is the case with the "Creole Coast" homeland that includes the Louisiana coast. Neighboring homelands are typified as the "Plantation South" and "Nouvelle Acadie."[2] In its early colonial phase, this Creole coast functioned not as a homeland but as "the rimland of the Caribbean culture area, an ecological zone linked to the Antilles in climate, flora, fauna, and a more or less common colonial cultural heritage." Homeland status for the *Creole Coast* is dated from the founding of the United States as an independent state (1783) to the ending of the Civil War (1865). While there has been little significant change over the decades ecologically, due to political, demographic, and other institutional shifts following the Civil War, what was a homeland became more fully assimilated into the mainstream United States and devolved into a "place." Homeland culture has been largely eclipsed and survives now as fragments of the "Romano-Caribbean culture that formerly provided the foundation of the homeland." Such fragments continue to lend "a regionalism and sense of place" to today's littoral.[3]

For much of this Creole Coast, the cultural items held in common with the Antilles were of a demographic, sociolinguistic, economic, or material order. For the Louisiana section of the coast settled by French Catholics, however, orthodox and alternative spiritual continuities with the Antilles were also significant. Anglo-American interests that assumed dominance over the entire state following the Purchase encountered a spiritual presence in New Orleans unlike any other in the acquired territory. The Catholic church was, of course, present, and so too were alternative agencies of ritual and devotion that did not openly oppose the church but related to it in an ambiguous fashion that privileged both coexistence and resistance.

At its core, the ambiguity that characterized such agencies encrypted an affinity toward alterity and resistance that was fundamental to an African-Creole identity forged and elaborated in the Antilles, as well as in the Creole Coast homeland. This identity drew heavily on the incidence of marronage, the earliest form of

---

2. Nostrand and Estaville, *Homelands*.
3. Jordan-Bychkov, "Creole Coast," 75–76.

communal resistance against and withdrawal from slave life in the hemisphere for its psychological-political model.[4] In addition, the capacity for entering and performing the altered state known as spirit-mediumship remained crucial to the attainment of religious well-being among Creoles with African forebears.[5] This latter came directly out of an African heritage that regards the body as an active symbol through which mediation between human beings and the higher entities they symbolize results in an actual exchange of vital energies.[6]

The Creole Coast no longer qualifies as an ethnic "homeland." The "Romano-Caribbean" cultural complex in which an African-Creole identity was forged has gone into decline under the steady press of Anglo-American institutional life and other exigencies since the Purchase. Yet New Orleans continues to be a place where Catholicism is deeply entrenched, and where the aura of alternative spiritualities to which the African-Creole presence contributes continues to make the city one of the more intense liminal centers of the country. In no public event is the special character of New Orleans more fully opened and centered than in the annual Mardi Gras.

This carnival, like other Mardi Gras festivals in the Antilles, is suffused in alterities grand and small that include the performance of integrated heritages in complex masquerades symbolizing both the process and attainment of Creole identity and spirituality. Among these masquerades the Mardi Gras Indian performed by and mainly for African-Creoles is an outstanding instance of a common cultural heritage linking New Orleans to the Antilles. A comparison of the Mardi Gras Indian performances in New Orleans and Trinidad also illustrates how differently this heritage plays out in these two sites located at the northern and southern limits of a historical Caribbean cultural area.

---

4. Lynne Guitar, "Criollos: The Birth of a Dynamic New Indo-Afro-European People and Culture on Hispaniola," *Kacike: Journal of Caribbean Amerindian History and Anthropology* 1, no. 1 (2000): 1–17.

5. Evan M. Zuesse, "Perseverance and Transmutation in African Traditional Religions," in Jacob K. Olupona, ed., *African Traditional Religions in Contemporary Society* (St. Paul, Minn.: Paragon House, 1991), 167–84.

6. Vincent Mulago, "Traditional African Religion and Christianity," in Olupona, *African Traditional Religions*, 119–34.

Historical Background

In 1534 Jacques Cartier founded the first French New World settlement in the Saint Lawrence River valley. This was followed by the colonial claim over New France, a vast continental territory, which by the end of the seventeenth century included the colony of Louisiana located in the Mississippi River basin. French efforts to establish a settlement on the Gulf Coast in the 1560s failed. A successful Gulf Coast settlement was not achieved until 1699 when Sieur d'Iberville and Sieur de Bienville entered the Mississippi from the Gulf of Mexico and established a permanent settlement at Biloxi. The settlements they founded were sustained and eventually became central to the colonial development of Southern Louisiana.[7] During the first half of the eighteenth century, New Orleans was founded (1718), African slaves were introduced to join and eventually displace Indians already enslaved by the French (1717–1721), sugarcane was introduced (1750s), yet by the 1790s Louisiana was not a profitable colony.

On the other hand, by the middle of the seventeenth century, the French had established colonies on the Caribbean islands of St. Christopher (1625), Dominica (1632), Tortuga (1634), Guadeloupe (1635), Martinique (1635), and St. Lucia (1660). Their great prize in the region, however, was Saint-Domingue, the western third of the island of Hispaniola ceded by the Spanish in the Treaty of Ryswick (1697). While fish, fur, and forest products were the principal production and trade items in the colonial development of New France, sugar and lesser plantation crops made the island colonies in the Lesser Antilles and Saint-Domingue more profitable: "By 1700 the French West Indies' population grew to an estimated 44,000 persons: 14 thousand from France and 30 thousand slaves. It was not until the 1720s and 1730s that conditions approached stability for the French residents in Louisiana."[8]

Economic development in the Caribbean colonies was based on intense African slave labor engaged in the production of plantation crops, sugar chief among them. Tobacco, cotton, indigo, and coffee were grown as well, but advancing into the eighteenth century, sugar came to be "worth its weight in gold," and Saint-Domingue was the

7. Frederick Quinn, *The French Overseas Empire* (Westport, Conn.: Praeger Publishers, 2000), 74–77.
  8. Ibid., 73.

largest producer in the world. Saint-Domingue was such a great economic success, the colony came to be known as France's "pearl of the Antilles" or "the Eden of the western world."[9] Yet the events following the French Revolution and the Haitian revolt showed that there were countercurrents at work in the colony. Among these were the divisive class lines between *grands blancs* ("great" landowners, military and government officers) and *petits blancs* (European tradespeople, clerks, minor officials, and renegades); a restive slave population and the incidence of marronage; and the growth of a mixed-blood population that, along with free blacks and lower class whites, constituted intermediate social and cultural segments between the grands blancs and the great number of Africans and their offspring who were held as slaves.[10]

In the hands of wealthy grands blancs—many of whom were representatives of absentee owners with nothing more than an economic interest in the colony—and with overheated economic conditions that led to a doubling of a large African slave population in less than twenty years,[11] and with the tensions that come with maintaining control in such a situation, eighteenth-century Saint-Domingue was a colony fraught with anxiety. Landowners were distrustful of any agency whose actions stimulated the impulse to liberty among the slaves. Instead of a Catholic colony such as that stipulated in the Bull of Pope Alexander VI, eighteenth-century Saint-Domingue was a colony where the "mission civilisatrice" was all but forgotten. The native Taino had all but disappeared, and it was accepted as an aspect of the human condition that African slaves did not have the intelligence to benefit from any civilizing instruction. Instead of being a colony based on the system of master-slave relations outlined in the Code Noir of 1685,[12] Saint-Domingue functioned under the thumbs of a totally secular and overly vigilant civil

9. Ibid., 83.

10. David Watts, *The West Indies: Patterns of Development, Culture, and Environmental Change since 1492* (Cambridge: Cambridge University Press, 1987), 350–52.

11. Ibid., 320.

12. The edict of Louis XIV (1685) was the basis for both the Code Noir adopted in Saint-Domingue in 1687 and the 1724 slave code applied to Louisiana. Among its declarations, rules, and orders, the edict stipulated that no religion other than Catholicism be practiced in the Catholic colony, that all slaves be instructed and baptized in the Catholic religion, and that no work for either master or slave should take place on Sundays and holidays. The edict also established that slaves had neither civil nor legal rights, and fugitives were to be dealt with harshly: cropping and branding for the first offense, hamstringing and further branding for a second offense, death for a third offense.

authority. Under these conditions the Catholic Church opted to construe itself as an agency that did not contest civil law and code; thus with mistrust an active force in the colony, and an amply evident ambivalence toward slavery among the clergy, the church did not prosper in this environment. Inevitably, variously individualized patterns of catechizing among the French clergy occurred. Also, given the importance of spiritual well-being among the slaves themselves, in instances where the Church could announce but not carry out its intention to be of service, self-appointed catechists arose from among them. Religious practices known among the Africans before they were shipped to the Antilles were revitalized. The practice of Voudou grew strong and reasonably widespread in eighteenth-century Saint-Domingue, sustained and refreshed by the regular arrivals of fresh groups of Africans as the slave trade burgeoned. Eventually, the colony would collapse in a bloodbath that resulted in the emergence of Haiti as the first black republic in the hemisphere, an event that led to the out-migration of a great number of refugees from Hispaniola to the Louisiana coast.

As Louisiana grew in the eighteenth century, French colonists who had experienced or had knowledge of the Antilles were attracted to the coastal region, and some key items from the islands were integrated into its economic and social development. Once New Orleans was established, trade and travel between this Gulf Coast port and the islands expanded, with African and Native American slaves being traded in both directions. Among travelers were fresh and seasoned émigrés seeking to establish themselves in the colonies, swashbucklers, adventurers, commercial agents, and a few functionaries of church and state. One writer described Louisiana society in the early eighteenth century as "an amalgam of partly reformed Caribbean pirates and somewhat settled coureurs de bois." Another scholar, in noting the difference between Louisiana and the rest of New France, summarized, "the notion of Louisiana as a legitimate child of Quebec was false. What had been established on the Gulf Coast was a colony similar to France's island possessions in the Caribbean. Lawless men of the buccaneer type who had conquered Saint Domingue formed the bulk of the early settlers, as against the solid Normans and Picards who had gone to Canada."[13]

13. Quinn, *French Overseas,* 73, 14; W. Adolphe Roberts, *Lake Pontchartrain* (Indianapolis: Bobbs-Merrill, 1946), 61.

Tobacco, indigo, rice, plus new varieties of sugarcane and cotton already well established in the Caribbean were adopted. Also, a crystallizing technique developed in Saint-Domingue helped propel sugar into becoming Louisiana's most profitable commodity. Plantations thrived on a steady supply of slave labor, and through the early decades of Gulf Coast colonization, shiploads of Africans were brought in—some directly from Africa, others by way of the West Indies. Economically, the colony showed progress. But in respect to formal religion, it remained relatively backward. In 1714 the Catholic bishop of Quebec appointed a vicar-general for Louisiana, and within the next decade the Jesuit, Capuchin, and Ursuline orders were engaged in missionary work in the territory. The colonists, however, were not particularly supportive of the church or diligent in their religious observations.

When Father Raphael du Luxembourg arrived to assume his duties as superior of the Capuchin Mission to Louisiana in 1723, he found "much poverty, suffering, and ignorance" amid a population that "seemed indifferent to all that savoured of religion."[14] For the rest of the century, conditions did not get much better so far as the Catholic mission was concerned. In 1763 the Louisiana territory was ceded to Spain. Under Spanish rule the church faced serious challenges not only in its mission to non-Christians and its unlettered and highly secularized congregation, but also within its own administration. The ecclesiastical province was first placed under the Bishop of Santiago de Cuba.

In 1787 the Diocese of Santiago de Cuba was divided, and Louisiana joined with Havana and Florida under the Bishop at Puerto Rico. In 1793 the See of St. Louis of New Orleans was established to include the Louisiana Province and Florida. French colonists resented the overlordship of the Spanish governor Ulloa and his administration, and this led to an alienation of Spanish congregants within the church. By 1795, in his report to his king, the bishop of the see complained of a general indifference to the practice of religion. "He condemned the laxity of morals among the men, and the universal practice of concubinage among the slaves," and he complained that the "toleration of the Government in admitting all

---

14. "I. Early Colonial Period," in Marie Louise Points, "New Orleans," in *The Catholic Encyclopedia* (New York: Robert Appleton, 1911); available online at www. newadvent.org (accessed November 12, 2007).

classes of adventurers for purposes of trade, had brought about dis-respect for religion."[15]

In spite of the Black Codes of 1724, the Catholic mission was no more successful in Louisiana than it was in Saint-Domingue, and for somewhat the same reasons. Economic development and trade dom-inated the colonizing effort, fragile and unstable political leadership undermined the sustenance of institutional security in the colony, and the church did not have the resources to make it an efficient agency in dealing with multiple cultural segments at an optimum level simultaneously. A further condition faced by the Catholic Church in Louisiana was the press of non-Catholic—and perhaps even anti-Catholic—sentiment filtering into the region with Anglo colonial competitors. Anglo hostility toward Catholics was etched in various laws passed against Catholics in the English colonies to the northeast,[16] and bloody conflicts between the Christian groups stretched from Europe to the Americas. This combination of circum-stances certainly fostered the pursuit of spiritual well-being in alter-native and maverick domains. Freemasonry emerged among the French elites, and the Sunday ritual of Congo Square was officially sanctioned as an alternative to surreptitious performances among the slaves.[17] Conditions were good for the survival and growth of Voudou.

Southern Louisiana remained under Spanish rule during the last two decades of the eighteenth century in which, as a result of the great slave revolt in Saint-Domingue, thousands of refugees dis-persed from that colony. A good percentage of these refugees even-tually settled in New Orleans. They amplified the Caribbean component of Louisiana's coastal culture in several ways,[18] among the most outstanding of which were plaçage and the rigorous color stratification that it spawned, the practice of Voudou, and a

15. "II. Spanish Period," in ibid.

16. E. Phillips Mantz and Michael J. Roach, "A History of Catholic America" (Hack-ensack, N.J.: C.E.S., 1975), 7, available online at http://www.franciscanfriarstor.com/friars/History_Catholic_America/catholic_america_history_part_I.htm (accessed Dec-ember 20, 2007).

17. "II. Spanish Period." On the significance of Congo Square, see Richard Brent Turner, "Mardi Gras Indians and Second Lines/Sequin Artist and Rara Bands: Street Festivals and Performances in New Orleans and Haiti," *Journal of Haitian Studies* 9, no. 1 (spring 2003): 124–56.

18. Jose Morales, "Fleeing the Nightmare: French Emigres in Cuba and Louisiana during the Haitian Revolution, 1791–1810," *MACLAS Latin American Essays* (Newark: University of Delaware and Middle Atlantic Council of Latin American Studies, 2000).

belligerent marronage. These prominent elements in coastal Creole culture all stood as alternatives to official orthodoxies in colonial institutions and culture.

Creole Identity and Marronage

What Jordan-Bychov labels the "Romano-Caribbean culture of the insular Caribbean" had its genesis within the creolized communities of the Antilles. The plantation, the Catholic church, and "Latin" style domestic practices charted the core of relations in which Creole sociocultural identity could be achieved, and from early on such identity could be disrupted by idiosyncratic interpretations and opposing attitudes both within and beyond the Creole category. Sidney Mintz notes that Caribbean creolization "began five centuries past, with migration and resettlement, forced transportation, the stripping of kinship and community, the growth of individuality on a new basis, and the appearance of the first true creoles—things of the Old World, born in the New."[19] Early on, the term *Creole* referred to those born of Old World parents in the colonies.

In time the meaning of the term was extended to include the mixed-blood offspring of conjugal relationships between Europeans (mainly male) and native islanders and Africans (usually women). Given that few European women immigrated to the colonies in the early days, the conquistadores found female partnership among the Indians and African slaves. This practice of interracial cohabitation was "made easier because of the Spaniards' widespread and long standing acceptance of miscegenation." A similar practice was noted among French colonists.[20]

In the Antilles, within sixty years after Columbus first landed at Hispaniola, the native population had gone into serious decline, and the mixed-blood population grew to be numerically dominant. Those who were accorded legitimacy by their fathers inherited mines, sugar estates, tobacco plantations, and cattle ranches. Legitimate or not, they were also supervisors, agricultural workers,

---

19. Sidney W. Mintz, "Enduring Substances, Trying Theories: The Caribbean Region as Oikoumene," *Journal of the Royal Anthropological Institute* 2, no. 2 (1996): 301.
20. Guitar, "Criollos," 4. See also Quinn, *French Overseas,* 89.

tradespeople, domestics, and altogether constituted a new and dynamic "multiethnic people and culture on Hispaniola."[21]

As generations passed, the culture complex developed out of an amalgam of European, Amerindian, and African elements among Creoles (or Criollos) on Hispaniola and elsewhere in the Antilles also came to be typified as Creole—meaning adaptive, flexible, related to preceding provenances but incomplete in this relation, invested unabashedly in rhythm and the sensuous body.[22]

However, Creoles on Hispaniola and elsewhere in the Antilles did not constitute a uniform social category. Early Caribbean Creole communities emerged on the island of Hispaniola in two opposed contexts: First, there was the colonial society at large, which was economically based on slave or otherwise unfree labor and was subject to administrative procedures propounded by European and English rulers and enforced by their military, ecclesiastic, and civil agencies. Second, there were Maroon enclaves that emerged simultaneously with the early colonial settlements and in opposition to them. Also, the patterns of discrimination that characterized colonial society were reflected in the hierarchies by which their hybridities were indexed: The French developed a mixed-blood chart with ten basic categories that combined into several more,[23] and some early Spanish censuses had no category for mixed-bloods, relying instead on "birthright, social status, and economic and political clout as categoric differentiators."[24]

Marronage got its start in the hemisphere when, to avoid the punitive deployment of Spanish rule, slave-raiding, and demand for tribute, native Arawaks on Hispaniola often deserted their villages and moved into the hinterland surrounding colonial settlements.[25] In time, Africans running away from the mines and plantations, as well as Spaniards who for one reason or another became renegades among their countrymen joined the natives in these enclaves, which became known as "cimarrones." It was in such cimarron communities where Ladinos (the black Spanish), West Africans, Tainos, and

21. Guitar, "Criollos," 6.
22. See Doris Garraway, "Race, Reproduction, and Family Romance in Moreau de Saint-Méry's Description . . . de la partie française de l'isle Saint-Domingue," *Eighteenth-Century Studies* 38, no. 2 (2005): 227–46.
23. Garraway, "Race," 230–31.
24. Guitar, "Criollos," 3–4.
25. Watts, *West Indies*, 92.

renegade Spaniards congregated in defiance against Spanish colonial authority that the early instance of Creole or Criollo culture evolved on Hispaniola.[26]

Marronage developed into a complex and well-sustained affair. Among eighteenth-century planters, two types of marronage were recognized: petit marronage and grand marronage. The historian Gabriel Debien likens the former to a sort of absenteeism among slaves who never drifted far from the plantations to which they belonged, and whose defiance against plantation rule, if any, was expressed mostly in the form of petty thefts. Grand marronage involved flight from the colonists' community by slaves with no intention of ever returning. These Maroons lived in bands in the hills and settled into a way of life that was almost "collective." They raided, pillaged, and terrorized certain areas. They drew the attention of the militia, mounted police, and even professional troops as the colonists tried to bring them back under control or get rid of them.[27] Out of the practice of grand marronage the legendary figures Makandal and Boukman emerged. In the narrative of Haitian independence, they play critical roles as inspirational leaders in the revolutionary movement that brought blacks to power. The Haitian revolution had the effect of confirming the Maroon as a principal agent of black liberation.[28] It also crystallized a sociocultural divide between those who were propertied and those who were or had been property among the Creoles. This divide turned on their different attitudes toward black empowerment, a difference that is well illustrated in how François Makandal and Dutty Boukman, two Maroons, and Vincent Ogé, a leading man of color, contributed to the liberation movement. These three eighteenth-century figures all fought against the royalist French plantocracy, Makandal the earliest. He was a runaway, a Maroon, and an herbalist with ritual skills who acquired a substantial following among the slaves on Haiti's northern plantations during the 1750s.[29]

26. Guitar, "Criollos," 3.

27. See Gabriel Debien, "Marronage in the French Caribbean," in Richard Price, ed., *Maroon Societies* (Baltimore: Johns Hopkins University Press, 1979), 107–34.

28. See John Stewart, "Culture, Heroism, and the Haitian Documentary," in Mbye Cham, ed., *Ex-Iles: Essays on Caribbean Cinema* (Trenton, N.J.: Africa World Press, 1992), 119–33.

29. See Hein Vanhee, "Central African Popular Christianity and the Making of Haitian Vodou Religion," in Linda M. Heywood, ed., *Central Africans and Cultural Transformations in the American Diaspora* (Cambridge: Cambridge University Press, 2001), 243–64.

Makandal is remembered as a skilled herbalist and spiritual leader who instigated a plan that called on slaves to exterminate their masters by surreptitiously serving them poisons prepared and distributed by himself. After a few deaths among the whites, his plan was betrayed by one of the slaves. Makandal was captured and burned at the stake in 1758. He was defiant to the end, and legend has it that before his body went up in flames, his essential self escaped as a bird (some say as an insect) to the hills, there to await the revolution proper, which erupted in 1791 when another Maroon, Boukman, emerged. Makandal is revered among Haitians as the spiritual father of the revolution that freed the slaves. He ranks among the most honorable of independent Haiti's founders.

In 1789 Vincent Ogé, a free man of color and wealthy merchant, journeyed from Saint-Domingue to Paris to represent the views of his class during debates on the fate of the colonists in the midst of the French Revolution. In the color-caste society of Saint-Domingue, free persons of color were not regarded as full citizens, and their privileges were commensurately limited. Ogé was there to present the view that a new constitution for the colonies should overturn current practice and establish their status as full citizens. He took pains to make it clear that his demands for equality did not favor any change in the condition of those who lived in servitude. Many of his class owned slaves. Aware of the restive condition among the slaves, he proposed that if the free colored were granted full equality with the white colonists, together they would become more successful in managing and controlling the enslaved. He was rebuffed and not allowed a seat with the Assembly in Paris. On his return to Saint-Domingue in 1790, he led the first outright rebellion and uprising against the planter regime. This was an entirely mulatto uprising; Ogé refused to recruit slaves to their cause. He and his band were defeated. He was captured, tried, convicted, and broken on the wheel. In the annals of the ultimate revolt, this uprising is cited as something of a precursor, but "only a few partisan historians have claimed a key role for survivors of Oge's rebellion in the great slave uprising of August 1791."[30]

Dutty Boukman, also a Voudou priest, is credited with a leading role in the ceremony at Bois Caiman in August 1791 that is generally

30. David Patrick Geggus, *Haitian Revolutionary Studies* (Bloomington: Indiana University Press, 2002), 94.

passed on as the igniting event for the massive slave uprising that plunged Saint-Domingue into a brutal series of wars over the twelve years preceding Haitian independence. A Maroon said to have been born in Jamaica, in legend he is recalled as a black man Herculean in size and strength and indomitable in battle. Boukman was captured and decapitated publicly in that year. His severed head was put on display at the public park in Cap Francais. At the time of his death, he is said to have had a following of six thousand slaves and Maroons.[31]

The Haitian revolution had far-reaching repercussions throughout the Antilles. Geographically, refugees from the fighting and destruction scattered through the islands from Trinidad to Cuba, and on to continental locations at Baltimore, New Orleans, St. Augustine, and other cities. New Orleans attracted the greatest number among these refugees, who came directly from Saint-Domingue, from Cuba, and even from France.[32] Culturally, the revolution had the effect of confirming black slaves-turned-Maroon liberation fighters into legitimate heroic figures. Marronage was already widespread throughout the Antilles and was not unknown on the mainland, but the success of the Saint-Domingue Maroons was unprecedented. They triumphed over substantive military and civilian forces in a conflict that lasted some ten years, and they gained control over a national territory. By comparison, the Maroons of Jamaica had settled for a self-defeating peace with the English that involved the transportation of a substantial number among them out of the colony.[33]

Revolutionary success in Haiti also had the effect of establishing religious practices that had sprung up among African slaves and been cultivated in Maroon enclaves as a legitimate source of empowerment. In fact, marronage is credited with playing a significant role in the development and preservation of these practices that together came to be known as Voudou.[34] Voudou priests and practitioners had successfully promoted the idea of invincibility among revolting slaves who often had little more with which to face well-armed

31. Leslie G. Desmangles, *The Faces of the Gods: Voudou and Roman Catholicism in Haiti* (Chapel Hill: University of North Carolina Press, 1992), 34.
32. Morales, "Fleeing," 1.
33. Carey Robinson, *The Fighting Maroons of Jamaica* (Kingston, Jamaica: William Collins and Sangster, 1969).
34. Desmangles, *Faces*, 35.

military forces than their bodies. In this way, the revolution as social drama openly displayed alternative attitudes among the combatting segments in respect to liberty and the black body with its extensions. The revolutionary war, then, was as much a war about color and culture as it was about territorial domain and political leadership.

Color and cultural discrimination among Creoles themselves was a disruptive condition, and there was a wide social and psychological divide between people of color whose Creole identity was based principally on their mixed blood and color (these were the *gens du couleur*), and the black masses who were Creole by virtue of their being born to the land and cut off from any vital contact with Africa. Most of the latter were slaves. Many of the upper classes among people of color were slave owners. Yet while there were differences and an antipathy between people of color and African-Creoles based on the different ways in which they perceived their destinies, both relied heavily on bodily symbols and performances as they construed their relationship with the dominant whites and projected their lives into the future. Among gens du couleur, plaçage was a critical structure in which women were agents of accommodation. On the other hand, African-Creoles for whom accommodation was not an option, the defiant male warrior served as agent of resistance.

Distinctions between people of color and African-Creoles in respect to bodily symbol and performance were no doubt amplified in the wider colonial social system in which European and Creole slaveholders could legitimately view the non-European body as little more than economic property, pertinent only to the production of labor, wealth, and suzerainty. Mixed-blood Creoles, among whom dissociation from their African progenitors was profitable, could hold that while slaves were and could be no more than property, the mixed-blood body, by virtue of that state, could be elevated to an equal status with elites on the basis of achievement. Social mobility was of prime importance. Maroons, and the mass of slaves from whom they had emerged—out of necessity it may be surmised, but also out of custom—were most mindful of the body as the source of the person who, irrespective of the economic and social negotiations in which it was engaged, proclaimed itself as existing beyond such negotiation and therefore an agent of a higher calling.

When emigrés from Saint-Domingue flooded into New Orleans and the surrounding countryside at the onset of the Haitian Revolution and later, not only did they meet a social structure and

Creole culture with which they were quite familiar (albeit in a lesser stage of development), but also they were enthusiastically though selectively integrated according to their color and social status. White refugees were welcomed and integrated among white colonists, and gens du couleur and African-Creoles both slave and free found their respective counterparts. Notably, while white refugees were expected to bring, and brought with them, industrial and agricultural economic knowledge, blacks and mulattos were expected to bring, and brought with them (along with whatever industrial, agricultural, and domestic skills they had), a rebellious attitude toward the elite slaveholding regime and a high potential for the armed pursuit of liberty.

Slave rebellions at Point Coupee in 1791 and 1795 were blamed especially on the free colored from Saint-Domingue and the slaves they brought with them. In 1803–1804, slaves among the Saint-Domingue refugees seeking asylum were forbidden to enter Louisiana. An 1807 act forbade entry to all colored persons regardless of origin.[35] Yet in 1811, what some scholars cite as the largest slave revolt in the United States occurred a few miles from New Orleans. "Charles Deslondes, a refugee from St. Domingue who worked as a slave driver on the plantation, organized the other slaves on the plantation. With the support of runaway slaves, or 'maroons,' who lived in the nearby swamps, Deslondes' band wounded Andry [the plantation owner] and killed his son. Seizing weapons on the plantation, they set off on the road along the river headed for New Orleans, gathering recruits from other plantations as they went. . . . On January 15, 1812, after one day of investigation, the tribunal condemned eighteen of the slaves. They were taken to the plantations of their respective masters, where they were shot and their heads cut off and mounted on poles as an example to the remaining slaves."[36]

Saint-Domingue refugees and "maroons" were cited in other bloody confrontations between slaves and slaveholders in Louisiana, but marronage did not grow to be as widespread and well developed in Louisiana as it had in Saint-Domingue. Fear of

35. Morales, "Fleeing."

36. "Slave Revolts and Insurrections," in "Historical Perspectives, 1682–1815," online at "The Louisiana Purchase: A Heritage Explored," educational resource from LSU libraries special collections, http://www.lib.lsu.edu/special/purchase/history.html# women4 (accessed December 20, 2007).

revolt fostered and perpetrated by emboldened Saint-Dominguans and those they inspired did remain tangible, however, through the first half of the nineteenth century, up to the Civil War. Following the Purchase, with Anglo investment and entrepreneurship, Louisiana blossomed economically. New Orleans swiftly grew into the fifth most populous city in the United States, the largest west of the Appalachians.[37] Yet the city, at the periphery of the culture zone with its historic center in the Greater Antilles, did not surrender its Creole character, which "Americans" found to be disorderly, violent, debauched, and conspiratorial. Most of all it remained resistant to the imposition of Anglo-American cultural preferences.[38] In this milieu, incubated in racial and color-distinct contexts spawned by the practice of slavery, the Maroon identified a deeply held attitude of resistance against slavery and its alternative structures for controlling black bodies.

Creole Spiritual Alterity

In the eighteenth century, when Catholicism was being seriously suppressed by Protestants in Maryland and New York,[39] "The Company of the West" charged with the colonial development of the Louisiana territory accepted the obligation to build churches wherever settlements were established, and "to maintain the necessary number of duly approved priests to preach, perform Divine service and administer the sacraments under the authority of the Bishop of Quebec."[40] It took several years before Louisiana became a well-settled colony, and during the early frontier days the church struggled, even though a number of religious orders—including the Jesuits, the Carmelite fathers, the Capuchin fathers, and the Ursulines—made their appearance in the colony.

The early missionaries did not always distinguish themselves from the common milieu. For instance, the Jesuits and the Capuchins

37. Peirce F. Lewis, *New Orleans: The Making of an Urban Landscape*, 2d ed. (Santa Fe: Center for American Places in association with the University of Virginia Press, 2003).

38. John G. Clark, *New Orleans, 1718–1812: An Economic History* (Baton Rouge: Louisiana State University Press, 1970).

39. Mantz and Roach, "History," 6–7.

40. "I. Early Colonial Period."

ministered to both whites and slaves, but they also owned slaves and profited from their labor.[41] Settler congregations were small and widely scattered. Settlers were not particularly avid in their support of the church and in their observation of ecclesiastical rules. They were neglectful in respect to official stipulations calling for the religious instruction of the slaves who, if they were baptized at all, were not allowed access to the other sacraments. Slaves were forced to work on holy days, received no religious instruction, and were discouraged from getting married. The Church was largely accommodating.

With the accelerated in-migration of Catholics of different nationalities, Louisiana emerged as a haven for not only French but also German, Spanish, Irish, Italian, and other European Catholics. Acadians, too, were numbered among the worshippers, as well as converted Native Americans and Africans. Anglo-Americans were allowed to immigrate into the territory on condition that they too would be converted to Catholicism.[42] The church served or attempted to serve them all as segregated communities. Yet by the end of the eighteenth century, anticlerical sentiments were popular in the colony, and Catholic practice was widely ignored.[43]

By 1809, following the influx of Saint-Domingue refugees, the New Orleans population doubled, and two-thirds of all New Orleanians were black or colored. This nineteenth-century influx of white, black, and mixed-blood Catholics from Saint-Domingue served to augment the church in New Orleans, and people of color were generous in their support. Forty years after the Louisiana Purchase, Bishop Anthony Blanc, who had ecclesiastical jurisdiction over the states of Louisiana and Mississippi, permitted the founding of the "Sisters of the Holy Family," a black religious order of women with the special duty of caring for "coloured orphans and the aged coloured poor."[44] This order, cofounded by the daughters of Haitian parents who migrated to the United States by way of Cuba, arose among people of color who were more French than African in inspiration, so that "there was no overt indication of an African American theme in their spirituality." Indeed, "taking the veil" served as a form

---

41. Cyprian Davis, *The History of Black Catholics in the United States* (New York: Crossroad Publishing, 1990).

42. Alfred E. Lemmon, John T. Magill, and Jason R. Wiese, *Charting Louisiana* (New Orleans: Historic New Orleans Collection, 2003).

43. Davis, *History*, 72.

44. "III. French and American Period," in Points, "New Orleans."

of rescue for young women of color who faced public disgrace for one reason or another.[45]

In the middle of the nineteenth century, Spanish Catholics campaigned against the laxity of morals and the practice of concubinage in the colony. But Creole flexibility in morals and rigidity in social structure continued unabated. Concubinage flourished. Among persons of color, many the offspring of genteel liaisons between elite white men and their concubines, ambiguous attitudes toward race and culture conditioned their religious practice.[46] Church wardens enforced the pattern of color discrimination that stipulated whites, persons of color, and slaves—when they were allowed to worship at all—worship separately and in that order. In addition, and of more profound concern, Catholic structures of belief and authority—as did such structures in all formal Western Christianity—did not endorse black religious experience and the practice among blacks of integrating elements from apparently disparate modes of expression in satisfying their spiritual needs. Creoles were not barred from worship in the Catholic Church. In fact, the church took an active role in helping to create the notion of "the Creole" by encouraging or forcing aboriginal Amerindians and Africans to give up their traditional ways of worship and become members of the Christian congregation. Institutionally, however, in its core belief and sacramental structure, the church was not prepared to do enough about the religious needs particular to the African-Creole heritage and experience.[47] African-Creoles could not rely on the church for their spiritual well-being. Voudou was a response to this circumstance in Saint-Domingue.

In New Orleans, Voudou never quite attained the level of development as a religious system that it did in Saint-Domingue. The practice got swept up into the popular culture of the city as a place where the mystique of the supernatural thrived.[48] During the nineteenth and into the early twentieth century, the practice of Voudou spread

---

45. Davis, *History,* 108–10.

46. Ibid., 73.

47. For a discussion of black experience and the symbolizing of God as an attribute of particular modalities of experience, see chapters 9–12 in Charles H. Long, *Significations: Signs, Symbols, and Images in the Interpretation of Religion* (Philadelphia: Fortress Press, 1986).

48. See Joseph Roach, *Cities of the Dead: Circum-Atlantic Performance* (New York: Columbia University Press, 1996).

beyond the African-Creole community to become a popular way of experiencing an alternative spirituality at secular, commercial sites open to whites and others in the city. New Orleans remains the principal continental site visited by many tourists and other part-time seekers in search of a Voudou experience.

Voudou belongs to a category of alternative homegrown rituals in the Antilles that are based on West African Orisha ritual elements at the core, with a structure open enough to accommodate, and in instances to accentuate, elements from other religious and nonreligious domains.[49] Santeria (Cuba), Cumina (Jamaica), and Shango and Spiritual Baptist (Trinidad) are other rituals in this genre. In Voudou ceremonies, chosen devotees transform into and perform as living embodiments of deific powers. Such transformation occurs as devotees enter into an "altered state of consciousness" or "spirit possession."[50] In such a state, worshippers temporarily transition from their everyday selves into the dedicated embodiment of transhuman powers. The body is fully co-opted as inscriptor by the deities, who perform corporeally in a communal atmosphere.

In the early colonial years, Voudou was condemned by the Catholic Church. The practice was demonized and driven to secrecy. In Haiti, clerical and official campaigns against Voudou, with persecution of practitioners and the destruction of sacred implements, occurred as late as 1941. The church has since abandoned its hostile stance for a policy of coexistence. Voudou was recognized as a religion on a par with all others in 2003. In Louisiana, Voudou came to be excessively secularized and performed as a commercial activity. It is interesting, however, that with the commercialization and fading of Voudou as an alternative spiritual experience, Afro-Creoles have developed fresh alternatives to formal Catholicism. One of these is the "Ceremony of Commemoration and Veneration of the Ancestors" developed by the Institute for Black Catholic Studies at

---

49. On the concept of a "deep structure" among Africans that is a spiritual antecedent to forms of religion, see Zuesse, "Perseverance."

50. Erika Bourguignon, "Ritual Dissociation and Possession Belief in Caribbean Negro Religion," in Norman E. Whitten Jr. and John F. Szwed, eds., *Afro-American Anthropology: Contemporary Perspectives* (New York: Free Press, 1970); George Brandon, *Santeria from Africa to the New World* (Bloomington: Indiana University Press, 1993); Melville Herskovits, *Life in a Haitian Valley* (New York: Doubleday, 1971); Leonard Barrett, "African Religions in the America," in C. Eric Lincoln, ed., *The Black Experience in Religion* (New York: Anchor Books, 1974), 311–40.

Xavier University, New Orleans. This annual ritual takes place on the Fourth of July and integrates BaKongo and Roman Catholic regard for the dead. The interweaving of BaKongo and Catholic ritual elements are perceived as "intercession for and to the Church Suffering and the Many Thousand Gone of the Middle Passage, for and to African and African American ancestors and those Black Catholic dead who are the seed of our church."[51] This ritual does not distance itself from the church the way Voudou did; it brings African elements into a formal Catholic setting. In a second recent alternative development to mainstream Catholicism, in 1989 Father George Augustus Stallings Jr. broke with the Catholic Church to launch the Imani Temple African American Catholic Congregation in Washington, D.C. Several branch temples have since been inaugurated— significantly, one in New Orleans and one in Lagos, Nigeria.

Within the caste system of New World plantation colonies, African-Creoles were required to fashion themselves culturally in a coercive system that privileged European enterprise, languages, and customs. African traditions were outlawed or customarily demeaned. They had to devise some protection from the steady, heavy-handed onslaught against the legitimacy of their unqualified existence, and they found ways to be secretive. Along with masking Orisha intentions in Catholic terminology and emblems,[52] Creoles developed the practice of associating dual or multiple meanings with given symbols in other contexts as well. In seeking to summarize this phenomenon as it is delimited in terms of national categories, Sheila Walker writes, "The categories American and African American/African Diasporan are sometimes mutually exclusive and sometimes overlapping, sometimes antagonistic and sometimes complementary, but always a source of at least 'two thoughts' of some kind of duality, or more likely multiplicity, of experience and/or perspective."[53] Along with hybridity, then, the recognition and performance of alter identities are foundational to African-Creole culture. Within this culture, the maintenance of multiple identities is less aberration than advantage.[54] The pattern

51. M. Shawn Copeland, "Tradition and the Traditions of African American Catholicism," *Theological Studies* 61, no. 4 (2000): 632–48.

52. Brandon, *Santeria*, 77.

53. Sheila S. Walker, ed., *African Roots/American Cultures* (Boston: Rowan and Littlefield, 2001), 19.

54. Rocky L. Sexton, "Cajun Mardi Gras: Cultural Objectification and Symbolic Appropriation in a French Tradition (1)," *Ethnology* 38, no. 4 (1999): 297–315.

of maintaining alternate identities that find their linkage in a spiritualized atmosphere is a feature that gives congregational performances a meaning among African-Creoles that may not hold for others.

Unique in its amalgamation of European, African, and Amerindian elements, African-Creole culture stands without a unitary antecedent and takes its particular character from the process of amalgamation itself, a practice far more in resonance with its African, rather than its European or Amerindian provenances. This stratagem resonates with what Evan M. Zuesse terms "those deep structures, which are likely to appear in African forms of religion even a thousand years from now," and, as he illustrates, underlie "the most central and pervasive concern of traditional African religions . . . the maintenance of life as the integral interflow of relationships."[55] In African-Creole culture, hybridity, mimesis, and alterity acquire substance and meaning in this maintenance of an integral interflow of relationships. Corporeal performances in which spiritual experiencing is scripted and communicated, the integrating of Orisha, Catholic, and other elements in Voudou and similar rituals, the practice of infusing secular observances with the ritual energy that summons religious experiencing, these are all emblematic of a process of "intermeshed transculturations" that is characteristic of Creole culture generally.[56]

William H. Green argues for a theory of religion in which the carnivalesque or party mode is recognized as a mode of religious activity. Within the vein of conventional theological notions, he observes, religion is defined in terms of belief, while the dimension that is performed by the body, ritual, is either ignored or downgraded. The history of religion, on the other hand, "presses towards a theory which is bodily, sensorial experience." In similar vein, Jim Perkinson writes, "Afro-diasporic rites of initiation and possession (such as those encountered in vodun, santeria, and candomble) represent a kind of

55. Zuesse, "Perseverance," 172, 173.

56. Jim Perkinson, "Ogu's Iron or Jesus' Irony: Who's Zooming Who in Diasporic Possession Cult Activity?" in Jennifer I. M. Reid, ed., *Religion and Global Culture* (Lanham, Md.: Lexington Books, 2003), 97–124. On the concept of "intermeshed transculturation," see Jon Beasley-Murray, "The Intellectual and the State: *Modernismo* and Transculturation from Below" (unpublished paper, Latin American Studies, University of British Columbia). See also Peter Hulme, "Travel, Ethnography, Transculturation: St. Vincent in the 70s," paper presented at the conference Contextualizing the Caribbean, University of Miami, Coral Gables, September 2000.

conjuration on the surface of Western culture. Older memories of other times are 'conserved' not so much in texts as in bodies in motion. The immediacy of contact with 'living and dying physicalities'... communicated an immediacy of spiritual contact."[57] Beyond the borders of performances categorized as "religion" in African-Creole culture, there are others in which the body is potently engaged in transmutations between the physical and the spiritual, and the Mardi Gras carnival is principal among them.

New Orleans, at roughly 30°N on the rim of the Gulf of Mexico, and Trinidad, approximately 10°N at the southeastern extreme of the Caribbean Sea, lie at the northern and southern boundaries of a Caribbean cultural region in the sense proposed by Jordan-Bychov. Hispaniola (Haiti and the Dominican Republic) and the rest of the Antilles lie in between. The cultural tradition coming out of the insular center of this region, which Jordan-Bychov labels Romano-Caribbean, might more accurately be referred to as Afro-Antillean, given that it varies somewhat from culture along the Venezuelan, Central American, and Mexican rimland, where a Native American presence has had a much fuller endurance. In the Antilles the aboriginal peoples and their cultural system did not last long once European colonists entered the region.[58] Although nationalist narratives in the Dominican Republic and Puerto Rico cite Arawakan foundations as central to local ethnicity, the native population of the islands was essentially displaced by Europeans and Africans by the end of the eighteenth century, in the wake of a series of wars and the establishment of the plantation economy. Colonist planters from early on found insular natives to be a fragile and unreliable workforce with unrelenting insurrectionist tendencies. African slaves were a preferred investment. Many natives who survived the wars were transported to the western rimland territory, and Africans were brought in great numbers. Following the wave of refugees fleeing the Haitian Revolution, Africans and their descendants (including mixed-bloods) were an important segment of the masses in the

---

57. William H. Green, "Capt'n Nat's Party: Religious Aspects of Carnage and Carnival in the Southampton Insurrection of 1831," paper presented at The Middle Passage: Reorientations in the Study of African American Religions, conference at the University of South Carolina, April 1998; Perkinson, "Ogu's Iron," 113.

58. Alfred W. Crosby Jr., *The Columbian Exchange: Biological and Cultural Consequences of 1492* (Westport, Conn.: Greenwood Press, 1972).

emerging homeland population. They were also principal among bearers of the Creole culture that coincided with Catholic colonial settlements from the Louisiana coast to Trinidad.

During the Creole Coast homeland era cited by Jordan-Bychov, the Dutch had a minor presence in the Caribbean, and the British were in authority in Jamaica, Barbados, and other sites in the Lesser Antilles. France and Spain were the dominant European presences in Trinidad, as they were in coastal Louisiana. Both Trinidad and Louisiana were under Spanish control and not yet developed when the 1776 "Cedula de Poblacion" issued by the king of Spain granted Spaniards and foreigners of the Catholic faith the right to settle in Spanish colonies. A second cedula, issued in 1783, granted similar rights for settlement in Trinidad. French and colored planters with their retinues flocked to Trinidad, and a "French landed aristocracy" was in place when the British took the island from Spain in 1797.[59] Spanish immigration policy resulted in a base population of ethnically and socially diverse Catholics coming together in both Louisiana and Trinidad. Under Anglo-American policy in Louisiana following the Purchase and British policy in Trinidad following 1797, immigration was no longer constrained by religious affiliation. Populations grew along with national and ethnic diversity. However, the civil and cultural ground rules of the Catholic forerunners persisted. Among religious institutions, the Catholic Church remained dominant, and in popular culture, the Mardi Gras carnival grew into the most significant public event on the annual calendar.

Perhaps it was propitious that the holy father accompanying Iberville said a mass when they entered the mouth of the Mississippi on Mardi Gras day.[60] The annual Mardi Gras has grown into an immense public ritual and spectacle for which New Orleans is internationally famous. This Mardi Gras is the only one of its kind in the United States. It draws thousands of revelers and tourists to the city each year and contributes substantially to a national sense of New Orleans as a liminal center.

No specific date for the founding of Mardi Gras as a public event has been fully established. A popular Mardi Gras narrative dates the founding in 1822, when some students brought the custom from

---

59. Errol Hill, *The Trinidad Carnival* (Austin: University of Texas Press, 1972), 6–7.
60. Encyclopedia Louisiana, http://www.enlou.com/time/year1699.htm (accessed December 8, 2007).

Paris.[61] A ban on black persons wearing masks or feathers and
attending night balls dated 1781 indicates, however, that the festival
in some early version was already well developed during the Spanish
administration.[62] Public pageantry and masquerade may have been
the lesser aspect of the festival when it was dominated by elites on
their plantations, in their salons, and at other private venues during
the eighteenth century. The celebration of 1857 is cited as the one in
which public pageantry and parade emerged as a major feature of
the carnival, with the organization and performance of the Mystic
Krewe of Comus.[63] Africans and African-Creoles were not welcome
in the parade of Krewes in the central part of the city. They developed their own celebrations in their neighborhoods where "Black
Indians" became the significant masquerade. The precise origins of
this masquerade is a contested issue. There is substantial evidence
that it emerged out of Native American–African American relations
in Louisiana.[64] This Indian masquerade is also said to have migrated
from Haiti, where it had developed prior to the revolution, with the
refugees who entered Louisiana during the early nineteenth century.[65]

Before the 1834 emancipation decree that put an end to slavery in
Trinidad, carnival was an affair restricted to whites and free coloreds.
White planters, government officials, and other elites held masked
balls and other entertainments in private. They drove through the
city streets masked on carnival days. The coloreds, though allowed to
celebrate, were required to do so separately from the whites. Slaves,
who could participate "as onlookers, or by special favour when
required to take part," were excluded from the celebrations.[66] Following the emancipation, the black populace did enter and eventually take over the carnival as the whites withdrew from participation,
and by the 1870s they were fully in charge of the street celebrations.
Their masquerades included localized versions of figures from

61. Herbert Asbury, *The French Quarter: An Informal History of the New Orleans Underworld* (New York: Alfred A. Knopf, 2003), 141.

62. Kalamu ya Salaam, "He's the Prettiest: A Tribute to Big Chief Allison 'Tootie' Montana's Fifty Years of Mardi Gras Indian Suiting," virtual book available online at Folklife in Louisiana, Louisiana's Living Traditions, http://www.louisianafolklife.org/LT/creole_books.html (accessed November 12, 2007).

63. Asbury, *French Quarter*, 141.

64. Salaam, "He's the Prettiest."

65. Samuel Kinser, *Carnival, American Style: Mardi Gras at New Orleans and Mobile* (Chicago: University of Chicago Press, 1990).

66. Hill, *Trinidad*, 10.

European popular and African ritual culture as well as figures from local history. Among the latter was the "Red Indian," a figure based on local contact with and knowledge of the Guajiro of coastal Venezuela who visited Trinidad regularly in those days.[67] It is also likely that émigrés from Haiti who had settled in Trinidad under the Spanish cedula brought the tradition with them.

The observation that many of the eighteenth-century settlers in Louisiana were "the flotsam and jetsam of European society,"[68] is mirrored in the comment that Trinidad in the same era became "a refuge for the rifraff of the Southern Caribbean." Once the carnival became principally a street festival in the hands of the populace, it didn't take long before its pointed caricaturing of authority and the violent and libidinous excesses drew serious disfavor among the Trinidad ruling class. Between the 1850s and 1890s, several attempts were made to stamp out the festival by force. This led to violent confrontations between revelers, and the police were backed up on occasion by military forces. It also fueled the cultivation of a warrior ethos within the carnival that was symbolized by several masquerades, the "Indian" among them.[69] Over the years, African-Creoles have come to dominate the carnival in all of Trinidad.

The same cannot be said for Louisiana. Within the city of New Orleans, however, African-Creoles have in their own neighborhoods maintained the "Black Indian"—later to become known as the "Mardi Gras Indian"—at the center of a powerful tradition of masking and parade. The similarities between this masquerade and the "Indian" masquerades of Trinidad are noted by some writers as evidence of the spread and influence of North American popular culture.[70] While such influence in the Caribbean is undeniable, a more feasible explanation would take into account the cultural foundations of Louisiana and Trinidad when both were essentially Catholic colonies with similar demographic bases, a similarly rigid class structure, a Creole culture in which charismatic freedom fighters were heroes, and public performance of spiritual actants with alternate domains a desirable attribute.[71]

---

67. Noted by the author while conducting field research in Trinidad in 1972.
68. Quinn, *French Overseas,* 73.
69. Hill, *Trinidad,* 8.
70. Helene Bellour and Samuel Kinser, "Amerindian Masking in Trinidad Carnival: The House of Black Elk in San Fernando," *Drama Review* 42, no. 3 (1998): 147–69.
71. In nineteenth-century Trinidad, leading stickfighters, or "bois-men," were

The Mardi Gras carnival at its pre-Christian roots harks back to certain rites of Egyptian origins in which the forces of "renewal" and "regeneration" were celebrated in mystery plays.[72] The contemporary carnival, however, is not wholly or perhaps even principally taken as being a religious event. Tourism, ethnicity, nationalism, and secular rebellion all compete for ritual performative space in the carnival. Yet while the festival may seem to be dominated by the glamor, glitter, and self-conscious excesses of secular celebrating, a spiritual element is sustained. The awareness of transhuman interaction is at times powerfully evident in the music and in the sensorial enactment of spiritual alterities in the costuming and congregational parade.[73]

Within the carnival, congregational alterities are based on the particularities that performing groups choose to celebrate. The appeal of the Native American figure among African-Creoles is associated with the incidence of courage, defiance, and independence in their own historical survival. The costume and ritual performance has less to do with taking on the special properties of "Indianness" than with extolling and paying homage to the common experience of resistance. This pattern is to be found among mulattos and mestizos as well. In the Dominican Republic, performing groups dressed up as Indians "stage historic dramas, based on some episodes involving the Conquistadores. One of the most popular dramas is the capture of Cacique Caonabo ... other street performances portray tainos' daily life episodes, such as areitos, ball games, and religious rites."[74]

The interweaving of blood and culture between Africans and Native Americans in the plantation regions may not have been as extensive as the interweaving between Africans and Europeans, but

---

charismatic folk figures both in their neighborhoods and in the streets at large. They marauded in bands on carnival days and fought bloody battles to the beat of kalinda drums.

72. Ian Isidore Smart, *Amazing Connections: Kemet to Hispanophone Africana Literature* (Washington, D.C.: Original World Press, 1996).

73. Peter Minshall, a Trinidadian designer and carnival bandleader, produced a series of bands in the 1980s with overtly religious themes. One of the most dramatic was "The Seven Deadly Sins," in which the seven deadly sins recognized in the Catholic cathechism were presented in costume and skits based on modern historical events. Also, the calypsonian David Rudder has consistently integrated religious themes and messages into his music. A most evocative rendition in this regard is the calypso "High Mas," composed for the carnival of 1998.

74. Dominican Secretariat of State Tourism, "By Way of History," http://www.dominicana.com.do/english/carnival.htm (accessed December 20, 2007).

it ran deep where it occurred, much deeper than is acknowledged in the average North American history.[75] In the islands and on the North American mainland, Africans fought as "members of the tribe" among the Caribs, Choctaws, Cherokees, Seminoles, and Natchez, as these native communities defended themselves against invading Europeans. In the 1730s, a group of defiant Bambara slaves "cooperated with the Natchez massacre of the French settlement" in Louisiana.[76] African-Creoles were among the Five Tribes who marched the Trail of Tears and among the Caribs who were exiled from their island homes in the Antilles to Roatan and the Central American coastland.

African-Creoles also fought alongside Europeans in these confrontations. Well-noted in this regard are the exploits of the "Buffalo Soldiers," African-American troops of the Ninth Cavalry deployed along the plains frontier after the Civil War, and nicknamed for their courage by the Kiowa, Cheyenne, and Apache against whom they fought. Black troops were among the colonial forces sent by the French governor of Louisiana to make war against the Natchez following an attack made by the Indians on some French settlers.

The African-Creole Mardi Gras Indian performance does not enshrine conquistadores, comment on the defeat of Native Americans, or present episodes from their daily lives. The African-Creole figure is a commemoration of triumph, in which performers do the dance of combat and victory in honor of ancestral valor. This is a spiritual not an ethnographic figure, one around which carriers of the tradition can congregate, one that can be imbued with the properties of a brave and protective ancestor. In American society, from the early days of colonization to contemporary times, the black male freedom warrior has been a source of unease and civic anxiety. It is customary, therefore, to have this black male image downgraded, outlawed, or at best, awarded minimal tolerance.

From Denmark Vesey to Malcolm X in North American annals, the figure of the black warrior engaged in the pursuit of freedom or liberty for blacks is downgraded to that of criminal, insurrectionist, or, at best, psychologically warped misfit with violent tendencies, as

75. See *Black Indians: An American Story* (video), dir. Steven R. Heape (Dallas: Rich-Heape Films), 2000.
76. Gwendolyn Midlo Hall, *Africans in Colonial Louisiana: The Development of Afro-Creole Culture in the Eighteenth Century* (Baton Rouge: Louisiana State University Press, 1992), 111.

in the case of Nat Turner.[77] On the other hand, Native American warriors in their personae as staunch enemies could be seen as brave and noble. The difference turned on the perception that Native Americans had lands and a way of life to defend, whereas the African blacks had neither. Disguising as Indians and miming Native American performance in the shape in which it existed in the popular mind, black performers, whether they had Indian blood in their veins (as some did) or not, could ritually bring a measure of legitimacy to sentiments and attributes that they in fact held but did not otherwise express.

In Haiti, where the tradition of "Indian masking" began, the Indian was largely a memory by the late eighteenth century. The Maroon provided the image of valor and prowess that is performed in carnival warrior figures. Marronage also produced images of warriors engaged in the pursuit of freedom and liberty, albeit in a style different from that of aboriginal Americans. Maroons in Haiti first bared their bodies to French weapons in numbers only when they were convinced by their priests that belief made them invincible and that death was merely a return to the African motherland. In time, they were inspired also by the imminence of victory, but guerilla warfare was more regularly the mode of combat on which they survived. Lacking any great store of military weapons, they developed and put to use certain psychological skills in facing superior colonial forces. Surreptitiousness and disguise were principal among these.

In spite of their valor and skill, through the eighteenth and nineteenth centuries continental Maroons never managed to secure dominion over any significant territory, and they were being largely eliminated when the Civil War took place.[78] With the decline of actual Maroon communities, other ways—some symbolic—in which to sustain the desired sentiments of defiance and endurance in struggle were found. The "badman" and the "trickster," well-known figures in African American folklore, emerged.[79] In Trinidad, the "bois-man" and the "smart man" took their places in the folk gallery.[80] The

77. William Styron, *The Confessions of Nat Turner* (New York: Vintage Press, 1967).

78. Herbert Aptheker, "Maroons within the Present Limits of the United States," in Price, *Maroon Societies,* 151–67.

79. See Alan Dundes, ed., *Mother Wit from the Laughing Barrel* (Englewood Cliffs, N.J.: Prentice-Hall, 1973).

80. Smart, *Amazing Connections.*

carnival provided an opportunity for the badman and the bois-man to perform. Often, inside the Indian costume in New Orleans was a badman who fought other badmen on carnival days, carrying the reputation of himself and his neighborhood into sometimes mock, sometimes real battle. In Trinidad, the bois-men fought real battles against the local constabulary and colonial military forces during the years following emancipation, when the government tried—unsuccessfully—to stamp out the celebration.

The altered state evoked among the Mardi Gras Indians of New Orleans is effectively captured in the work of Samuel Kinser. He has made several astute observations about Mardi Gras Indian performances and the cultural emphases they reveal: "Masking Indian is not costume art; the performance is unified by the rhythmized body, to which all else—sequins and gestures and tambourine sounds and chants—are subordinated." The "orally-centered culture" out of which masking Indian comes "is rooted in the body's down-flowing, gravity-centered kinetic feel . . . this culture aims at unifying reality from the bottom up rather than from the head down." "What is sought is directness of communication," and "Black culture"—the wider set of traditions in which "masking Indian" is situated—"is 'soul' culture, but this spirituality has little to do with the ineffable supernaturalism of white Western traditions. . . . The Spirit accosts black worshippers, it moves them totally, without and within. The path to God is no quiet removal from the world's temptations in silent inward prayer. Inspiration comes directly to the true worshipper, and it moves from one believer to another. The trancing possessed ones share their glory with the congregation."[81]

The release of the self to possession in the active miming of otherness is a feature of the Mardi Gras carnival. This is the processional path to the "oneness" or *communitas* that is to be attained through reveling in the celebration.[82] For African-Creoles the carnival was more than a preamble to the holy core of Catholic tradition—the Passion. They seized on the festival as an opportunity to pay homage to ancestral and other cultural elements of a complex heritage, and cultivate among themselves various identities that were disapproved of or accorded little legitimacy in the society at large. In a broad

81. Kinser, *Carnival,* 171, 173.
82. Victor Turner, ed., *Celebration: Studies in Festivity and Ritual* (Washington, D.C.: Smithsonian Institution Press, 1982).

sense, the carnival brings with it space for relational experiencing that dissolves barriers and brings a beneficent overseeing power within reach. It is an occasion for great congregational achievement.

Mardi Gras Indians as Congregation

In costume, song, dance, and other ritual traditions, the Mardi Gras Indians document and commemorate the dramatic contact between Africans and the other exploited people in the New World colonies—the Native Americans. This contact was at times hostile, at times friendly; at times it was collaborative and domestic, at other times limited to the battlefield. Mardi Gras Indians in their costuming and performance edit the history to eliminate the ethnic divide between those of the dispossessed and the enslaved who found common ground in the spirit of aggressive resistance. As with other forms of celebration in African-Creole culture, the Mardi Gras Indians emerged as an instance of the spirit world in performance. The figure of the Native American holds a firm place in this world as one through whom divine or occult powers may be channeled. Among Spiritual Baptists in Trinidad, devotees who undertake the dream traveling that occurs as part of the mourning ground ritual frequently report encounters with Native American among other spirit figures from whom special instructions and directions are received. Similarly, in the Spiritual churches in New Orleans, the historical figure of Black Hawk, who led a rebellion against whites in Illinois in the 1830s, has been integrated into their pantheon of saints and regarded as a spirit guide who inspires the warrior within.[83]

Mardi Gras Indians sing, dance, and display their regalia in performance. They also compete with one another. In their earlier performances during carnival time, Mardi Gras Indians in New Orleans reflected the violent world in which African-Creole males weathered constant assaults against the legitimacy of their manhood. Bands constituted themselves as rivals, and rivalry often resulted in bloody fights when they encountered each other on the streets. The injuries, and sometimes deaths, that resulted from these violent confrontations led to the bands being treated as "gangs" that required special

83. Jason Berry, *The Spirit of Black Hawk* (Jackson: University of Mississippi Press, 1995), 19.

attention from the police. Ritual violence, particularly when it involves the shedding or exchange of human blood, is a powerful magnet around which congregations assemble. In Trinidad, masking Indians also engaged in ritual confrontations against each other, but these were of a more individual character than in New Orleans, with much less likelihood that blood would be shed.[84] Bloody confrontations were the province of the "bois-men," or stickfighters, who were communal warriors. They were the ones around whom congregational sentiments developed. In New Orleans, the Mardi Gras Indians were communal representatives.

Actual bloodletting has been dropped from contemporary performances, but ritual confrontation still serves as the dramatic core. In costume, with their chants and marches and ready with their ritual boasts, the New Orleans Mardi Gras Indian bands parade, meet, and compete with each other in speech and display, then return to their home sites where the celebration continues on the order of a thanksgiving authored by the band, on behalf of the band's community. Band members do not take their membership lightly, and bands are generally constructed as social clubs that have a claim on participants that reaches beyond performance on carnival days. Organized around a big chief and a number of lesser officers, bands meet at their exclusive sites throughout the year. Members socialize with each other regularly, and bands participate in other public events such as Super Sunday, St. Joseph's Day, and St. Patrick's Day parades. At meetings they conduct the business of mutual aid, plan and work on their participation in upcoming events, and engage in ritual practice through which congregational faithfulness and fervor are sustained. Above all, to congregate is to evoke and encourage an aura of family in the spirit that is exclusive and not readily accessed by outsiders.[85]

Central to and preceding the congregational family are the more conventional families who hold the trust of the Mardi Gras Indian heritage. They sponsor the big chiefs around whom bands congregate. It is within the context of such families that the dedication required in the making of expensive and meticulously worked costumes is to be found. Within such families, knowledge of the historical experience in masking and the reverence in the task are maintained. The values in costume elements and the art of costuming,

84. Hill, *Trinidad*.
85. Kinser, *Carnival*.

plus the "tribal chants" with their meanings to be expressed in song and dance, are passed on from generation to generation.[86] This is a pattern characteristic among African-Creoles, where alternative rituals that bring the spirit world within reach are sustained.

In Trinidad, contemporary bands are smaller, fewer, and tend to be made up principally among members of extended families. Bands no longer seek out each other for ritual confrontation, and where they happen to cross paths, such confrontations seldom unfold into minidramas of competitive speech-making, dancing, and physical combat as they did in the past. Bands mostly take their places in the general parade where the focus is on pageantry, costume, and mass congregation in which participants gather for the moment, bringing no investment of heritage or culture, and expect nothing from the experience beyond a good time. The decline of the "Wild Indian" and the "bois-man" as carnival figures coincides with the legitimating of Orisa and other homegrown forms of worship based on African antecedents. In the past, Orisa worshippers have been known to "hide" their rituals in the public carnival, but the need for such covert public performance no longer exists. Orisa worship is no longer an outlawed activity, and the religion is being openly revitalized.[87]

The shift of spiritual content away from the carnival to a more openly religious context would seem to account for a noted deritualizing within the Trinidad carnival in general. The same is less true for the Mardi Gras Indian tradition in New Orleans (although commercialization has made some inroads here too) which may have benefited from being sustained as a neighborhood festival, rather than as an aspect of the touristy extravaganza that characterizes the main New Orleans Mardi Gras.[88] Mardi Gras Indians do not parade along one exclusive route. Yet when they are encountered, their ritual evokes a heritage of resistance: "Of all the second line parades in the black community today, those of the Mardi Gras Indians most clearly retain the essential features of the early processions of Afro-Creole people from their various sanctuaries and workplaces in and

86. Salaam, "He's the Prettiest."
87. Frances Henry, *Reclaiming African Religions in Trinidad: The Socio-Political Legitimation of the Orisha and Spiritual Baptist Faiths* (Norman: University of Oklahoma Press, 2003).
88. Michael Smith, "Mardi Gras Indians: Culture and Community Empowerment" (Baton Rouge: Louisiana Division of the Arts, Department of Culture, Recreation, and Tourism, 1999).

around the city to the central marketplace. . . . Such marches would have constituted a unified and formidable form of resistance to hostile authority, and over the years they have become closely associated with the idea of freedom and political advancement among blacks in New Orleans."[89] This is the heritage around which they form their dedicated congregations. It is a heritage on which much of African-Creole culture, both in the Antilles and on the mainland, was founded.

Carnival and Religion in the Creole Complex

At its salient core, Creole culture constructs, or resurrects perhaps,[90] the resource for developing alternative spiritualities where such constructions elaborate meanings of themselves that might be otherwise constrained. Perhaps the need to address racial and cultural ambiguity and the need to be politically surreptitious were powerful incentives in this regard. In the early years of contact, Creoles were a fresh category without precedent. With their affiliations to opposed traditions always open to subversion, and isolated from any natal homeland where "home" was profound and automatic, the capacity for performing alterities was a social and cultural necessity among them. Alterities limited the angst with which the amalgamated self could be confronted in sharply polarized sociocultural situations. It also facilitated the process of transculturation through which sense could be brought to the amalgamation of discordant elements by appeal to abstract actants. This pattern is well documented in current treatises on Orisha and generically related Creole religions.[91] Not much attention is given, though, to the numen in its less specifically religious forms.

89. William Schafer and Richard B. Allen, *Brass Bands and New Orleans Jazz* (Baton Rouge: Louisiana State University Press, 1977), 12. Quoted in Michael P. Smith, *Mardi Gras Indians* (Gretna, La.: Pelican Publishing, 1994).

90. Zuesse, "Perseverance," 182.

91. See Perkinson, "Ogu's Iron"; Henry, *Reclaiming*; Brandon, *Santeria*. See also Joseph M. Murphy and Mei-Mei Sanford, eds., *Osun across the Waters: A Yoruba Goddess in Africa and the Americas* (Bloomington: Indiana University Press, 2001); and Margarite Fernandez Olmos and Lizabeth Paravisini-Gebert, *Creole Religions of the Caribbean: An Introduction from Voudou and Santeria to Obeah and Espiritismo* (New York: New York University Press, 2003).

Resistance and creativity are fundamental forces in Creole culture. They infuse liberating social and political performances and are in turn fostered by a deeply rooted and boundary-disrupting numen in both symbolic and practical domains. The carnival, with its openness to alterities within the context of a community's submission to forces of *communitas* greater than its own, is an instance in which this numen is richly performed. The Mardi Gras Indian is a performance of singular significance. The figure harmonizes racial and cultural complexities, and it images a historical stance against the depredations of European colonialism. The violent confrontations between individual masquerade bands in early performances also mirror the angst among Creoles who experience tension between the different agencies and elements out of which they and their culture were founded.

For early Creoles, conditioned to functioning within severely constrained social frameworks, and with limited access to documenting media, bodily performance became a reliable way of awakening and sustaining communal alterities that represented forces greater than any individual, greater than the community itself. That practice is also celebrated in the carnival. Through decoration, dance, song, and other signifiers, the body becomes the great instrument of inscription in congregational performances. Among Mardi Gras Indians, and other costumed masquerades, the body becomes a spiritual anagram, and bodily performance an engagement with the sublime in congregation.

From New Orleans to Trinidad, spirit performances in both religious and secular contexts demonstrate the diffusion and survival of a foundational directive that steers toward the experiencing of spiritual alterities in multiple contexts. Recognizing such a directive lends substance to Zuesse's proposition that African "civilization's religion . . . runs deeper than 'religion.'" It also brings to attention Long's treatise in which he asserts that traditions of creolization among what he calls "cultures of contact" may serve as "the basis for renewal and critique" as the crisis of self and meaning in the contemporary world is contemplated.[92]

---

92. Zuesse, "Perseverance," 170; Charles H. Long, "Indigenous People, Materialities, and Religion: Outline for a New Orientation to Religious Meaning," in Reid, *Religion and Global Culture*, 178–79.

New Orleans as an American City
Origins, Exchanges, Materialities, and Religion

CHARLES H. LONG

Introduction

New Orleans is rightly thought of as the most exotic city in the United States. In the midst of a dominating Protestantism as the style of the culture of the United States, New Orleans has continued its Spanish, French, Mediterranean, and African Caribbean traditions. Given this characterization, New Orleans has been looked upon as somewhat apart from the culture of the United States—an extra, surd, or surplus in the midst of a sea of "other Americans." While affirming much of this characterization, I wish to show how *essential* New Orleans is for an understanding of the formation of this country and its culture.

New Orleans forces us to ask other questions regarding our origins. By asking new and different questions, research into the meaning of New Orleans will reveal a novel perspective not only on this city but also on the culture of the United States. Everything looks different from the point of view of New Orleans. Research into the religious significance of this place will necessarily involve an interdisciplinary approach moving us beyond the touristic exotica into the fundamental meanings of this site and space of American cultural reality.

Through such a study, a new and different emphasis might be given to what this country might and could mean when it speaks of diversity and pluralism. In other words, a shift from our New England and Virginia origins to a contemplation of our origins in

New Orleans might prove to be quite salutary at this juncture of our cultural history.

The Founding of the Republic: Civil Religion, Settlement, and the Land

With the publication of Sidney Mead's article "The Nation with the Soul of a Church" and continuing in Robert Bellah's article "Civil Religion," published in *Daedalus* the same year, a new locus for the understanding of American religion was set forth.[1]

The notion of "civil religion" or the "religion of the Republic" moved beyond the study of American churches and denominations by combining an older perspective on religion with newer Enlightenment meanings, especially as these latter meanings found expression within what became the United States. The older notion of religion embodied in "civil religion" is derived from the founding documents, the Declaration of Independence and the Constitution, and their analogues with the mores and customs in ancient societies. This is expressed most profoundly in the founding rhetoric, ideology, and myth-story of the founding. Examples of this meaning in ancient societies may be seen in *The Ancient City,* by Fustel de Coulanges, and in *The Idea of a Town,* by Joseph Rykwert.[2] From the point of view of the founding of ancient cities and states, the act of founding consisted of a new and fundamental orientation in time and space and thus the evocation of the gods of that place and relationship of the gods of that place to the techniques of orientation. Joseph Rykwert's text is one of the exemplary discussions of the founding of Rome and the Romulus and Remus myth. Rykwert shows how the civil society of Rome was undergirded by the founding gods in the establishment of Rome as a fit place for human habitation.

In light of these myths and techniques of ancient foundings, the novel meaning of civil religion creates a paradox as it is related to the

1. Mead's essay, "The Nation with the Soul of a Church," was originally published in *Church History* 36, no. 3 (September 1967): 1–22; the essay was republished in Sidney Mead, *The Nation with the Soul of a Church* (New York: Harper, 1975); see also Robert Bellah, "Civil Religion in America," in *Daedalus: Journal of the American Academy of Arts and Sciences* 96, no. 1 (winter 1967): 1–21.

2. Numa Denis Fustel de Coulanges, *The Ancient City* (Baltimore: Johns Hopkins University Press, 1980); Joseph Rykwert, *The Idea of a Town: The Anthropology of Urban Form in Rome, Italy, and the Ancient World* (Princeton: Princeton University Press, 1976).

American Republic. The rational Enlightenment ideology in the founding rhetoric of the republic led to an explicit separation between any *empirical* church, denomination, or religious institution and the founding "God" of the republic. Thus, in Mead's language, there is a "God of the Republic" and this "God" lies at the heart of the "religion of the Republic." This "God" is not, however, identical to the Jewish or Christian God of Revelation.[3]

It is clear that the "men of the Revolution" took seriously their break from the order of being colonists. The Declaration of Independence was supposed to outline and give reasons to the world for such a radical break. In the Declaration there is the appeal to the abstract meanings of freedom and equality as ordained by "Nature and Nature's God," that is, the "god of reason." Outside of the class of revolutionaries and entrepreneurs, there is little or no mention of the actual situation of this part of the North American continent, of the issues of the aboriginal populations and their rights and obligations to the land, of the existence of chattel slavery, or of those in their same class, who, while having grievances with England, saw a revolutionary break as a foolhardy exercise.

Catherine Albanese has described the structure of this civil religion from the pre-Revolutionary days through to the twentieth century. In all the phases of this civil religion, attempts are being made to come to terms with the formation of a civil society created by colonists, who, after their independence, assume the role of colonialists, deriving their legitimate populations from a steady stream of new immigrants. I should like to refer to three modes of the more recent discussions of civil religion in the United States. Robert Bellah's meaning of civil religion rehearses the basic documents and what he considers in those documents that express the rhetoric of the American republic. These would include the Declaration of Independence, the Preamble to the Constitution, Abraham Lincoln's

3. One cannot say that this is a far-fetched notion. The founders were indeed familiar with the myths and ceremonies of the founding of Rome. See Catherine Albanese, *Sons of the Fathers: Civil Religion of the American Revolution* (Philadelphia: Temple University Press, 1976). See Hannah Arendt, *On Revolution* (New York: Viking, 1971), especially chapters 4–6. Arendt continued this discussion in her Gifford Lectures published as *The Life of the Mind*, 2 vols. (New York: Harcourt Brace Jovanovich, 1978). The issues of revolutionary time and beginnings are addressed in vol. 1, *Thinking*, in section 4, "The gap between past and future, the nunc stans," and in vol. 2, *Willing*, in section 4, "The abyss of freedom and the novus ordo seclorum." Her injection of the meaning of the hiatus between the revolution and the founding is especially important.

Second Inaugural Address, and so on. For Bellah, these documents set forth the raison d'être of the American republic, its status quo, but equally a critical meaning for the notion of a continuing democracy in the future. Will Herberg's rather descriptive understanding of the American republic as consisting of and being held together through the socioreligious symbolics of Protestant-Catholic-Jew points both to the religious and immigrant nature of American civil society. Whatever religious meanings that lie subliminally in the United States must express some mode of monotheism, and here we are reminded of some of the formulations of Roger Williams, but Herberg's formulation makes clear that his formulation would encompass only those from a European immigrant background.[4]

Sidney Mead, in "Nation with the Soul of a Church" and in his later formulations of the frontier experience, attempts to keep alive the pre-Revolutionary Puritan sentiments of the settlers within the context of their movement across frontiers. Mead's is the only formulation of a meaning of civil religion that mentions the land or people other than those of European descent.

I would like to set forth another framework for American civil religion. In one sense it carries some of the style of Herberg in its demographic dimensions, and it extends meanings related to Mead's notion of the land but from other perspectives. My formulation is that the culture of the United States of America is an Aboriginal-Euro-African culture. I set this forth as a structural, foundational, and primordial order of this culture. There are certain implications attendant to this formulation. In each case—of the Aborigines, the Europeans, and the Africans—we might ask what meaning of "land" is implied and how, at any particular time, this issue of land is adjudicated among and between them; we can also seek to understand their perception of this entity of the land. Again, the structure indicates that there have been relationships, contacts, among and between all these groups. This is a critical meaning, for as a normative order it specifies the country as having in all of its important aspects a multicultural orientation and thus the changing demographies should be seen within the context of this structure rather than understood as a new and additive dimension to the normativity of the American reality.

4. See part 2, chapter 13, in Catherine Albanese, *America: Religion and Religions*, 3d ed. (Belmont, Calif.: Wadsworth, 1999); and Will Herberg, *Protestant-Catholic-Jew: An Essay in American Religious Sociology* (Chicago: University of Chicago Press, 1960).

For such a meaning to have validity, it must be located in a space/place where it is able to evoke new and different forms of cultural historical data. I have chosen New Orleans as that space where new meanings and data regarding a meaning of American civil religion might be forthcoming. In this proposal the temporal/spatial arena defined as New Orleans will be the locus in which several different peoples and orientations find themselves at various historical periods, thus allowing this historical, geographical space, time, and situation to become a place in which the issues of exchange, adjudications, reciprocities, tensions, powers, and realities work themselves out. Thus, the religious significance is not defined by any one of the specifications; rather, that significance is defined by the manner in which the relationships create and enable persons and communities to become aware of powers of being that orient all of them in their specific worlds. The so-called Southwest may be another important place for this rethinking and reevaluation. New Orleans became a part of the United States as a part of the Louisiana Purchase in 1803, expanding the country into a continental nation and doubling its original size.

Historical Geography of the New Orleans Area

Fernand Braudel, in his magisterial *The Mediterranean and the Mediterranean World in the Age of Philip II*, demonstrated how the destinies of peoples and nations are determined in multiple and complex ways by the almost cosmic and empirical/practical modalities of that large body of water that is the Mediterranean Sea. Braudel does not put forth a notion of geographical determinism, however; he is more precise and specific. He suggests various temporal rhythms that interact on the historical stage, thus enabling us to see how the nonhuman structures of reality enter into the creation of human community at the same moment that the human community is altering and changing these nonhuman orders.[5]

Neither New Orleans nor the Gulf of Mexico is analogous to the Mediterranean and Mediterranean cultures. The Mississippi River, the Mississippi Delta, and the city of New Orleans might well

---

5. Fernand Braudel, *The Mediterranean and the Mediterranean World in the Age of Philip II*, 2 vols., trans. Sian Reynolds (New York: Harper and Row, 1972).

represent, however, a unique and other place for the meaning of an American orientation and memory.

Just as studies stemming from New England and the American Revolution have always been prominent in any history of American Christianity, on the one hand, and American civil religion on the other, New Orleans offers very different possibilities for the significance of another form of religious orientation in the United States. The peculiar geography of New Orleans and the exchanges embedded in its history—involving the Aboriginal populations, the Spanish, French, Africans, and finally the Euro-Americans—force us to deal with its situation as a most important structure of memory. In New Orleans, these memories have not been erased; indeed—they continue to constitute the mundane practical rituals of the city. The cultural geographer Peirce F. Lewis has commented on New Orleans as a geographical site:

> The apparent paradox between excellent location and miserable location merely illuminates the distinction between two terms, "site" and "situation"—which urban geographers use to describe the location of cities. Site is the actual real estate which the city occupies, and New Orleans' site is wretched. Situation is what we commonly mean when we speak of a place with respect to neighboring places. New Orleans' situation is her location near the mouth of the Mississippi, and the fact that a million people work and make a living on this evil site only emphasizes the excellence of the situation. If a city's situation is good enough, its site will be altered to *make do*.[6]

The historical geographical transformations that took place in New Orleans over an almost three-hundred-year period have not disappeared. The structure of empirical and popular languages, the specific and unique musical traditions, the forms of religious rituals, as well as the architecture and cuisine, combine to make New Orleans a distinctively different kind of American city. The broad usage of the term *Creole* is indicative of the amalgam of the various traditions that have taken place in this city.

While many might agree with the distinctiveness of New Orleans, they might also suggest that the city is at the same time exotic and

---

6. Peirce F. Lewis, *New Orleans: The Making of an Urban Landscape,* 2d ed. (Santa Fe: Center for American Places in association with the University of Virginia Press, 2003), 19.

peripheral to the main currents of American life and thought. One could almost feel comfortable with this notion since New Orleans is seldom evoked in any of the founding stories. But the importance of New Orleans as a site of major geographical orientation is attested to by the double exchanges of the city between the Spanish and the French. As far as the United States is concerned, New Orleans has been strategically important since the end of the eighteenth century. The successful slave revolt of Toussaint-Louverture in Santo Domingo (Haiti) in the 1790s that influenced a number of slave insurrections in the Chesapeake area prompted many slave owners to sell slaves literally "down the river" to reduce the density of the slave populations in the Chesapeake. These Chesapeake slaves came into contact with African slaves who had been directly imported into New Orleans from Africa.

Peirce F. Lewis has divided New Orleans into three major periods. He calls the period from 1718 to 1810 "New Orleans as a European City," the period from 1810 to 1865 "America's Western Capital," and the period from 1865 to 1945 "A City Adapting to the Twentieth Century." Lewis's divisions are centered around the development of New Orleans as an urban form; another classification, that of Thomas N. Ingersoll, divides the city along cultural historical periods. His divisions are as follows: 1) "The French Regime, 1718–1769"; 2) "The Spanish Regime, 1769–1803"; and 3) "The Republican Period, 1803–1819." Let me trace the history of New Orleans by overlapping the divisions of Lewis and Ingersoll.[7] I begin in 1682, when Pierre Le Moyne, Sieur d'Iberville, established a post and brought French colonists into the site.

EARLY PERIOD, 1699–1810

Though the Spanish made claims to this region based on the explorations of Hernando de Soto in the early 1540s, no sustaining post was established in this area by them. The choice of the site of New Orleans was a strategic decision based on two centuries of exploration in the region. The Spanish were the first Europeans to

7. Thomas N. Ingersoll, *Mammon and Manon in Early New Orleans* (Knoxville: University of Tennessee Press, 1999), has much to say about the originality and brilliance of Law's monetary theories (see below).

claim and explore the lower Mississippi Valley, but the only mark they left was a bitter memory among the local Native Americans. Partly because the Spanish found no treasure and partly because Spanish ships could not navigate the narrow waterways, European colonization did not occur until much later. The site of present-day New Orleans must be attributed to the French. New Orleans implodes as a city from the inland continent; it is an offshoot of French settlements in Canada. Prior to Iberville, La Salle had sailed down the Mississippi establishing outposts from Detroit to St. Louis, Petit Roche (Little Rock), and Baton Rouge, Mobile, and New Orleans. He and his fellow explorers named the territory "Louisiana" after King Louis XIV.

The French made peaceful alliances with the Native Americans, since they were dependent on them for their food supply. It was Iberville's plan to expand the Louisiana outpost as the base for driving the English from North America. During this period, members of the French gentry as well as woodsmen and fur-trappers joined the French colony in Louisiana. The hopes for the establishment of a significant French base were dashed by the death of Iberville from fever in 1706. He was succeeded by his bother Jean-Baptiste Belville. The Louisiana outpost fell on arduous times, suffering from lack of provisions and neglect by the French government. The colonists became increasingly dependent on the Native Americans for their survival in this new landscape.

No plan was developed in France for the exploitation of the French outpost in the Lower Mississippi. The king had appointed a commoner, one Antoine Crozat, to see to the administration of the colony. Crozat was primarily interested in the fur trade, and after exploiting the colony for all he thought was valuable in furs, he turned the colony back over to the crown. During this period the French were sending vagrants, convicts, and undesirables to the colonies. Hoping against hope to be able to establish viability through the cultivation of tobacco and indigo, the French had begun the importation of African slaves. Given the benign neglect of the crown, the colony was quickly becoming a métis colony, in fact and in reputation, the population rapidly becoming a racial mixture of French, Native Americans, and Africans.

At this point, let us remember a geographical fact. When Peirce Lewis referred to the "wretched site" that is New Orleans, he was pointing out the significance of this particular site, one of the many turns in the sinuous river that flowed into the Gulf of Mexico one hundred miles below. Those treacherous miles of muddy water south of the river bend discouraged enemy intrusion. The site of New Orleans was a crescent in the shoreline of an old Indian portage to a series of huge lakes that provided an eastern backdoor route to the Gulf. The Indian trail was tremendously important, as it was the key controlling the entire Mississippi River delta on the underbelly of North America, a region that contained some of the richest soil in the world. Moreover, the whole region lying between the lakes and the river was protected by a natural, reinforceable levee bordering the river.

With the death of Louis XIV in 1715, Louis XV became king but did not reach his majority until 1723; the affairs of state were taken over by a regent, Phillippe II, duke of Orleans. It was the duke of Orleans, in league with the brilliant Scottish economist John Law, who schemed to bring new life into the colony of Louisiana. In 1719 they formed the new Compagnie des Indes. The crescent city would bear the name of the duke of Orleans, for it was to become a part of a grand design to link Canada, Louisiana, and the Antilles into a strong economic cordon. Emboldened by John Law's new monetary theories of the economy and the desire of nobles to venture into the "world of money-making,"[8] they set forth to convince colonists to immigrate to the colony and sell stock in the company. Their campaign was too successful, and in 1720 the shares in the stock of Louisiana's future that promised only 5 percent annual interest lured the greedy gamblers of the upper class into a frenzy of speculation. Neither the government nor the national bank could cover the stock and thus the "Mississippi bubble" burst.

There are two lasting effects of the Orleans-Law debacle: 1) the notion that the colony of Louisiana should have a wider impact on the fortunes of the French in the Atlantic world, and 2) during this period of speculation, seven thousand French citizens and over nineteen hundred African slaves were imported to the colony. The sudden population increase was too much for the crescent city, and many of the French and slaves were forced to live with the Biloxi and Pascagoula Indians.

8. Joseph A. Schumpeter, "Ancestor of the Idea of a Managed Currency," in *History of Economic Analysis* (New York: Oxford University Press, 1986), 321–22; see also Jack Weatherford, *The History of Money* (New York: Three Rivers Press, 1997), 130–32.

NATIVE AMERICANS

From the earliest French period, Native Americans had an intimate relationship with the French fur traders and settlers. Given the geography of the area, the French were unable to exploit the richness of the soil, for they did not understanding the shifting structures of the levees. For the most part, they depended on the occasional provisional ship from France, but they were more basically dependent on the Native Americans for a sustaining food supply. During the nascent period of agricultural experimentation, the French had enslaved Native Americans as the labor force for their agricultural ventures.

For the most part, the relationship of the French and the Native Americans was highly ambiguous. Sometimes the Indians were considered allies, other times they were enslaved, and other times they engaged in legal marriages and in various other forms of sexual unions with the French. Whereas the French claimed the land as a mode of sovereignty, it was clear that the Native Americans knew the land and had the greater capacity to live on and with the land. The French were attempting to remain sovereign over the Native Americans while they were dependent upon them for a sustaining food supply, and the relationships were never stable. During the period of the Compagnie des Indes, large numbers of Africans were brought into the colony in the hope of sustaining a much larger population of French immigrants as well as providing a stable and totally dependent labor force. These Africans in many cases recapitulated many of the relationships that the French had with the Native Americans. When in 1729 the Natchez revolted against the French, many Africans were to be found in the ranks of the Natchez. while other Africans were pressed into military service by the French. The Natchez revolt, along with the financial debacle of the "Mississippi Bubble," signaled the end of the influence the Compagnie des Indes held on the colony.

AFRICANS IN NEW ORLEANS

The great influx of Africans in the colony of New Orleans occurred during the Compagnie des Indes period.[9] The company,

9. For a history of the Africans in Louisiana, see Gwendolyn Midlo Hall, *Africans in Colonial Louisiana: The Development of Afro-Creole Culture in the Eighteenth Century*

though propelled by the economic potential of the New Orleans colony, had much broader interests in Africa and the Caribbean. As a matter of fact, one might say that it was African slavery that brought the peculiar meaning of *Creole* into prominence. To understand this, one must understand some details of the African slave trade. The Portuguese were the first to establish themselves as slave traders on the west coast of Africa. The slave trade was not an episodic venture; it was an institution, a major business of the Atlantic world that was engaged in by every maritime nation of the Atlantic—the Portuguese, Dutch, English, French, Spanish, Danes, and Swedes; it was also engaged in by Africans. For the trade to be viable, several enclaves, factories, or in the Portuguese, *feitorias,* were established along the coast of West Africa. These were places where enslaved Africans were stored and processed for the Atlantic trade. These factories produced a peculiar and distinct form of culture. The Africans who worked in them were no longer under the obligations of their kinship groups, and the Europeans were equally distant from their lands of birth. A new language of buying and selling of human beings as commodities and items of trade was beginning to develop in these entrepôts. Europeans and Africans were engaged in all forms of intercourse with human matter including sexual matters. A distinct Creole culture and language was thus being created in these spaces. This is the same arena identified by William Pietz in his famous articles on the creation of the fetish and how the meaning of the fetish as a religious discourse is directly related to the new economy of the Atlantic world in its usage of the term *commodity.*[10] In passing, we should note that the similarity between the Portuguese terms *feitorias* and *feitiço;* both terms emerge simultaneously from the same context.

The Compagnie des Indes had secured the rights necessary to carry on the slave trade on the West African coast of Senegambia. This meant that they had easy access to the Dogon and Bambara

---

(Baton Rouge: Louisiana State University Press, 1992).

10. For a discussion of these African Creole societies, see the prologue and introduction to Ira Berlin, *Many Thousand Gone* (Cambridge: Harvard University Press, 1998). For a sustained discussion of the meaning of the fetish emerging from the African trade, see William Pietz, "The Problem of the Fetish," *RES* 9 (spring 1985): 5–17; William Pietz, "The Problem of the Fetish II: The Origin of the Fetish," *RES* 13 (spring 1987): 23–45; and William Pietz, "The Problem of the Fetish, IIIa: Bosman's Guinea and the Enlightenment Theory of Fetishism," *RES* 16 (autumn 1988): 105–23.

peoples. In fact, a large number of Bambara were enslaved into the factory system. The French became especially interested in enslaving Dogon and Bambara peoples when they discovered that these Africans knew the technique of rice cultivation. They were also adept at building dikes and controlling levees. By chance, the French had discovered barrels of rice in a shipload of Africans from the Bambara area. A great demand for Bambara, Mandingo, and Dogons ensued in the colony. And it is clear that large numbers of Bambara were sold into the New Orleans area. Since they were from the same tribe in Africa, they were able to maintain their language and many of their customs and memories.

Enslaved Africans brought into the colony were regulated by the Code Noir enacted by Louis XIV in 1685. Most of the provisions of the code specified the kinds of legitimate punishment that owners could mete out to slaves, and they were severe. In comparison to other criminal codes of the time, for example, in early-nineteenth-century England, juveniles were hanged for stealing a handkerchief, and a Frenchman convicted of stealing animals or crops would be sent to the gallows, the Code Noir might be considered mild. There was one provision that made it distinct in comparison to Anglo-American slave treatment: While the code vested a slave owner with power that could be exercised directly on the body of a slave, it also established authority over the slaveholder by limiting the degree of violence that he could use. In other words, because the code's final authority rested with the monarch and not with the slave owner, it made all humans in the realm subject to the authority of the monarchy.

The influx of Africans into the colony during the later third of the first French period created New Orleans as a *slave society*. A slave society differs from a society with slaves. In a society with slaves, the slaves and slavery are peripheral to the overall maintenance and productions within the society. In a slave society, slaves and the institution of slavery constitute the central meaning of the maintenance and productions of the society; this was the case in New Orleans by 1762. The issue for the colony of New Orleans was how to obscure the importance of the meaning of slaves and the institution of slavery while still maintaining its necessity and viability. A similar issue was present in the Chesapeake area, but it cannot be so clearly noted given the rhetorics of the Middle Colonies.

Africans in the New Orleans colony discerned their situation in various ways. First, there was the multicultural nature of the colony itself; second, the Code Noir allowed slaves to purchase their freedom; and, third, Africans occupied the spaces of the plantation and of the bayous and swamps. Given these modalities and the power through language and memory of Africa, slaves were quick to exploit any and all gaps in their situation of servitude and to create another form of culture. While originating with the Africans, this style would permeate the colony. The slave culture thus becomes the stylistics through which what began as an African creolization is translated and transformed into a specific form of North American culture.

THE SPANISH PERIOD, 1769–1803

Thomas Ingersoll has written concisely of the motives behind the transfer of Louisiana from France to Spain:

> In the series of bargains that made up the Treaty of Paris in 1763, Louis XV finalized his gift of Louisiana to Charles III of Spain. After the fall of Montreal in 1760, the French crown saw Louisiana as an expensive liability and used it as a pawn to induce Spain to join in the war against England in 1762. While Charles III was not at all sure he really wanted the colony, it was clear that Louis would abandon it, and Charles knew he must take it to prevent it from falling into the hands of Britain; it was potentially the gateway to Mexico for the Anglo-American colonies.[11]

I will not take too much time in the discussion of the Spanish period. Suffice it to say, that no major structural changes took place. One might surmise that the residual possibilities of New Orleans that were present in the French period came to fruition during the Spanish period. The Spanish rule, especially after the takeover by the Spanish captain Alejandro O'Reilly, was without turbulence. During the Spanish period, sugarcane production was introduced into Louisiana, thus requiring the import of more African slaves.

The Spanish version of the Code Noir was the Coartacion. While the Spanish code followed closely many of the provisions of the Code Noir, the Coartacion was supplemented with seventeen new

11. Ingersoll, *Mammon*, 247.

provisions as it related to Africans and slaves. "Significantly, they removed many of the impediments to manumission that had been present in the Code Noir. The Spanish law of coartacion allowed a slave who had accumulated money equivalent to his or her market value to purchase freedom—further it required owners to accept payment."[12]

The cultivation of sugarcane and the change in the legal codes served to bring many free Africans into the colony from other parts of the Caribbean, thus increasing the number of persons of color in a slave society that was to be dominated by persons of European ancestry.

By 1800, France under Napoléon had revived the dreams of a North American empire. Napoléon schemed with Spain for the return of Louisiana to France. Control of Louisiana would halt the westward expansion of the United States and supply France's other colonies in the Western Hemisphere with the supplies they needed. In 1800 Napoléon signed a secret treaty with Spain, the Treaty of Ildefonso, that stipulated that France would provide Spain with an Italian principality for the son-in-law of the Spanish king, Charles IV, if Spain would return Louisiana to France. Napoléon's vision was for Santo Domingo to become the breadbasket for a flow of French immigrants into the Louisiana Territory. The successful revolt of the African slaves in Santo Domingo under Toussaint-Louverture in 1803–1804 ended the dream of a North American empire for France.[13] The American diplomats in France heard rumors of the French/Spanish deal; knowing that with the loss of Santo Domingo, Napoléon lacked funds for his various European ventures, the Americans realized he was more than open to an offer to sell the Louisiana Territory.

Americans and the Louisiana Purchase

D. W. Meinig offers a broad perspective on the tremendous growth and accompanying aspirations of the young nation:

12. Lynn Stewart, "Louisiana Subjects: Power, Space, and the Slave Body," *Ecumene* 2, no. 3 (July 1995): 227–46.

13. For the impact of the revolt in Santo Domingo on the French Revolution, see C. L. R. James, *The Black Jacobins: Toussaint L'Ouverture and the San Domingo Revolution,* 2d ed., revised (New York: Vintage Books, Alfred A. Knopf, 1963).

In 1800 the United States was one of the world's largest states. Extending broadly inland from the Atlantic, spanning the Appalachians and fronting upon nearly the entire length of the Mississippi, its boundaries encompassed about 900,000 square miles. In simplest geographic terms, apparent to all at the time, it was a country divided into two parts: east and west, seaboard and interior, old and new. The American people were eagerly expanding into the newly opened and nearly empty lands of the western interior, and the prospects of national growth and enrichment seemed unlimited in a country blessed "with room enough," as Thomas Jefferson said in an inaugural flourish, "for all descendants to the 1,000 & 1,000 generation."[14]

The great expanse of this new country presented several geographic problems related to its coherence and security. First, how could the East and West be bound together, divided as they were by such a broad corrugation of mountains and so divergent in their alignments on the grand waterways of nature? Second, how could the young nation secure geographic positions deemed essential to the development of its territories; especially, how could it secure unrestricted use of the Mississippi River, upon which the traffic of the western half of the nation must move? And third, how could the union of states maintain the delicate geopolitical balances of federation, as the spreading population became formed into an array of new western states?

None of these issues were lost in the vision of Thomas Jefferson. Even before his presidency, in 1790, as secretary of state, he had rehearsed the possibilities of American access to the Gulf of Mexico. While Americans had access to the Mississippi all the way through the Mississippi Delta, access to the Gulf of Mexico, which meant going through New Orleans, was not open to them. New Orleans was under the rule of Spain, and though Spain never denied Americans access through New Orleans, the fact that another nation controlled New Orleans meant that the United States lacked total power over this vital waterway, so essential to the coherence and security of the new nation, and was a situation that Jefferson felt could not be tolerated for too long.

---

14. D. W. Meinig, *The Shaping of America: A Geographical Perspective of 500 Years of History,* vol. 2, *Continental America, 1800–1867* (New Haven: Yale University Press, 1993), 4.

While the United States was relatively content with Spanish control of the mouth of the Mississippi, rumors began in 1795 that Spain was conducting diplomatic talks with France for a transfer of New Orleans back into French hands. From the American perspective, this was troubling news, for the French claimed a vast territory on the North American continent, and control of New Orleans was their access to this large piece of the continent. Jefferson's role in the Louisiana Purchase allows us another perspective on the author of the Declaration of Independence and *Notes of Virginia*. Read from this point of view, Jefferson must be seen as our first expansionist and geopolitical president. As would become clearer both in the career of Jefferson and with the expansionist policies of the country, America seemed destined to become a continental country peopled by persons from Northern Europe.

When the United States heard of the impending transfer of New Orleans back to France, Jefferson sent Robert Livingston as a special envoy to France to inquire about the purchase of New Orleans. Napoléon initially refused, but he later consented to the sale in April 1803. At this point Napoléon offered to sell not only New Orleans but also the entire territory of Louisiana to the United States. The United States purchased Louisiana for $11,250,00 and assumed claims of its own citizens against France up to $3,750,000 for a total of $15,000,000. On November 30, 1803, Spain's representatives transferred Louisiana to France's representatives in New Orleans. On December 20, 1803, France officially transferred New Orleans and the territory of Louisiana to the United States.

Several radical steps were taken in the purchase of Louisiana. With Louisiana, the United States acquired a foreign city and people without their consent and without the rule of conquest. Was this a legal act? But beyond the issue of legality were the practical issues incumbent upon making this foreign city into an American place. To be sure, New Orleans possessed a planter class, but its citizenry was from French, Spanish, Canadian, African, Italian, and Greek backgrounds—more Mediterranean than the Northern European immigrants in the other parts of the States. There was initial tension in the adjudication of legal codes and in the creation of a lingua franca, but these caused few major problems.

The leveling catalyst proved to be the radical institutionalization of slavery and racism as the basis for the unity of the citizens in the city. There had been many free Africans in the city under both the

French and Spanish administrators; many of these free Africans were themselves slave owners. The institutional form of chattel slavery under a republican white superiority meant that class, as far as persons of African descent were concerned, could not become the foundational basis for this unity. Many of the free African slave owners left with their slaves for a return either to Santo Domingo or to Vera Cruz in Mexico. This adaptive strategy of racism foretold one of the issues of the Louisiana Territory: the Americanization of the territory was synonymous with a commitment to the extension of African slavery as a fundamental institution of American society. While there was some concern about the adaptation of the foreign Europeans in New Orleans, no serious thought was given to the millions of Native Americans whose fortunes had changed over the last two hundred years through purchases and diplomatic treaties of Euro-American powers. The issue of whose land this was or, more fundamentally, "what is the land?" was solved through the assertion of ownership and conquest.

New Orleans, Civil Religion, and the Founding

It is not my intention to pose New Orleans and the Louisiana Purchase as an alternative in lieu of the reigning historical mythology of the Puritans and the American philosophes. In proposing New Orleans as a structure of civil religion, I am not setting forth a binary—"good New Orleans" as opposed to a "bad New England." I mistrust most binaries and especially this one. What I am saying is that New Orleans is as necessary for an understanding of American civil religion as was the control of New Orleans and the mouth of the Mississippi for a coherent geographical, political, and economic order of the nascent American republic.

Obviously, there is a great deal more to say about New Orleans. I have not even touched upon the spectacle of the Mardi Gras, the traditions of music, the cuisine, the layout of the city and the levees, or the specific and general characteristics of Creole and creolizations. I have been at pains to present a schematic historical geography of a very propitious time/space as an entrée to a discussion about foundings, civil religion, and religion in general.

The backdrop to my portrayal of New Orleans is the presence of empirical and symbolic bodies of water—the Mississippi River, the

Gulf of Mexico, the Caribbean, and the waters of the Atlantic. All the persons and demographies in this history have been formed in relationship to these waters. In another place I have spoken of the symbolisms of water and religions:

> On the conventional level, it is clear that the Mediterranean seems to be the womb for the gestation and birth of religions. . . . [T]he Atlantic is, however, not a revealer of deities, seers, and prophets; it is not under the sign of revelation but of reason, civilization, and rational orders. This world manifests no regard for the layered thickness of time. It is a world justified by the epistemologies of Descartes and Kant, the English empiricists, and the ethical economies of Adam Smith and Karl Marx. The world of the Atlantic lives under the rhetoric and mark of freedom—a freedom that was supposed to banish the specter of the ancient gods and reveal a deeper structure to the meaning of human existence.[15]

The revolutionary democracy of the United States boasts the honor of being not only the first modern nation but also the only one that did not found itself upon a religious tradition. Are such foundings so easily accomplished? Hannah Arendt has explored the political and symbolic meanings of the founding of a state, especially of a revolutionary state. Arendt gives us two sustained discussions of the American founding; the first is contained in her book *On Revolution* and is taken up in chapter 4, "Foundation I: Constitutio Libertatis," and in chapter 5, "Foundation II: Novus Ordo Saeclorum." She returns to this theme in her posthumously published *The Life of the Mind*, volume 2, *Willing*. Arendt is at pains to make the case that the revolutionary founders were very much aware of the problematic of founding something anew.

Arendt tells us that there is a temporal hiatus, an abyss, between the act of liberation and the actualization of freedom. This hiatus or abyss was a moment and time of discernment, a moment in which one might divine those heretofore "powers of being" that had always been there but had never been perceived until the act of liberation; these modes, actions, and materialities would be those resources that might give body and material meaning to the act of revolution. She implies that this is where the founders "blew it." Anyone who has

---

15. Charles H. Long, "Passage and Prayer," in *The Courage to Hope*, ed. Quinton H. Dixie and Cornel West (Boston: Beacon Press, 1993), 13–14.

spent time with cosmogonic myths will recognize the problem being presented here by Arendt. What, if any, perfumes waft over the founding of the American republic? The founding fathers tended not to think sensuously nor redolently about their revolution.

My interest in New Orleans as a meaning and locus for the renewal of the discussion about civil religion is related to another possibility of our common origins. While we like to characterize ourselves as now concerned about diversity and multiculturalism, there is no fundamental structure of our culture that has ever affirmed either diversity or the multicultural as constituting an empirical situation in the country. Untold Native Americans, Africans, Chinese, and others, have stories about diversity and the multicultural that few wish to hear. The Louisiana Purchase takes place in the same generation as the adoption of the Constitution. As the most significant singular acquisition of geographical space in our history, it offered a new possibility for the forming of a true revolutionary democracy. In presenting New Orleans as a datum, I am proposing that in that abyss and hiatus between the act of liberation and the actualization of freedom we inject the time/space and meaning of New Orleans as a fundamental structure of our origins. New Orleans becomes a part of this nation only thirteen years after the adoption of the Constitution; its acquisition is presided over by the author of the Declaration of Independence and a "founding father."

New Orleans, however, does not carry with it a master narrative, of either the triumph of Protestants or the excellence of reason. Its reason for being is not justified by high moral principles, and, as Peirce Lewis put it, the site was indeed "wretched," but it is also a mundane situation in which over a million people carry on their lives. It is the second largest port after New York, and it is our opening to the rest of the Americas and the world. It is the place that is conscious of the fact that, for over three hundred years, Chickasaws, Choctaws, French, Spanish, Canadians, Bambaras, Dogons, Africans from the Chesapeake, and U.S. citizens from Tennessee and Philadelphia, have met and exchanged. It is a place that admits to no mastery of human agency—the levees have never been completely tamed, shifting in unfathomable ways according to their own rhythms. And this admixture of people is interlaced with the cultivation of rice, indigo, and sugarcane, and now shipping and the oil industry.

It is again the place to ponder the economic theories of John Law, who originated the notion of credit as an asset and was the author of the Mississippi bubble. New Orleans makes a triangle with the Chesapeake and with Santo Domingo; the revolt of Toussaint-Louverture in Santo Domingo and the dashing of the hopes of Napoléon for a French empire in North America thus led to the Louisiana Purchase. From the perspective of New Orleans, we would have to face the matter and materiality of our founding and realize that if America is a "discourse," it is a discourse about something other than discourse. Mixed into every formulation about the American reality, whether it be about race, gender, religion, economics, or politics, there is the specificity of a meaning and modality of materiality that is avoided in most statements. This avoidance of the sensuous nature of reality as matter has forced most Americans to hide from themselves what has happened and is happening in this country. Attention to New Orleans as an important ingredient in the discussion of civil religion might allow us to mature as a nation and begin to deal with our issues as genuine human problems and not as "dilemmas" that will be overcome by a happiness that is coincidental with an infinite progressive future.

My research on New Orleans and this paper were undertaken long before the devastation of Hurricane Katrina. This nation must now come to terms with New Orleans in a new manner. Again we have the possibility of making New Orleans into more than an authentic American city; I hope that in the rebuilding of the city, we might be reminded again of its cultural significance for our national life.

Contributors

RICHARD J. CALLAHAN, JR., is Assistant Professor in the Department of Religious Studies at the University of Missouri–Columbia, where he specializes in American religious history, culture, and folklore. He is the author of *Work and Faith in the Kentucky Coal Fields: Subject to Dust.*

DOUGLAS HENRY DANIELS is Professor of Black Studies and History at the University of California, Santa Barbara. Trained as a historian, his works include *Pioneer Urbanites: A Social and Cultural History of Black San Francisco; Lester Leaps In: The Life and Times of Lester "Pres" Young;* and *One O'clock Jump: The Unforgettable History of the Oklahoma City Blue Devils.*

PAUL CHRISTOPHER JOHNSON is Associate Professor in the Department of History and at the Center for Afroamerican and African Studies at the University of Michigan–Ann Arbor. He is the author of *Secrets, Gossip, and Gods: The Transformation of Brazilian Candomblé* and *Diaspora Conversions: Black Carib Religion and the Recovery of Africa.*

ELAINE J. LAWLESS is Curators' Distinguished Professor, English and Women's Studies (Adjunct Religious Studies and Anthropology) at the University of Missouri–Columbia. She has published four books on women and religion and numerous articles; her more recent research and one book has been on women's narratives of domestic violence. Lawless is Director of the Center for Arts and Humanities at UMC and is President of the American Folklore Society.

CHARLES H. LONG is Professor Emeritus of History of Religions at the University of California, Santa Barbara. He is also Former Director of the Research Center for Black Studies at UCSB. Prior to his appointment at the University of California he held professorships in History of Religion at the University of Chicago, the University of North Carolina, Chapel Hill, Duke University, and Syracuse University. Among his publications are *Alpha, The Myths of Creation, Myths and Symbols: Essays in Honor of Mircea Eliade* (ed. with Joseph Kitagawa); and *Significations: Signs, Symbols, and Images in the Interpretation of Religion.*

AMANDA PORTERFIELD is Robert A. Spivey Professor of Religion and Director of Graduate Studies in Religion at Florida State University. Her recent books include *Protestant Experience in America; Healing in the History of Christianity;* and *The Transformation of American Religion.* She currently serves as coeditor of the quarterly journal *Church History: Studies in Christianity and Culture.*

CAROLE LYNN STEWART is Assistant Professor of English at the University of Maryland, Baltimore County. She specializes in American and African American literature, primarily from the nineteenth century, and interdisciplinary American cultural studies of political space and religion. Stewart's publications include "Civil Religion" in *The Encyclopedia of Religion* (2005), and "Challenging Liberal Justice: The Talented Tenth Revisited," in *Re-Cognizing W. E. B. Du Bois in the Twenty-First Century.* She is currently completing a book manuscript on civil religion and civil society in the literary imaginations of Jonathan Edwards, Herman Melville, and W. E. B. Du Bois.

JOHN STEWART, anthropologist and writer, is Professor Emeritus of African American and African Studies, University of California, Davis, and lives and works in Davis, California. He is a past Director of African American Studies at the University of Illinois and UC Davis, and his work has focused on cultural continuities across the African diaspora in the Americas.

PETER W. WILLIAMS is Distinguished Professor of Comparative Religion and American Studies at Miami University in Oxford, Ohio. He is the author of *Popular Religion in America, Houses of God,* and *America's Religions* and is coeditor of *The Encyclopedia of Religion in America,* to be published by Congressional Quarterly in

2010. His special interests are the built environment of American religion and the Episcopal Church and American culture.

MICHAEL J. ZOGRY is Assistant Professor in the Department of Religious Studies at the University of Kansas. An affiliated faculty member in the Center for Indigenous Nations Studies, his research interests are in the areas of First Nations religions, ritual studies, and religions of the United States.

Index